Social Monitoring
for Public Health

Synthesis Lectures on Information Concepts, Retrieval, and Services

Editor
Gary Marchionini, *University of North Carolina at Chapel Hill*

Synthesis Lectures on Information Concepts, Retrieval, and Services publishes short books on topics pertaining to information science and applications of technology to information discovery, production, distribution, and management. Potential topics include: data models, indexing theory and algorithms, classification, information architecture, information economics, privacy and identity, scholarly communication, bibliometrics and webometrics, personal information management, human information behavior, digital libraries, archives and preservation, cultural informatics, information retrieval evaluation, data fusion, relevance feedback, recommendation systems, question answering, natural language processing for retrieval, text summarization, multimedia retrieval, multilingual retrieval, and exploratory search.

Building a Better World with Our Information: The Future of Personal Information Management, Part 3
William Jones
2015

Click Models for Web Search
Aleksandr Chuklin, Ilya Markov, and Maarten de Rijke
2015

Information Communication
Feicheng Ma
2015

Social Media and Library Services
Lorri Mon
2015

Analysis and Visualization of Citation Networks
Dangzhi Zhao and Andreas Strotmann
2015

The Taxobook: Applications, Implementation, and Integration in Search: Part 3 of a 3-Part Series
Marjorie M.K. Hlava
2014

The Taxobook: Principles and Practices of Building Taxonomies, Part 2 of a 3-Part Series
Marjorie M.K. Hlava
2014

Measuring User Engagement
Mounia Lalmas, Heather O'Brien, and Elad Yom-Tov
2014

The Taxobook: History, Theories, and Concepts of Knowledge Organization, Part 1 of a 3-Part Series
Marjorie M.K. Hlava
2014

Children's Internet Search: Using Roles to Understand Children's Search Behavior
Elizabeth Foss and Allison Druin
2014

Digital Library Technologies: Complex Objects, Annotation, Ontologies, Classification, Extraction, and Security
Edward A. Fox and Ricardo da Silva Torres
2014

Social Monitoring for Public Health

Michael J. Paul and Mark Dredze

ISBN: 978-3-031-01183-2   paperback
ISBN: 978-3-031-02311-8   ebook

DOI 10.1007/978-3-031-02311-8

A Publication in the Springer series
SYNTHESIS LECTURES ON INFORMATION CONCEPTS, RETRIEVAL, AND SERVICES

Lecture #60
Series Editor: Gary Marchionini, *University of North Carolina at Chapel Hill*
Series ISSN
Print 1947-945X   Electronic 1947-9468

Social Monitoring
for Public Health

Michael J. Paul
University of Colorado

Mark Dredze
Johns Hopkins University

SYNTHESIS LECTURES ON INFORMATION CONCEPTS, RETRIEVAL, AND SERVICES #60

ABSTRACT

Public health thrives on high-quality evidence, yet acquiring meaningful data on a population remains a central challenge of public health research and practice. Social monitoring, the analysis of social media and other user-generated web data, has brought advances in the way we leverage population data to understand health. Social media offers advantages over traditional data sources, including real-time data availability, ease of access, and reduced cost. Social media allows us to ask, and answer, questions we never thought possible.

This book presents an overview of the progress on uses of social monitoring to study public health over the past decade. We explain available data sources, common methods, and survey research on social monitoring in a wide range of public health areas. Our examples come from topics such as disease surveillance, behavioral medicine, and mental health, among others. We explore the limitations and concerns of these methods. Our survey of this exciting new field of data-driven research lays out future research directions.

KEYWORDS

social media, web data, public health, data science

For Dad. –MJP

For Chava, Gilah, Hadar, and Micah. –MHD

Contents

Preface

In October of 2010, Michael was a new computer science Ph.D. student at Johns Hopkins, Mark was his research adviser, and we were both attending the conference on Empirical Methods in Natural Language Processing (EMNLP). Sitting in a Boston restaurant one night of the conference, we started talking about this new website called "Twitter" and what interesting research we could do with millions of tweets. One of us wondered if anyone talked about health on the new social media platform. At the end of the conference, Mark sent an email to Michael:

> *I did a quick search out of curiosity. I looked at half of 1% of our twitter collection…to pull out all tweets that have the word "sick"…You can see that there are lots of tweets where the author [writes] sick, but of course it's not such a simple problem.*

That email led to Michael's class project, which led to our first paper together at the International Conference on Weblogs and Social Media (ICWSM) [Paul and Dredze, 2011]. That paper contained many of the ideas we'd follow in subsequent years: structured topic models, topic analyses for social media, influenza surveillance, drug and tobacco use, health behaviors, mental health, and geo-locating tweets. Since then, it's been a whirlwind of research, and we've each developed a deeper interest in public health.

In some sense, the field of social monitoring for public health has followed a similar path. Initial work on using Google and Twitter for influenza surveillance progressed to surveillance for other infectious diseases, and quickly branched out to a wide range of public health topics. Before we knew it, an entire field of research had grown around us.

As we read newly published papers in this area, we were amazed by the creativity and breadth of what was being achieved. We collected our observations and began to notice common themes and structures across research areas, structures that could organize the field and allow it to move forward. It made sense to write down what we observed, and before we realized it, we had a book.

This book is a reflection of the past decade of research, a summary of how we reached this point and what has been done so far in this fast-paced field. We can't predict the future, but by understanding what we have achieved so far, we hope to provide researchers with a foundation on which to build the future of this field.

Michael J. Paul and Mark Dredze
August 2017

Acknowledgments

This book would not have been possible without the help and inspiration from too many people to name: our colleagues at our universities, including our students; people we've met at conferences and workshops; people we've talked to in government, NGOs, and companies working in this field; and the hundreds of people we've learned from, through papers, talks, emails, and conversations over dinner. This has been an amazing education for us, and we continue to learn all the time.

As for getting this book written, we thank Emre Kiciman and the anonymous reviewers for their incredibly thorough and insightful feedback, and Jimmy Lin for encouraging us to do this.

Michael J. Paul and Mark Dredze
August 2017

CHAPTER 1

A New Source of Big Data

We can only see a short distance ahead, but we can see plenty there that needs to be done.

Alan Turing

Protecting Health, Saving Lives—Millions at a Time

Mission of the Johns Hopkins Bloomberg School of Public Health

You've likely seen a public health awareness campaign. Perhaps you've seen an advertisement from New York Health (the Department of Health and Mental Hygiene) on the subway warning about the dangers of synthetic drugs. Maybe you've seen a billboard in Baltimore warning that children with influenza should stay home from school. You may have seen a social media advertisement from Los Angeles's "Break Up With Tobacco" campaign.

These are just some of the advertisements you may come across as part of public health awareness campaigns. These programs promote breast cancer screenings, testing for HIV, counseling for depression. Public health awareness campaigns are organized efforts to promote awareness of a health issue through the use of advertising, news and social media. There are hundreds of public health awareness campaigns organized every year, from well-known topics like "World Immunization Week," "World AIDS Day" or "The Great American Smokeout," to lesser known ones like "Global Handwashing Day" or the "National Bone Health Campaign." All share the same goal: increase awareness in the hopes of combating a public health problem. A simple question: do these campaigns work?

For the moment, let's consider another topic: vaccines. One of the great public health victories of the last century has been the development and dissemination of a wide range of vaccines. Thanks to vaccines, we've saved 5 million lives a year by eliminating smallpox. We've essentially eliminated many other diseases in the developed world, including diphtheria, whooping cough, measles and polio. In the United States, with the introduction of the first measles vaccine in 1962, the number of measles cases went from roughly half a million a year to only a handful by the end of the 20th century [Orenstein et al., 2004].

Yet this great public health victory is slowly being eroded with an uptick in cases over the past 5 years, including 667 measles infections in 2014.[1] The return of the measles can be attributed to the growing vaccine refusal movement, which advocates against childhood vaccination, including the MMR vaccine (measles, mumps, and rubella). While many of us have heard the arguments of this movement against vaccines, why are they so effective with a small but significant fraction of parents? What reasons for skipping childhood vaccines are most convincing to different types of parents? How can physicians best address the concerns of parents?

One final topic. One of the leading causes of death in the United States is suicide. It's a staggering figure, but over 40,000 Americans die by suicide each year.[2] While our understanding of mental health disorders and factors that influence suicide has advanced tremendously, we remain especially poor at predicting who will follow through on a suicide attempt. We have been unable to identify unique predictors of suicide [Murphy, 1984]. Instead, we can identify a large at-risk population, a small percentage of which will actually attempt. Treating this group is generally effective for suicide prevention, but too many cases are missed since we cannot further focus our efforts. With such a large number of deaths each year, it is natural to ask: are there other unknown predictors of suicide we are missing?

These are just a few of the numerous questions for which we need better answers. Given the importance of these public health topics, issues that effect millions of lives, why don't we have an answer? Why can't we do the research necessary to provide actionable information?

Like all scientific pursuits, our ability to answer health questions depends on our access to relevant data. Without evidence from data, we can't provide meaningful answers. What about "big data" research, the popular buzzword that encompasses all manner of new research efforts from physics to psychology, from linguistics to literature? Where might we find big data for public health?

A patient visits a doctor, and the interaction is documented in a clinical record. This interaction happens over *a billion times* in the United States each year.[3] Surely this is enough to qualify as big data! These clinical records taken together have the potential to answer many important questions in medicine. Among the many goals of the Affordable Care Act passed by the United States Congress in 2010 was to digitize these records by incentivizing physicians to switch to electronic health records (EHRs). While the primary goal of the initiative was to reduce costs, an additional goal was to create a vast digital resource for health research [Adler-Milstein et al., 2014]. In large part, this has worked—the number of physician offices using EHRs has grown from around 50% in 2010 [Hsiao et al., 2012] to nearly 87% in 2015.[4] Millions of digital records for patients throughout the United States have created opportunities for secondary use of electronic medical records [Safran et al., 2007] that can help answer questions about adverse drug events or measure the quality of health care delivery.

---

[1] http://www.cdc.gov/mmwr/publications/index.html
[2] http://www.cdc.gov/nchs/fastats/leading-causes-of-death.htm
[3] http://www.cdc.gov/nchs/fastats/physician-visits.htm
[4] http://www.cdc.gov/nchs/fastats/electronic-medical-records.htm

Yet even if we had full access to an EHR with a billion clinical visits each year, we may not be able to answer the questions for the three topics posed above. Increased awareness of a health topic doesn't necessitate a clinical visit, parents come to believe in the dangers of vaccines outside of doctors' offices, and the indicators that may suggest suicide are likely not being recorded by a health professional. Where can we find big data to answer these and many other public health questions? What digital records can be analyzed to support research on these topics?

Perhaps surprisingly, we already have a large source of patient information outside of the doctor's office: **user-generated content** from the Web. This type of data includes, but is not limited to, blogs and microblogs, forum discussions, online reviews of products and services, and queries issued to search engines. But how does **social media** tell us anything about health? How can any of these online activities be used to answer important public health questions?

That is the topic of this book: how can large quantities of (often freely and publicly accessible) social media data inform public health? Public health—the area of medicine focused on the health of a population as a whole—depends on people's behaviors: what people do in their everyday lives. Public health topics are often more about what happens outside than inside of a doctor's office. Social media chronicles the lives of a population, recording their beliefs, attitudes, and behaviors on a wide variety of topics. Since health is an important part of people's lives, social media reflects these health topics. By analyzing social media we can gain new insights into public health.

Who is this Book for?

Analyzing social media for public health requires two broad areas of expertise: computer science and public health. We hope that academics, researchers, and practitioners from both areas will find value in this book. Maybe you're a data scientist who knows machine learning or natural language processing and wants to learn how to apply it to public health, or a health informaticist who wants to learn more about harnessing social media as an alternative data source, or a public health researcher who wants to learn about how new technologies offer new research possibilities. If so, you're the intended audience for this book.

For computer scientists, we expect that Chapter 2 will provide a summary of the core principles of public health, and Chapter 5 will survey the areas of public health most suited for work in social monitoring. For public health experts, we hope that Chapters 3 and 4 will summarize the major types of social media data and relevant analytics. All readers should benefit from Chapter 6, which describes limitations and concerns of this type of research. Of course, we encourage you to read the entire book and share in our amazement over what has been achieved so far, and what new research may yield.

We expect that you're coming into this field with one set of training and expertise, either on the computational side or public health side, and want to start learning more about the other area. This book is aimed at people in this stage, who want to know a little bit about the other side and how it can intersect with their own background. What this book will not do is make you an expert in a new area—this field is too broad and diverse to cover everything comprehensively in one book. For instance, this book won't teach you enough to go off and build a machine learning system if you don't already have that expertise—but it will introduce you to the common types of tools that are available and how they are used in social monitoring, which in turn will inform you about solutions available for your problems. And while this book can't possibly do justice to decades of public health research in so many areas, it will at least make you aware of the major areas of public health, why they are important, and how social media can help. The goal is to equip you with enough knowledge to start thinking and having conversations about how you can benefit from, or contribute to, this rapidly growing field.

Why a Book? Why Now?

This new field of social monitoring for public health is quite new, with the earliest foundational papers barely ten years old. In fact, many of the data sources we discuss in this book haven't even been around for that long. So why write a book now? While research in this area is fast paced, with new avenues of research yet unexplored, clear patterns have emerged to form a recognizable research landscape. We have some idea of what works, and what doesn't work. What characteristics of public health questions are best suited for social media analysis, and which computational tools are most suited for answering these questions. Our goal is to provide a firm footing on which new researchers, as well as experienced experts, can base new research projects that build on what we've learned so far. We cannot possibly foresee all of the exciting new advances in this field, but we hope this book provides a basis on which these advances can start.

Another goal of this book is to promote rigor when working with social data. Methods for careful study design and validation that are common in traditional public health research have sometimes been ignored in research using social media, especially in earlier work, in part due to disciplinary differences in methodologies and a lack of community norms and expectations about how this kind of research should be done. The entire field came under scrutiny after it was noticed in a widely publicized study that Google Flu Trends, a popular digital flu monitoring system that we discuss throughout this book, had started performing inaccurately and severely misfired in a recent year [Lazer et al., 2014b]. Researchers have made a lot of progress in addressing the limitations of social data, but there are unresolved concerns about reliability, validation, and ethics with this kind of research. We raise these issues in this book, particularly in Chapter 6, and we hope our discussion of these issues will encourage more thoughtful work in this area.

The Scope of this Book

This book focuses on public health surveillance applications: tasks in which we can learn about public health topics by passively analyzing existing social media data. We term this **social monitoring**, a term that is inclusive of a wide range of online data sources, from new social media platforms, to more traditional web forums, and to search engine queries.

There is a growing and promising area of research that examines how social media and electronic interventions can change health behaviors and improve health outcomes. However, while related in spirit, the tools, topics, and approaches of interventions have significant differences with public health surveillance and social monitoring. This book focuses on the latter to ensure a more comprehensive presentation.

CHAPTER 2

Public Health: A Primer

Sandra is a college student. One morning during the fall semester, Sandra wakes up with a fever, cough, and headache. She feels sick enough that she decides to go to her campus's student health services. At the clinic, a doctor diagnoses Sandra with influenza—the seasonal flu. For a young healthy person with no complications, the treatment is easy enough: drink plenty of fluids, stay in bed, and take ibuprofen or acetaminophen to help with the fever. After a few days, she will hopefully feel better and return to class.

Was it inevitable that Sandra contract the flu or could she have done something to prevent it? For many people, flu is a preventable disease. The seasonal flu shot offers remarkable protection against contracting influenza. The exact rates of immunity vary year to year, but on the whole, it is the single most effective step one can take to prevent a disease that infects tens of millions of Americans, hospitalizes hundreds of thousands, and kills thousands each year.[1] Many universities organize vaccination campaigns at the start of the academic school year, offering free vaccines to students to prevent flu outbreaks. For those who are medically able to receive the vaccination, momentary discomfort and minor side effects are a small price to pay for protection against a potentially deadly virus.

Both of these cases—Sandra receiving treatment for the flu and Sandra receiving a vaccine—are clear examples of healthcare and medicine. However, they are also within the scope of *public health*.

What exactly is public health and how does it differ from medicine in general? As a rough guide, medicine deals with the interaction of a single doctor and patient: Sandra receiving care from her doctor for influenza. On the other hand, public health focuses on an entire population and asks what can be done to improve the health and prevent disease in mass. How can we inoculate a population to a disease, and track an outbreak as it develops?

How many patients do you need to treat before you are in the domain of public health? After all, developing a new cancer drug can save millions of lives, but we wouldn't consider it public health. Conversely, an effective public health intervention may only impact a few hundred people. The distinction between the two isn't a matter of numbers.

Furthermore, the choice of topic alone doesn't determine if work is considered public health. Some areas of medicine fall almost entirely under the domain of public health, such as controlling environmental pollution to limit negative health outcomes or improving vehicle

---

[1]Flu has such a low mortality rate that many people are surprised to learn that influenza is a leading cause of death in the United States. Since it infects so many people, even a low mortality rate leads to thousands of deaths.

safety to prevent traffic fatalities. Other areas fall outside of public health research, such as new surgical or radiology techniques. But many domains touch both public health and traditional medicine, including drug overdoses, mental illness, and our example above: infectious disease and vaccinations.

What makes an area a public health topic isn't the disease or ailment: it's the types of interventions and goals.

Consider the vaccine example above. If Sandra had visited her doctor earlier in the semester, the physician might have recommended she receive her annual flu shot during her visit. This interaction isn't in the domain of public health. Furthermore, the research that goes into developing the vaccine isn't necessarily public health either. Her campus deciding to launch a vaccination campaign with the goal of reaching hundreds or thousands of students, or working with local clinics to ensure they distribute vaccine information—that is public health.

If what defines public health is a set of methods and goals, then what are they? This chapter provides an answer. We will outline the basic goals and principles of public health. Our goal is to provide basic fluency with the field to set the stage for understanding how social media can advance public health understanding.

Before we get into specifics, we should step back to consider the amazing success public health has had so far. Public health efforts have led to safer roads and cars to dramatically reduce traffic deaths, improved workplace safety, reduced pollutants to create safe drinking water, reduced infant mortality, dramatically reduced tobacco use to prevent lung cancer, reduced cavities through water fluoridation, improved our ability to control disease outbreaks, and nearly wiped out several infectious diseases with vaccines.[2]

Let's consider the seasonal influenza vaccine as just one example. Many of us are accustomed to our annual flu shot, but it's worth admiring this marvel of our modern public health system. We often forget just how unique it is to have a treatment that *entirely prevents* a disease from ever infecting a patient. After all, the first vaccine (for smallpox) was only invented at the turn of the 19th century. In the case of the seasonal flu shot, there are a number of challenging factors.

We'll focus for a moment on the United States. First, for a variety of reasons, each season's influenza strain requires its own vaccine. This means that researchers must develop a new vaccine each year. Second, in order to allow enough time to produce millions of doses of vaccines, decisions on what influenza strains should be included in the annual vaccine must be made many months before the start of flu season. Researchers make educated guesses based on currently circulating strains, as well as looking at countries in the southern hemisphere. Since these countries have winter during the U.S. summer, we can gain clues as to what strains may be circulating by looking at their flu season. As an aside, often times the reason that a flu shot is less effective is because unanticipated strains are circulating. Third, rapidly manufacturing safe and effective vaccines for the start of the flu season requires careful coordination between man-

---

[2] http://www.who.int/about/role/en/

ufacturers and government agencies. Finally, vaccines rolling off the manufacturing line isn't enough. Health organizations need to decide how many to order, and how to run vaccination campaigns. Should they run lots of advertising early in the season against a possible early seasonal peak, or should they run a longer campaign in anticipation of a late flu season? Will this season be mild, in which case they may not heavily advertise, or will it be a particularly severe season? It is a remarkable feat of the modern public health system that all of this comes together each year and results in tens of millions of Americans receiving a vaccine, preventing numerous infections, hospitalizations and deaths.

With a sense of amazement, let's proceed to discussing the techniques and goals of public health.

2.1   THE PUBLIC HEALTH CYCLE

Broadly speaking, public health focuses on two distinct goals. First, to monitor and assess the health of a population, including the identification of health problems. Second, to craft health policies to address the identified health problems, including the task of ensuring the population has access to appropriate care. Rather than being distinct goals, they are intertwined. As policies and healthcare practices are revised, public health researchers must reassess the population to understand the effectiveness of the policies and practices and adjust accordingly.

These two goals are reflected in the public health cycle, which consists of ten different components [Harrell and Baker, 1994].[3] Figure 2.1 illustrates how these components can be organized around three main activities.

- **Assessment:** monitoring the health of a population, and identifying and evaluating health issues.

- **Policy development:** education and development of community partnerships to come up with policies that address the results of assessment.

- **Assurance:** enforcing policies, providing access to care, and evaluating the results of the policies.

Social monitoring has a role to play in all three activities. It can be used to learn about a population, to help develop partnerships and debate policy, and to provide care. In disease prevention, we can measure infection prevalence in a population (assessment), network to create new partnerships with healthcare organizations to disseminate influenza information (policy development), and provide information on care, for example by sharing links to organizations providing vaccines (assurance). There are numerous examples of social media aiding health communication [Hawn, 2009, Moorhead et al., 2013] and various health interventions [Korda and Itani, 2013]. Many health agencies use social media for broadcasting information [Bartlett and

---

[3]http://www.cdc.gov/nphpsp/essentialservices.html

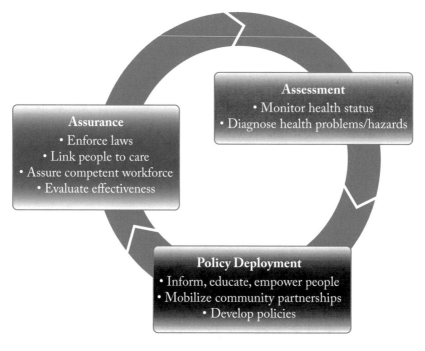

Figure 2.1: The three main stages of the public health cycle, along with their respective public health activities, as proposed by the Core Public Health Functions Steering Committee [Harrell and Baker, 1994].

Wurtz, 2015, Harris et al., 2013, Neiger et al., 2013], and doctors use social media to engage patients and the public [Lee et al., 2014b].

As we said at the end of the previous chapter, this book will focus on **assessment**, which in the case of social media typically involves the passive monitoring of data to learn about health issues, and their prevalence, in a population. Social media is ideally suited for surveillance: it provides a constant stream of information on a population that can be monitored for topics of relevance to public health. Additionally, monitoring tasks is a more accessible type of research for computer scientists looking to work in public health. The main tools in this domain are data collection and analysis, as opposed to designing interventions or working with patients. That's not to say that there aren't many examples of computer scientists working successfully in policy development or assurance. Rather, we find plenty of interesting problems in assessment, and we're sure you will too!

2.1.1   PUBLIC HEALTH SURVEILLANCE

Public health surveillance concerns the "continuous, systematic collection, analysis and interpretation of health data."[4] This includes monitoring for existing identified health concerns as well as discovering new issues. You may also hear the term *syndromic surveillance*, which is surveillance of a specific syndrome (a set of related symptoms).

Consider infectious disease surveillance, which is one of the largest and most widespread examples of public health surveillance. The United States has a fairly robust national surveillance system for infectious diseases. Perhaps the largest surveillance system is FluView,[5] the Centers for Disease Control and Prevention's (CDC) national influenza monitoring system. FluView encompasses several sources of data, including ILINet, a network of thousands of clinics throughout the United States that report weekly statistics on patients presenting with influenza-like illness. These reports, along with virology reports and other sources, make up a weekly CDC report that tracks the rate of influenza infection. A similar process is replicated on the state and local level in many jurisdictions, and many U.S. states produce regular flu reports. Due to its popularity as an application for the use of social media data, we'll discuss influenza surveillance in detail in Section 5.1.1.

National infectious disease surveillance extends to other notifiable infectious diseases, illnesses in which a physician is required to notify public health authorities of an infection. Examples include measles, ebola, and dengue.[6] Surveillance also extends to discovering new illnesses. This is how AIDS was originally identified, by the CDC pro-actively investigating unexplained infections [Curran et al., 2011].

Surveillance goes well beyond infectious diseases. Surveillance can identify novel tobacco products [Ayers et al., 2011a, Stanfill et al., 2011] and adverse reactions to medications [Budnitz et al., 2006], both of which have been achieved using social media (see Sections 5.2.2 and 5.4.2, respectively).

2.2   SOURCES OF DATA

Public health depends on data about populations to support its goals. Traditionally, public health draws data from two main sources.

The first is **surveys**, in particular telephone surveys, which have long been the backbone of public health. There are several, large-scale surveys run on a regular basis (typically annually) that provide a steady supply of public health data. Examples include the Behavioral Risk Factor Surveillance System (BRFSS) and the National Immunization Survey. BRFSS is run annually and collects detailed data from more than 300,000 Americans on a wide variety of public health topics, including access to medical care, mental health, exercise, and tobacco use. Some large-scale surveys rely on in-person interviews, such as the annual U.S. National Survey on Drug

---

[4]http://www.who.int/topics/public_health_surveillance/en/
[5]http://www.cdc.gov/flu/weekly/
[6]https://www.cdc.gov/mmwr/mmwr_nd/

Use and Health (NSDUH). Beyond these repeated surveys, many researchers commission one-time telephone or in-person surveys. These can include focus groups, which provide more free-flowing sources of information on public beliefs and attitudes. Online surveys are also growing in popularity due to their low cost, though numerous quality challenges remain [Cook et al., 2000, Dredze et al., 2015, Eysenbach and Wyatt, 2002]. Finally, many private polling companies also conduct health-related phone surveys. For example, Gallup uses phone surveys to measure the well-being of Americans.[7] A growing thread of work with social media data consider methods for enhancing or replacing traditional survey mechanisms [Benton et al., 2016b].

The second primary source of data come from **clinical encounters**. The influenza surveillance network described above, ILINet, is the largest such example. Large-scale surveillance networks require significant coordination as they rely on active reporting from clinics. More recently, researchers have turned to automated methods run on electronic medical records that enable scalability and reduce the strain on manual reporters.[8]

While these are the most common data sources for public health, the field has a tradition of seeking new and creative sources of data suited to specific analyses. These include monitoring drug sales and pharmacy records [Heffernan et al., 2004, Magruder et al., 2004] to track gastrointestinal illness [Edge et al., 2004] and use of nicotine replacement therapies [Metzger et al., 2005]. Others have used insurance company billing records to track mammographies [Smith-Bindman et al., 2006] and cardiovascular disease [Lentine et al., 2009]. Some unusual data sources include counting cigarette butt waste in cities [Marah and Novotny, 2011] and estimating community drug abuse by wastewater analysis [Irvine et al., 2011, van Nuijs et al., 2011, Zuccato et al., 2008].

2.2.1   LIMITATIONS OF TRADITIONAL DATA

Monitoring practices that rely on traditional data sources have their advantages and limitations. In general, these methods are well understood and are viewed as reliable, provided they are properly analyzed with biases corrected. Furthermore, many of these data sources go back many years (e.g., annual survey questions), allowing for comparisons over time.

However, we wouldn't be writing this book if there weren't disadvantages to traditional methods and thus opportunities for social media data to make improvements. In the case of telephone surveys, they are becoming *less accurate* over time, as fewer people use landline phones, and the response rate drops [Kempf and Remington, 2007]. This introduces particular bias against low-income and young adults in survey results [Blumberg and Luke, 2007]. Surveys are also expensive to conduct, especially if the survey size is very large or requires in-person interviews [Iannacchione, 2011]. The NSDUH survey mentioned above takes nine months to complete each year.

---

[7]http://www.well-beingindex.com/
[8]http://www.cdc.gov/ehrmeaningfuluse/syndromic.html

Clinical records address some of these issues, but are still expensive and complex to set up. Many of the topics covered in surveys do not appear in clinical records, or if they do, they are in unstructured text and thus hard to analyze. Both of these methods can be slow. We cannot measure today's influenza rate when we do not get clinical records or sentinel site reports more frequently than once a week. Finally, these methods can only cover certain topics, as discussed in Chapter 1. Many areas of public health are understudied because they lack sufficient data to support research.

2.2.2   OPPORTUNITIES FOR SOCIAL MONITORING

These limitations create opportunities for researchers and practitioners to use social media as a data source for learning about health and medicine [Grajales III et al., 2014]. Compared to traditional public health monitoring, social media-based monitoring is fast, cheap, covers a large population, and provides data on topics with little coverage from traditional sources.

One of the most popular social media platforms for health research has been Twitter [Williams et al., 2013], which provides real-time streams of public data, often for free. This type of data creates the potential for real-time health surveillance, which is generally unattainable with traditional methods.

Certainly social media is not a panacea for all problems, and will not replace traditional data sources. We'll discuss some of these limitations in detail in Chapter 6. However, social media can play a complementary role to traditional monitoring. For example, social media analysis can be used for hypothesis generation [Parker et al., 2015]: rapidly testing out ideas that are not yet worth the time and effort of traditional data collection. The most promising ideas can be forwarded to a more in-depth phase of traditional investigation. Social media can also complement survey data with respect to its demographic coverage. Young adults are overrepresented on Twitter [Duggan et al., 2015] yet underrepresented in telephone surveys, an especially important characteristic for topics like electronic cigarettes and illicit drug use.

A growing chorus of researchers argue that social media will play an important role in public health and epidemiology [Brownstein et al., 2009, Dredze, 2012, Salathé et al., 2012, 2013b]. The U.S. government has taken notice and has started to consider how social media data can aid public health efforts. This has included hosting competitions for building social media-based systems for disease surveillance [Biggerstaff et al., 2016].[9] [10] With social media adoption expanding,[11] and with new advancements in technology, social media is likely to have an increasing impact on public health.

---

[9]http://www.nowtrendingchallenge.com/
[10]https://nowtrending.hhs.gov/
[11]http://www.pewinternet.org/fact-sheets/social-networking-fact-sheet/

CHAPTER 3

Social Data

What constitutes "social data" and how can this type of data be used for public health monitoring? This chapter describes different types of social media, including well-known platforms like Twitter and Facebook, as well as other online platforms that may be less known but still valuable. We take "social data" as an broad term that includes a variety of the types of online data.

Before embarking on any social monitoring project, it is important to understand the social media landscape and the options for data sources. For example, it may surprise you to learn that Facebook, despite being the world's largest social network, is rarely used for social monitoring. This is due to a variety of factors, including how the platform is used by people and the tools available for data collection. In contrast, Twitter dominates the social monitoring community, for reasons that are scientifically motivated (it provides a large and relatively representative sample) and reasons that are not (the data is free and convenient). We'll compare different platforms, describing the affordances of different data sources and data types, their strengths and weaknesses, and their appropriateness for different health applications.

Finally, we briefly describe how to obtain data from a few popular platforms, with pointers to tools and tutorials.

3.1 WHAT IS SOCIAL DATA?

Social data refers to data that is created by people with the goal of sharing the data with others. For example, when people post messages or photos online to share with others, the text and images of the messages and photos are considered social data. **Social media** websites are the platforms through which social data is created. Examples of popular social media platforms include Twitter and Facebook. In general, social data is created by ordinary people, rather than professional writers or domain experts (e.g., clinicians).

This book will also use "social data" to refer to data that is created by people on the Web but not necessarily intended for social sharing, including search query data, because this data is prominently used for public health monitoring in addition to standard social media data. We also include data generated by people's online activities other than intentionally posted messages, like location information—the "digital traces" left behind by people's online behavior [Welser et al., 2008]. What we don't generally include is data created specifically for researchers (like survey responses), although we do discuss how new technologies can facilitate collection of that kind of data.

3.2   MONITORING OF SOCIAL DATA

Social monitoring refers to the act of analyzing social data—either by manually reading the data, or automatically using computational tools—to learn about the world. Many people use social media platforms to publicly share information about what they are currently doing and thinking. By analyzing social data, it is possible to infer what is happening around the world and within populations.

Social monitoring is also a form of *infodemiology*, or information epidemiology, a term introduced by Eysenbach [2002] to describe the study of health determinants and the sharing of health information on the internet. Some of the earliest studies of health on the internet looked at the quality of health information on available websites [Davison, 1996, Impicciatore et al., 1997]. Social monitoring focuses on studying user-generated content to learn about a population.

It is possible to measure and understand all sorts of population opinions and behaviors through social monitoring. For example, social media can be monitored to measure consumer sentiment [Bian et al., 2016, Chamlertwat et al., 2012] and political sentiment [O'Connor et al., 2010]. Social monitoring has been used for forecasting sales [Asur and Huberman, 2010], predicting financial markets [Bollen et al., 2011], forecasting elections [Digrazia et al., 2013, Tumasjan et al., 2010], and estimating crowd sizes [Sinnott and Chen, 2016] and traffic congestion [Tse et al., 2017]. It is also a rich resource for interdisciplinary work, such as combining health and economics [Althouse et al., 2014, Ayers et al., 2012b] or health and politics [Dredze et al., 2017].

Social monitoring can be used to answer scientific questions, often in social science [Cioffi-Revilla, 2010, Lazer et al., 2009], including learning regional dialects [Eisenstein et al., 2010] and learning associations with personality traits [Schwartz et al., 2013].

We mention all these examples from different areas to give a taste of the enormous potential of social data. Of course, this book will focus on applications in public health, which we'll survey throughout.

3.2.1   ACTIVE VS. PASSIVE MONITORING

Social monitoring can take an active or passive approach. **Active** monitoring requires explicit participation from users, while **passive** monitoring makes use of data already published by users, without requiring user interaction. An example of active monitoring is asking a sample of Twitter users which presidential candidate they favor, while a passive monitoring approach might analyze what Twitter users are writing about the candidates and infer sentiment toward candidates from the messages alone. Passive monitoring represents the bulk of research into social monitoring due to its relative ease and low cost.

We will focus on passive monitoring in this book, but will mention active approaches when relevant. See Hill et al. [2013] for a discussion on the utility of active approaches to public health surveillance compared to passive monitoring.

3.2.2   TYPES OF USERS

This book focuses on monitoring of people in a population, and we therefore focus on messages written by individuals. However, large swaths of social data are produced by organizations, bots, and spammers. These messages also have value in public health analyses. Heldman et al. [2013] considered how public health agencies can use social media and others discuss how the medical profession can use social media to communicate with the population [Moorhead et al., 2013, Thackeray et al., 2008]. McCorriston et al. [2015] introduce automated methods for differentiating Twitter accounts between individuals and organizations. Whether to detect and remove spammers in analyzing health messages in social media is the subject of debate [Allem and Ferrara, 2016, Kim et al., 2016], but certainly the presence of such messages should be considered when designing research studies.

3.3   TYPES OF PLATFORMS

Social data comes in many forms. Different online platforms and websites exist for different audiences and different purposes, and different platforms may be better suited for particular public health goals. This section will describe the different types of social media, and will discuss the types of health applications for which they are appropriate.

3.3.1   GENERAL-PURPOSE SOCIAL MEDIA

Blogs and Microblogs
Blogs (short for weblogs) are websites where individuals post messages and articles. Popular blogging platforms include Tumblr, WordPress, and Blogger.

Microblogs, such as Twitter and its Chinese counterpart, Sina Weibo, are social media platforms where users share brief "status updates." The defining characteristic of microblogs is the short message length, in contrast to standard blogs. For example, Twitter messages can be no longer than 140 characters, a restriction that has been in place since its inception (though it has been loosened in various ways, first by using URL shortening, and more recently by not counting usernames toward the limit). Other platforms like Facebook have higher length limits, but messages still tend to be short. Smaller specialty platforms often have specific features that can change how they are used, such as the now defunct app YikYak which offered users anonymity [Koratana et al., 2016].

Microblogs are popular avenues for sharing news as well as the current status, beliefs, and activities of users, making them desirable for social monitoring. These platforms are intended for broadcasting information, often to a general, public audience. As such, content on these platforms is most often public, even though private accounts are possible.

Microblog users will often share messages written by others, called "retweets" in Twitter. Retweets are repostings of previously-published messages, rather than original content, and are often handled separately in systems that use social media data, since retweet activity can differ from original tweet activity.

Social Networks

Social networking platforms, such as Facebook and LinkedIn, are websites where users can connect with one another. In contrast to microblogs, where users typically publicly broadcast information, information published on social networking platforms is typically shared with a limited audience, such as friends and coworkers. Such websites are primarily designed for maintaining relationships and accounts are often private, although there are plenty of public accounts on Facebook that share general news. For these reasons, social networks are used less commonly for public health surveillance. However, social network data can be valuable for research that investigates social factors [Cobb et al., 2011].

Media Sharing Platforms

Some social media websites primarily serve as platforms for sharing visual media, such as videos (e.g., YouTube) and photos (e.g., Instagram, Flickr) [Vance et al., 2009]. Media can reveal population attitudes and behaviors, such as dietary choices revealed through photos [De Choudhury et al., 2016a] and drug use captured in videos [Morgan et al., 2010]. Additionally, the comments on sites like YouTube can be helpful for some health applications [Burton et al., 2012a, Freeman and Chapman, 2007].

General-purpose sharing websites include Reddit and Digg, where users submit links to other websites and articles, in addition to media such as images and videos. These websites are typically organized into different categories of discussion, such as politics and science. For example, Reddit is organized into thousands of topic-specific "subreddits" which are created and moderated by users.

For social monitoring, often the text comments and discussions on these platforms are used as data rather than the media itself.

3.3.2   DOMAIN-SPECIFIC SOCIAL MEDIA

In addition to general-purpose social media, some websites exist for more narrow purposes, including in the domain of health.

Review Websites

Online reviews are a focused type of social media, where users write reviews (usually including numeric scores) of products and services. Some review websites are quite broad, like Yelp, which is most commonly used to review businesses and restaurants. However, many review websites are domain-specific, including in the domain of health. For example, RateMDs.com is a website where people can post reviews of their doctors, and Drugs.com allows users to write reviews of medications.

In the domain of public health, researchers have monitored review websites to detect food poisoning outbreaks (from restaurant reviews) [Harrison et al., 2014] and drug side effects (from medication reviews) [Yates and Goharian, 2013].

Patient Communities

There are many web-based communities designed for patients to share information and experiences with one another. Online communities often use **discussion forums**—websites where users can create and respond to threads of conversation and discussion—as the mode of communication. Forums can be used to communicate information as well as to provide social support. Some patient forums also function as support groups, such as the websites DailyStrength and MedHelp.

A well-known patient community is PatientsLikeMe, where patients share information, especially regarding treatment options. In a famous experiment, hundreds of PatientsLikeMe members experimented with a novel treatment for amyotrophic lateral sclerosis (ALS) and shared their results, functioning as an informal, grassroots clinical trial [Wicks et al., 2011].

Additionally, some grassroots patient communities have developed in general-purpose platforms. For example, people create "group chats" on Twitter, where interested users agree on a particular hashtag and meeting time, and regularly have a conversation on a topic (e.g., cancer support chat on a weekly basis). Approximately 10% of Twitter group chats are about health [Cook et al., 2013].

3.3.3   SEARCH AND BROWSING ACTIVITY

While most social media data consists of information that is *broadcast* by users, other useful sources of information are *activities* performed by users on the Web.

One of the most common types of web activity is **search**. A query in a search engine suggests an interest in a topic, and thus by analyzing what people are searching for, researchers can infer what people are interested in. In public health, search data was most famously used by the Google Flu Trends system (Section 5.1.1), which estimates flu prevalence based on the number of people who are searching for flu-related information, under the assumption that those who are interested in flu are probably experiencing flu.

Search engines, such as Google, Bing, and Yahoo, log the queries that are searched by users. Raw query logs are private data, but some engines make aggregate statistics about query volumes publicly available through services such as Google Trends, described in Section 3.5.

Search data can also be analyzed from domain-specific websites, such as PubMed [Yoo and Mosa, 2015], often through private services not publicly obtainable, in contrast to Google Trends. For example, researchers from the National Cancer Institute partnered with Ask Jeeves to understand the information needs of cancer patients [Bader and Theofanos, 2003], and Santillana et al. [2014a] obtained search data from UpToDate, a disease database used by clinicians, to infer disease prevalence from clinician activity.

Another useful type of activity is **browsing**—a trace of the web pages that are visited by a user. Such data can come from detailed logs recorded by browsers such as Google Chrome and Microsoft Internet Explorer, but this data is private and, as such, is typically limited to researchers working at these companies [schraefel et al., 2009]. Outside researchers can obtain browser activity logs directly from the machines of participants, but obtaining such data requires the recruitment of consenting volunteers, and thus such research will typically be small scale [Fourney et al., 2014].

A public source of browsing data comes from Wikipedia, which public health researchers have utilized. Wikipedia publicly publishes timestamped logs of visits to each article, and this data can be used to measure levels of interest in articles such as "Influenza" or "Dengue fever" [McIver and Brownstein, 2014, Tausczik et al., 2012]. A limitation of Wikipedia logs as a data source is that they do not contain information about the locations of the readers, unlike most of these data sources (Section 3.4.2). Instead, researchers have used the language of articles as proxies for location [Generous et al., 2014], such as resolving French-language articles to France. However, this approach is coarse and unreliable, as many languages are widespread.

3.3.4   CROWDS AND MARKETS

Crowdsourcing is a method of obtaining feedback and assistance from large numbers of people using online services. For example, Amazon's Mechanical Turk service is a general-purpose platform where users can post tasks to be completed, and other users are paid to complete the tasks [Buhrmester et al., 2011, Callison-Burch and Dredze, 2010, Goodman et al., 2013, Paolacci et al., 2010, Shapiro et al., 2013]. Crowdsourcing platforms allow for large-scale recruitment of workers to participate in projects.

Domain-specific crowdsourcing systems exist for health. For example, Flu Near You [Baltrusaitis et al., 2017, Crawley et al., 2014, Smolinski et al., 2015] is an application where users are periodically asked to share their health status—whether they are experiencing the flu—and this data can be used to estimate flu prevalence.

Crowd-based systems are a form of *active* monitoring, as discussed in Section 3.2.1. That is, learning about a population through crowdsourcing requires active involvement of the community, in contrast to the other platforms described above, in which publicly accessible information can be passively monitored.

Prediction markets are another way of harnessing crowds. Prediction markets are markets where future outcomes are traded—essentially, participants bet on what they think will happen—and prices can be used to measure the likelihood of different outcomes, according to the beliefs of the crowd. A few studies have shown prediction markets to be effective for forecasting diseases [Li et al., 2016, Polgreen et al., 2007, Tung et al., 2015].

3.3.5   COMPARISON OF PLATFORMS

The choice of data source in this diverse landscape is motivated by the type of application. **General-purpose** social media is a good source for identifying common, real-time trends. Topics such as influenza and vaccines are often discussed in the population at large, and so are well-represented in general-purpose social media. Furthermore, the nature of this type of platform provides real-time data, making it a good resource for studying current trends. Moreover, general-purpose platforms include discussion on a variety of topics outside of health, which allows one to study how people's habits and behaviors across a variety of domains interact with their health.

There are many general-purpose social media platforms, each with their own characteristics, features, and user populations. See Osborne and Dredze [2014] for a comparison of some of these platforms.

In contrast, **domain-specific** social media is best suited for an in-depth study of a specific health condition, especially those that are not common in the general population. The communities surrounding specific diseases and health topics provide rich details into the thoughts and behaviors of people engaged with the particular topic. Furthermore, many of these forums go back years, allowing for analysis of trends over a long period of time.

Search activity provides both real-time and historical capabilities. For example, Google Trends[1] provides historical data back to 2004, as well as daily updates of search activity (and in some cases, hourly). Additionally, search queries cover a wide range of subjects and so can provide information on low-prevalence health conditions. However, search activity often misses the "why" of health behaviors. While we can sometimes ascertain the reason behind a query based on the keywords in a search, often times it is impossible to know the user intention. In short, search traffic can answer "what," but not always "why." Additionally, because search activity in the form publicly available to researchers is aggregated across users, we cannot undertake the type of user analysis, or the linking of multiple queries to a single user, that may be needed for fully understanding the data.

We note that not only are different platforms used in different ways, but they are used for different **topics** of health discussion. De Choudhury et al. [2014b] compared the prevalence of mentions of health issues in tweets vs. search query logs, finding that more serious and stigmatizing conditions (e.g., sexually transmitted disease) are more prevalent in search logs than tweets, while certain benign conditions (e.g., jet lag) are more prevalent in Twitter. The authors thus suggest using caution when using Twitter to study high-stigma conditions, due to the apparent self-censorship being applied in public social media. However, a study of privacy settings in Facebook did not find large differences in content posted by public accounts vs. private accounts, which suggests that public social media data may not be as biased as previously believed [Fiesler et al., 2017].

---

[1]https://www.google.com/trends/

Finally, the users of different platforms have different **demographic** characteristics; see Duggan et al. [2015] for a summary.

3.4   TYPES OF DATA

We will now discuss the various forms of data available from social media, such as text (e.g., from tweets or search queries), locations (e.g., precise coordinates or geographic entities), and social network information (e.g, friends and followers).

3.4.1   CONTENT

The bulk of web content is in the form of **text**. Text can often be analyzed by searching for messages containing particular words or phrases of interest. More sophisticated analyses of text require *natural language processing*, described in Section 4.1.1, which is a computational approach to automating linguistic analysis of language. Most social monitoring uses text, and this book will focus on text.

Other content may come in the form of **images** (such as through Instagram) and **video** (such as through YouTube), which are often also accompanied by text in the form of captions, descriptions, and user comments. Images and video can be automatically analyzed and categorized using *computer vision*, a computational approach to analyzing imagery. For example, Garimella et al. [2016] found that automatically extracted tags of Instagram images can be useful for some health applications, like detecting excessive drinking. However, these types of tools are limited, so most research using this type of media have relied on manual analysis by people.

3.4.2   METADATA

Metadata, such as the time and location of messages, are crucial for social media analysis, in order to understand variation in populations.

Time

Almost all data on the Web is timestamped, and this information is typically trivial to collect. Often individual messages will come with timestamps, typically at the granularity of seconds. For some types of data, individual messages are unavailable, and only aggregate information over an *interval* of time, such as a day or month, is available. This is the case with services like Google Trends, which do not share individual search queries, but will provide the number of queries issued within various time intervals.

Location

Obtaining the location of a message—that is, the location of the author who wrote it—is often more difficult to obtain than time information, yet is often critical for health applications [Burton et al., 2012b]. Sometimes location information is provided by the social media platform.

For example, Twitter allows users to provide detailed location information in the form of latitude and longitude **coordinates**, which are sometimes available when users participate with a GPS-enabled device. Additionally, users can tag a location in their tweet, such as a city, neighborhood or specific point of interest. Unfortunately, this type of location data is rare; only a small percentage of tweets contain coordinates. For example, roughly 1–3% of Twitter messages are geocoded.

To increase the amount of geolocated data, researchers have developed a range of methods for automatically inferring location from available user data [Han et al., 2014]. There are a variety of methods for inferring location information, and we summarize these techniques in the next chapter in Section 4.3.1.

Location stability   Some location data is **dynamic**, meaning that it is updated to the current location for each message that is sent. GPS-tagged tweets and IP address geolocation are dynamic: they describe the location of the user when the activity was performed. Other information is **static** and may stay the same as a person moves around. For example, the location field of a user profile typically describes a user's primary home location, and does not change as a person travels. In general, the location of a user can be difficult to quantify, as locations can change and their accuracy can be subjective. For example, the identification of a user as residing in New York City, but who actually resides across the river in New Jersey, may be sufficient for many applications, even though the identification has the wrong state. Similarly, for a user who resides in El Paso, Texas, United States and works in Juarez, Chihuahua, Mexico, either city would be an accurate location despite being in different countries. In contrast, confusing a state or country would be a major geolocation error in most cases. See Dredze et al. [2013] for some of the challenges with evaluating geolocation.

3.4.3   SOCIAL NETWORK STRUCTURE

Another useful type of data is the network structure of a social platform, meaning the links or relationships between platform users. Social network structure is important for certain types of public health surveillance, such as predicting the spread of disease [Sadilek et al., 2012a,b] or understanding social support for healthy behaviors such as smoking cessation [Cobb et al., 2011].

Many platforms **explicitly** encode relationships between users. For example, in Facebook, users become "friends" upon mutual agreement. In Twitter, users "follow" other users, meaning that they subscribe to read the content of their followers. Following a user on Twitter is an asymmetric act and does not require mutual consent.

It is also possible to **implicitly** construct a social network. For example, one might infer a relationship between users if they communicate on a social network [Rao et al., 2010]. Even if explicit network information is available, implicit communication networks may also serve as a useful alternative, as these networks imply a different type of relationship. For example, Twitter users who communicate with each other may have a stronger relationship than users who follow each other but do not communicate. An "affiliation network" connects two users who share a common activity, like reading the same article or purchasing the same product [Mishra et al., 2013].

Network relationships can be either directed or undirected. **Undirected** relationships are symmetric, such as "friend" relationships in Facebook. **Directed** relationships flow from one user to another, such as a "follow" relationship in Twitter, in which one user follows another. Directed relationships can always be treated as undirected, if needed for a task, by removing the directionality.

3.5   DATA COLLECTION

We provide a brief summary of some of the most popular data sources in the social media research community and their associated APIs (application program interfaces) to serve as a starting guide. We encourage readers to visit the developer pages of the platform of interest for more information. Working directly with an API may be beyond the ability of researchers without technical training, although there are some guides written specifically for non-technical researchers (see Denecke et al. [2013], Yoon et al. [2013], Schwartz and Ungar [2015]). Some of the platforms described below make data available in easy-to-use formats, such as comma-separate values (CSV), usually including a rich variety of metadata, and others sell data in formats suitable for non-technical researchers.

Twitter   makes it very easy to obtain a wide variety of data using their API.[2] The streaming API provides a constant real-time data feed (approximately 1% of all tweets), while the REST API allows for searching through (limited) historical data. This allows researchers to collect targeted datasets based on specific keywords, locations, or users. There are a variety of tutorials and tools available for quickly starting a Twitter data collection.[3] Commercial options for larger data collection are available through Gnip, Twitter's enterprise API platform, which can provide samples larger than 1% and historical data matching specific queries. Gnip also provides data from other platforms, including Instagram and YouTube.[4]

Facebook   also has a robust API that allows for a number of different data queries,[5] including the Graph API, which is the primary way to read from the Facebook social graph. However, unlike Twitter, most Facebook data is not publicly available, and so it is not available unless one has explicit permissions from the data author. Additionally, Facebook provides various search methods but not a streaming method, making it difficult to obtain random samples of data. An alternate approach is to develop a Facebook app that obtains explicit sharing permissions from

---

[2]https://dev.twitter.com/
[3] For example, see http://socialmedia-class.org/twittertutorial.html and https://github.com/mdredze/twitter_stream_downloader.
[4]https://gnip.com/sources/
[5]https://developers.facebook.com/

users. While time consuming to develop and promote, investments in Facebook apps can yield valuable datasets [De Choudhury et al., 2014a, Schwartz et al., 2013].

Reddit   is a popular online forum and content-sharing service, where users can submit content and leave comments. It is one of the most popular forum sites, and therefore hosts content on a wide range of topics including health. Reddit provides an API that makes it easy to download content.[6]

Google Trends   provides aggregated keyword search data going back to 2004, with the ability to show trends specific to a location, time or category.[7] The site also suggests related queries, so that users can expand their search to find other queries relevant to their topic of interest. Google allows data to be exported in CSV format. Bing provides a similar tool, though it is aimed at advertisers.[8]

Additionally, some health-specific data resources are described in Section 5.1.4 for the purpose of disease surveillance.

---

[6]https://www.reddit.com/dev/api
[7]https://www.google.com/trends/
[8]http://www.bing.com/toolbox/keywords

CHAPTER 4

Methods of Monitoring

This chapter surveys methodology: the types of information that can be analyzed and how to do so, covering machine learning, statistical modeling, and qualitative methods. We will start by discussing quantitative methods—statistical analysis of data—including large-scale computational approaches to categorizing and extracting trends from social data, both at the level of populations and individuals. We also discuss validation, how you know when to trust your analysis. We then briefly discuss qualitative methods as a potentially richer but smaller-scale methodology. Lastly, we discuss different issues involved in designing a study, including methods for inferring population demographics, an important component of public health research.

This chapter touches on some advanced concepts in machine learning that won't be taught in depth in this book—though we do provide a few pointers to other tutorials and tools. Our aim is to provide a high-level overview of these methods, introducing important terminology, surveying different ways of approaching a problem, and giving examples of typical pipelines for conducting social monitoring.

4.1   QUANTITATIVE ANALYSIS

We begin by surveying the common quantitative methods for analyzing social data. We will summarize methods for identifying and filtering for relevant data, then analyzing the data, for example by extracting trends, and then validating the extracted information. This pipeline of quantitative methods is illustrated in Figure 4.1.

We will use one of the most common social monitoring uses, **influenza surveillance**, as our running example of social monitoring (with other tasks mentioned as needed) in order to illustrate the quantitative methodologies, but these methods are applicable to other public health problems as well.

The goal of influenza surveillance (described later in Section 5.1.1) is to measure the prevalence of influenza (flu) infection in a population. Official monitoring by government health agencies is delayed by at least one to two weeks, so social media has been used as a real-time supplementary source of monitoring. If you are familiar with social monitoring of influenza, you may find it strange that we chose to use it as our running example: the most popular system, Google Flu Trends, has been widely criticized for being unreliable. However, keep in mind that Google Flu Trends was one of the earliest systems to do this, using methods that are limited by today's standards. While the system resulted in substantial errors, they are errors that could have been avoided using more sophisticated techniques, including those implemented by Google Flu

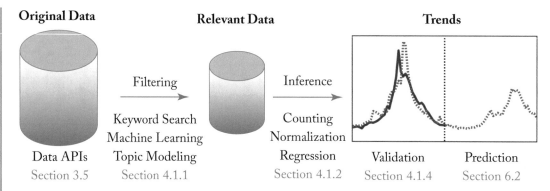

Figure 4.1: A standard pipeline of quantitative methods for inferring trends from social data. The various steps are described in the indicated sections.

Trends itself in later iterations [Santillana, 2017]. The takeaway is not that social monitoring for flu doesn't work, but that it must be done thoughtfully and validated extensively. We will point out potential pitfalls as we go along, discussing validation in Sections 4.1.4 and 4.2.1, with general limitations discussed extensively later in Chapter 6.

4.1.1   CONTENT ANALYSIS AND FILTERING

The first step in any data driven project is to ensure you have the data! When it comes to social monitoring, and the data comes in the form of tweets or messages on a variety of topics, it may be challenging to know if the available data support your research aims. Before investing time into planning a project, or collecting and processing data, you should determine if the data supports your goals. We typically advise researchers to identify 10 messages (by hand or through keyword search) that exemplify the data needed for the project. For example, Twitter provides a web search interface that makes these types of explorations easy.[1] This process can also help you decide the best method for filtering the data. If you can't find enough data at this stage, it's unlikely you'll be able to automatically mine the needed data.

When you know what you are looking for, you are ready to filter the data down to the subset of data relevant to the public health task at hand. For example, if the task is to conduct disease surveillance, then one must identify content that discusses the target disease (e.g., influenza). Approaches to filtering include searching for messages that match certain phrases, or using more sophisticated machine learning methods to automatically identify relevant content. We now describe these approaches in a bit more detail.

---

[1]https://twitter.com/search-home

Keyphrase Filtering or Rule-based Approaches

Arguably the simplest method for collecting relevant content is to filter for data (e.g., social media messages or search queries) containing certain **keywords or phrases** relevant to the task. For example, researchers have experimented with Twitter-based influenza surveillance by filtering for tweets contain words like "flu" or "fever" [Chew and Eysenbach, 2010, Culotta, 2010, 2013, Lampos and Cristianini, 2010]. For Twitter data, tweets matching certain terms can straight-forwardly be collected using Twitter's Search API, described in Section 3.5. We note that there exist clinically validated sets of keywords for measuring certain psychological properties, such as emotions [Pennebaker et al., 2001].

Keyword and phrase-based filtering is thought to be especially effective for search queries, which are typically very short and direct, compared to longer text, like social media messages [Carmel et al., 2014]. Search-driven systems like Google Flu Trends [Ginsberg et al., 2009] rely on the volume of various search phrases. Most research that uses search query volumes is in fact restricted to phrase-based filtering, as data available through services such as Google Trends (described in Section 3.5) come as aggregate statistics about certain search terms, rather than the raw text that is searched, which is private data.

A special type of keyword is a **hashtag**. Hashtags are user-created labels (denoted with the # symbol) used to organize messages by topic, used primarily in status updates (e.g., on Twitter) or photo captions (e.g., on Instagram). Because hashtags are widely used by different users, they can serve as useful filters for health monitoring. For example, if one was interested in understanding physical activities in a population, one might search for hashtags such as #workout or #running. However, additional filtering may be needed to distinguish between messages by ordinary users and by advertisers or media outlets, e.g., "I had a great #workout today!" vs. "Top 10 #Workout Tips." Rafail [2017] cautions that hashtag-based samples of tweets can be biased in unexpected ways.

Beyond searching for keywords or hashtags, other **rules** can be applied to filter for data. For example, one might choose to exclude tweets that contain URLs, which are less likely to be relevant for flu surveillance [Lamb et al., 2013]. By using machine learning, described in the next subsection, systems can learn which characteristics to favor or disfavor, rather than defining hard rules by hand.

Machine Learning Classification

Keyword-based filtering is limited because it does not distinguish between different contexts in which words or phrases appear. For example, not all tweets that mention "flu" indicate that the user is sick with the flu; a tweet might also discuss influenza in other contexts (for example, reporting on news of laboratory experiments on influenza) that are not relevant to surveillance.

A more sophisticated approach is to use **machine learning** to categorize data for relevance based on a larger set of characteristics than words alone. An algorithm that automatically assigns a label to a data instance (e.g., a social media message) is called a **classifier**. A classifier takes a message as input and outputs a discrete label, such as whether or not a message is relevant. For example, Aramaki et al. [2011] and Achrekar et al. [2012] constructed classifiers to identify tweets that are relevant to flu surveillance. Others have built classifiers to identify tweets that are relevant to health in general [Paul and Dredze, 2011, Prieto et al., 2014, Yin et al., 2015]. Lamb et al. [2013] combined multiple classifiers for a pipeline of filtering steps: first, a classifier identifies if a message is relevant to health, and if so, a second classifier identifies if a message is relevant to flu.

Classifiers *learn* to distinguish positive and negative instances by analyzing a set of labeled examples, and patterns learned from these "training" examples can then be used to make inferences about new instances in the future. Because training data is provided as examples, this approach is called **supervised** machine learning.

Common classification models include *support vector machines* (SVMs) and *logistic regression*, sometimes called a maximum entropy (MaxEnt) classifier in machine learning [Berger et al., 1996]. Logistic regression is commonly used for public health, traditionally as a tool for data analysis (see discussion of regression analysis in Section 4.1.3) rather than as a classifier, which predicts labels for new data. Recent advances in neural networks—loosely, models that stack and combine classifiers into more complex models—have made this type of model attractive for classification [Goldberg, 2017]. While more computationally intensive, neural networks can give state-of-the-art performance for classification.

Classifiers treat each message as a set of predictors, called *features* in machine learning, typically consisting of the words in a document, and sometimes longer phrases as well. Phrases of length n are called n-grams, while individual words are called unigrams. One can also use additional linguistic information as features. **Natural language processing** (NLP) is an area of computer science that involves processing human language, and a number of NLP tools exist to parse linguistic information from text. For example, Lamb et al. [2013] showed that classification performance can be improved by including linguistic features in addition to n-grams, like whether "flu" is used as a noun or adjective, or whether it is the subject or object of a verb.

We won't get into the technical details of classification in this book, but many of the common toolkits for machine learning (a few of which are described at the end of this section) provide tutorials.

Unsupervised Clustering and Topic Modeling

An alternative to classification is **clustering**. Clustering has the same goal as classification—organizing messages into categories—but the categories are not known in advance; rather, messages are grouped together automatically based on similarities. This is a type of **unsupervised** machine learning.

A popular method of clustering for text documents is **topic modeling**. In particular, probabilistic topic models are statistical models that treat text documents as if they are composed of underlying "topics," where each topic is defined as a probability distribution over words and each document is associated with a distribution over topics. Topics can be interpreted as clusters of related words. In other words, topic models cluster together words into topics, which then allows documents with similar topics to be clustered. Probabilistic topic models have been applied to social media data for various scientific applications [Ramage et al., 2009], including for health [Brody and Elhadad, 2010, Chen et al., 2015b, Ghosh and Guha, 2013, Paul and Dredze, 2011, 2014, Prier et al., 2011, Wang et al., 2014].

The most commonly used topic model is *Latent Dirichlet Allocation* (LDA) [Blei et al., 2003], a Bayesian topic model. For the domain of health, Paul and Dredze developed the *Ailment Topic Aspect Model* (ATAM) [2011, 2014], an extension of LDA that explicitly identifies health concepts. ATAM creates two different types of topics: non-health topics, similar to LDA, as well as special "ailment" word distributions with words that are found in dictionaries of disease names, symptom terms, and treatments. Examples of ATAM ailments are shown in Figure 4.2.

An advantage of topic models over simple phrase-based filtering is that they learn many words that are related to concepts. For example, words like "cough" and "fever" are associated with "flu." When inferring the topic composition of a document, the entire context is taken into account, which can help disambiguate words with multiple meanings (e.g., "dance fever"). A disadvantage is that they are typically less accurate than supervised machine learning methods, but the tradeoff is that topic models can learn without requiring annotated data. Another consideration of topic models is that they discover broad and popular topics, but additional effort may be needed to discover finer-grained issues [Prier et al., 2011].

Another use of topic models, or unsupervised methods in general, is for **exploratory** analysis. Unsupervised methods can be used to uncover the prominent themes or patterns in a large dataset of interest to a researcher. Once an unsupervised model has revealed the properties of a dataset, then one might use more precise methods such as supervised classification for specific topics of interest.

The technical details of probabilistic topic models are beyond the scope of this book. For an introduction, we recommend reading Blei and Lafferty [2009].

Which Approach to Use?

We have mentioned a variety of approaches to identifying social media content, including keyword filtering, classification, and topic modeling. These approaches have different uses and tradeoffs, so the choice of technique depends on the data and the task.

Most research using a large, general platform like Twitter will require keyword filtering as a first step, since relevant content will be such a small portion of the overall data, whether that requires keywords related to a particular topic like flu or vaccination, or health in general—for example, Paul and Dredze [2014] used a few hundred health-related keywords to collect a broad range of health tweets, which is still only a small sample of Twitter. Keyword filtering can be reasonably reliable for obtaining relevant content, although it may miss data that is relevant but uses terminology not in the keyword list, or it may identify irrelevant data that uses terms in

Figure 4.2: Examples of ailment clusters discovered from tweets, learned with the Ailment Topic Aspect Model (ATAM) [Paul and Dredze, 2011]. The word clouds show the most probable words in each ailment, corresponding to (clockwise from top left) allergies, dental health, pain, and infuenza-like illness.

different ways (e.g., slang usage of "sick"). Classifiers can overcome the limitations of keyword filtering, but are time consuming to build, so they are generally considered as a next step if keywords are insufficient. Topic models, on the other hand, are most often used for exploratory purposes—understanding what the content looks like at a high level—rather than looking for specific content.

These techniques are not mutually exclusive, and it is not unreasonable to combine all three. Let's illustrate this with an example. Suppose you want to use social media to learn how people are responding to the recent outbreak of Zika, a virus that can cause birth defects and had been rare in recent years until a widespread outbreak in 2015 originating in Brazil. (In fact, several researchers have done just that [Dredze et al., 2016c, Ghenai et al., 2017, Juric et al., 2017, Miller et al., 2017, Muppalla et al., 2017, Stefanidis et al., 2017].)

You decide to study this on Twitter, which captures a large and broad population. The first step is to collect tweets about Zika. There aren't a lot of ways to refer to Zika without using its name (or perhaps its Portuguese translation, Zica, or its viral abbreviation, ZIKV). You might therefore start with a keyword filter for tweets containing "zika," "zica," or "zikv," which would account for a tiny fraction of Twitter, but probably nearly all tweets about Zika, at least explicitly.

If you don't already know what people discuss about Zika on Twitter (since it was not widely discussed until recently, after the outbreak), you might use a topic model as a starting point to identify the major themes of discussion in your dataset. After running and analyzing a topic model, you might find that in the context of Zika, people use Twitter to talk about the latest research, vaccine development, political and funding issues, pregnancy and birth issues, and travel bans and advisories.

Suppose you are interested in using social monitoring to learn how people are changing their behavior in response to the virus, so you decide to focus on topics related to pregnancy and travel. To narrow down to tweets on these topics, you could construct a list of additional keywords for filtering, maybe using the word associations learned by the topic model, or using your own ideas about relevant words, perhaps gained by manually reading a sample of tweets. Finally, if you need to identify tweets that can't be captured with a simple keyword list (for example, you want to identify when someone mentions that they are personally changing travel plans, as opposed to more general discussion of travel advisories), then you should label some of the filtered tweets for relevance to your task and train a classifier to identify more such tweets.

Tools and Resources

A number of free tools exist for the machine learning tasks described above, although most require some programming experience. For a guide aimed at a public health audience rather than computer scientists, see Yoon et al. [2013]. For computationally oriented researchers, we recommend the following machine learning tools.

- **scikit-learn** (`http://scikit-learn.org`) is a Python library for a variety of general purpose machine learning tasks, including classification and validation.

- **MALLET** (`http://mallet.cs.umass.edu`) is a Java library for machine learning for text data, supporting document classification and topic modeling.

- **NLTK** (`http://www.nltk.org`) is a Python library for text processing, supporting tokenization and classification.

- **Stanford Core NLP** (`https://stanfordnlp.github.io/CoreNLP/`) is a set of natural language processing tools, including named entity recognition and dependency parsing.

- **HLTCOE Concrete** (`http://hltcoe.github.io/`) is a data serialization standard for NLP data that includes a variety of "concrete compliant" NLP tools.

- **Twitter NLP** (`https://github.com/aritter/twitter_nlp`) is a Python toolkit that implements some core NLP tools with models specifically trained on Twitter data.

- **TweetNLP** (`http://www.cs.cmu.edu/~ark/TweetNLP/`) is a toolkit implemented in Java and Python of text processing tools specifically for Twitter.

- **Weka** (`http://www.cs.waikato.ac.nz/ml/weka/`) is a machine learning software package that supports tasks like classification and clustering. It has a graphical interface, making it more user-friendly than the other tools.

4.1.2   TREND INFERENCE

We will now describe methods for extracting trends—levels of interest or activity across time intervals or geographic locations—from social media. First, we discuss how raw volumes of filtered content can be converted to trends by normalizing the counts. Second, we describe how filtered content can be used as predictors in more sophisticated statistical models to produce trend estimates. Examples of these two approaches, as applied to influenza surveillance, are contrasted in Figure 4.3.

Counting and Normalization

A simple method for extracting trends is to compute the volume of data filtered for relevance (Section 4.1.1) in each point (e.g., time period of location), for example the number of flu tweets per week [Chew and Eysenbach, 2010, Lamb et al., 2013, Lampos and Cristianini, 2010].

It is important to **normalize** the volume counts to adjust for variation over time and location. For example, the system of Lamb et al. [2013] normalizes influenza counts by dividing the volumes by the counts of a random sample of public tweets for the same location and time period. Normalization is especially important for comparing locations, as volumes are affected by regional differences in population and social media usage, but normalization is also important for comparing values across long time intervals, as usage of a social media platform inevitably changes over time.

Note that the search volume counts provided by Google Trends are already normalized, although normalization is plot dependent, and values cannot be compared between plots with establishing baselines for comparison. See Ayers et al. [2011b] for details.

Statistical Modeling and Regression

A more sophisticated approach to trend inference is to represent trends with statistical models. When a model is used to predict values, it is called **regression**. Regression models are used to fit data, such as social media volume, to "gold standard" values from an existing surveillance system, such as the influenza-like illness network from the Centers for Disease Control and Prevention (CDC).

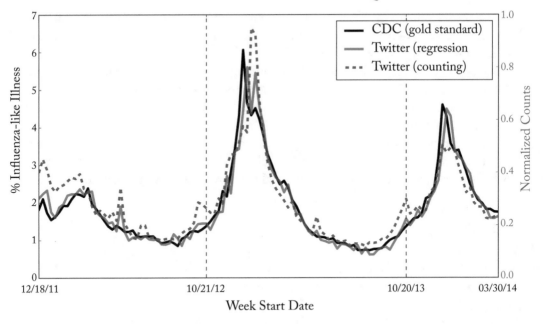

Figure 4.3: Estimates of influenza prevalence derived from Twitter (blue) alongside the gold standard CDC rate (black). The dashed Twitter trend is the normalized count of influenza-related tweets, estimated with the method of Lamb et al. [2013]. The solid Twitter trend uses the normalized counts in a regression model to predict the CDC's rates. The regression approach is based on research by Paul et al. [2014], in which an autoregressive model is trained on the Twitter counts as well as the previous three weeks of CDC data. Predictions for each season (segmented with vertical lines) are based on models trained on the remaining two seasons. The regression predictions, which incorporate lagged CDC data, are a closer fit to the gold standard curve than the counts alone.

The simplest type of regression model is a univariate (one predictor) linear model, which has the form: $y_i = b + \beta x_i$, for each point i, where a point is a time period such as week. For example, y_i could be the CDC's influenza prevalence at week i and x_i could be the volume of flu-related social media activity in the same week [Culotta, 2010, Ginsberg et al., 2009]. The β value is the regression coefficient, interpreted as the slope of the line in a linear model, while b is an intercept. By plugging social media counts into a regression model, one can estimate the CDC's values.

Other predictors can be included in regression models besides social media volume. A useful predictor is the trend itself: the previous week's value is a good predictor of the current week, for example. A kth-order **autoregressive** (AR) model is a regression model whose predictors are the previous k values. For example, a second-order autoregressive model has the form $y_i = \beta_1 y_{i-1} + \beta_2 y_{i-2}$. If predictors are included in addition to the time series data itself, such as the social media estimate x_i, it is called an autoregressive *exogenous* (ARX) model. ARX models have been shown to outperform basic regression models for influenza prediction from social media [Achrekar et al., 2012, Paul et al., 2014].

A commonly used extension to the linear autoregressive model is the autoregressive integrated moving average (ARIMA) model, which assumes an underlying smooth behavior in the time series. These models have also been used for predicting influenza prevalence [Broniatowski et al., 2015, Dugas et al., 2013, Preis and Moat, 2014].

Regression models can also be used for **forecasting** trends into the future. For example, rather than training models to predict y_i, one might train models to predict y_{i+k}, which corresponds to flu activity k weeks into the future, in the case of influenza surveillance.

4.1.3   INDIVIDUAL ANALYSIS

While trend prediction involves the modeling of populations through aggregate data, there are some applications where it is appropriate to build models that describe attributes of individuals.

One reason to use individual-level models is to make **predictions** about individuals, for example, predicting whether a person will become sick with the flu [Sadilek et al., 2012a,b] or predicting if a person is at risk for suicide [Thompson et al., 2014].

In addition to making predictions, individual-level models can also be used to **analyze** the individuals, to learn what characteristics are predictive of an attribute. For example, De Choudhury et al. [2014a] analyzed what types of Facebook activity are correlated with depression. This approach is called **regression analysis** because regression models are used to analyze and understand a fixed set of data, rather than to make estimates about new data, as in Section 4.1.2. This is a standard methodology in public health, e.g., to learn correlates of health outcomes, but in this case the data come from social media rather than traditional means (e.g., surveys or medical records).

In general, individual-level analysis with social media is less common than trend analysis, in part because this type of data is harder to obtain.

4.1.4   VALIDATION

An important part of social monitoring is to evaluate the validity of the information extracted from social media. We now summarize common methods for validation and evaluation.

Comparison to External Data

When possible, one should validate social media systems by comparing to data from gold standard surveillance systems, for example surveillance from the Centers for Disease Control and Prevention (CDC) in the United States. Most studies on social media influenza surveillance in the United States compare to CDC data.

Different metrics exist for comparing social media trends to gold standard trends. Perhaps the most commonly used metric for comparing two trends is the Pearson **correlation** coefficient, which measures the degree to which two trends have a similar shape.

If trends exhibit *autocorrelation*, meaning that a trend has similar values at nearby points in time or space, then the correlation between trends may be overstated, because such trends are more likely to have similar shapes by chance. In time series data, one can reduce autocorrelation by replacing the original value at each time point with the *difference* between the value and the value of the previous time point. These modified values now reflect the changes between consecutive points in time. This differencing procedure can be repeated multiple times until autocorrelation is removed, and then correlation can be measured between the modified trends with differenced values [Box and Jenkins, 1990]. This approach was used to evaluate influenza prevalence in Broniatowski et al. [2013].

Correlation metrics are appropriate when the trends are on different scales. For example, if a trend is produced using only counts on Twitter (Section 4.1.2), the values will be very different from the values in CDC data, but we can still measure whether the values rise and fall at the same time. In contrast, if trends are meant to be directly comparable to external data, for example by plugging Twitter values into a regression model that predicts the CDC data, then a more direct evaluation is to measure the **error** or difference between the predicted values and the true values. A common error metric is mean squared error (MSE), which is the average of the squared error at each point. Other error metrics include mean absolute error (MAE) and mean absolute percentage error (MAPE), where the error is normalized by dividing the absolute error at each point by the true value [Hyndman and Koehler, 2006, Lazer et al., 2014b].

MSE and MAE are similar, but MSE is weighted more heavily toward large errors, since the errors are squared. If a system makes small errors on average, but has some very large errors, then those large errors will affect MSE more than MAE. This can be a useful property if you care about having no or few large errors, even if that makes other errors slightly worse. Percentage error with MAPE measures error relative to the size of the value. For example, during the off-season of influenza, a small raw error might be very large relative to the overall flu prevalence. A metric like MAPE may better capture the performance in both low and high points of a season, while MAE and MSE may give more weight to the larger errors made during high season.

Another category of metrics measures **model fit**—how well the model explains or matches the data. Closely related to mean squared error is the **log-likelihood** of the true values under the regression model. Akaike information criterion (AIC) [Akaike, 1974] is a common metric that is based on log-likelihood, but adjusts the score to penalize models with larger numbers of parameters, since more complex models may not generalize well to future data (see below). Variants of AIC exist, such as Bayesian information criterion (BIC) [Schwartz, 1978].

Table 4.1 summarizes the metrics described above and provides their mathematical definitions.

Table 4.1: Definitions of commonly used validation metrics, described in Section 4.1.4. We assume the x values are predictions (e.g., by a social media system) and the y values are gold standard. N is the number of data points and K is the number of free parameters in the prediction model. For the correlation metric, σ_x denotes the standard deviation and $\bar{x}$ denotes the mean. For the last three metrics, it is assumed that the log-likelihood is of a Gaussian model, as in linear regression.

Metric	Definition	Objective
Correlation	$\dfrac{1}{N} \dfrac{\sum_{i=1}^{N} (x_i - \bar{x})(y_i - \bar{y})}{\sigma_x \sigma_y}$	Maximize
Mean squared error	$\dfrac{1}{N} \sum_{i=1}^{N} (x_i - y_i)^2$	Minimize
Mean absolute error	$\dfrac{1}{N} \sum_{i=1}^{N} |x_i - y_i|$	Minimize
Mean percentage error	$\dfrac{1}{N} \sum_{i=1}^{N} \dfrac{|x_i - y_i|}{y_i}$	Minimize
Log-likelihood	$-\sum_{i=1}^{N} (x_i - y_i)^2$	Maximize
Akaike IC	$2K + 2 \sum_{i=1}^{N} (x_i - y_i)^2$	Minimize
Bayesian IC	$K\log N + 2 \sum_{i=1}^{N} (x_i - y_i)^2$	Minimize

In addition to comparing the entire trends, one might wish to evaluate specific characteristics of a trend. For example, the CDC's "Predict the Flu" competition [Biggerstaff et al., 2016, Centers for Disease Control and Prevention, 2013] (described in Section 2.2.2) evaluated trend predictions based on certain features of the influenza season: the week the season starts, the week the season ends, the week the season peaks, and the prevalence at the peak.

Out-of-sample validation   An important issue with validation is whether the metrics described above are computed on *in-sample* data—the data that the model or algorithm is estimated with, called **training** data in machine learning—or *out-of-sample* data, called **test** data in machine learning, which is held-out data that the algorithm has never seen before. Evaluating a system on in-sample data creates false confidence in model accuracy, because a model that fits current data well may do a poor job of predicting data in the future. A model that trivially memorizes the expected predicted values for the training data has learned nothing about out-of-sample data. This issue is called **over-fitting**. While some metrics, like AIC, try to correct for this, a more robust approach is to evaluate how well a model predicts trends on data it has never seen before.

One method for creating test data is **cross-validation**, in which the data is partitioned into distinct subsets for training and testing, and the evaluation metrics from different test subsets are averaged to produce a final score. *K-fold* cross-validation is when $\frac{1}{K}$ of the data are held-out for testing, and this process is repeated K times on different held-out partitions. Common choices are 5-fold and 10-fold cross-validation, where 20% and 10% of data are held-out for testing, respectively. Model fit metrics like AIC are typically applied to in-sample data, although AIC is asymptotically equivalent to *leave-one-out* cross-validation, where only one instance is left as test data in each fold [Stone, 1977].

When evaluating time series trends, data can often be naturally partitioned into train and test sets. For example, when evaluating influenza trends, one might train on earlier seasons, and evaluate on the latest season available [Paul et al., 2014]. When only one season of data is available, one might train on the first half and evaluate on the second [Culotta, 2010].

Often, one needs to evaluate models not just to estimate performance, but also to compare competing models or to tune parameters of a machine learning algorithm. In such cases, the best practice is to use multiple sets of held-out data. One held-out set, usually called the **development** set in machine learning, is used for comparing models and tuning parameters, and models can be evaluated on development data multiple times during research. Separately, a test set should be used for evaluation after all tuning and model selection is done. This two-step process is used to avoid over-fitting by tuning models to the evaluation data. Cross-validation can also be used for the development phase, with a separate held-out test set used at the end of the process.

Added value of social media   When evaluating trends from social media data, it is important to compare to fair baselines that contextualize the gains made with social media. For example, influenza surveillance research has found that simple autoregressive models (Section 4.1.2) using only CDC data are often better than social media trends alone, though combining both still leads to improvements [Goel et al., 2010, Lazer et al., 2014b, Paul et al., 2014]. It is therefore a good practice to compare social media systems to systems using only traditional surveillance, to fairly measure the value added by incorporating social media.

Intrinsic Evaluation of Filtering Quality

Another important type of evaluation is measuring the quality of the filtering step (Section 4.1.1). For example, if one is estimating influenza prevalence by filtering for flu-related tweets, then it is important to know how many tweets identified by the filter (e.g., a machine learning classifier) are actually relevant to influenza surveillance [Aramaki et al., 2011, Lamb et al., 2013]. This type of evaluation is especially important for tasks that do not have existing surveillance data to compare to.

Simply computing the accuracy of positive and negative classifications is usually not appropriate for evaluating filtering, since often the labels are highly imbalanced: if 99% of tweets are irrelevant, then a filter that labels all tweets as negative will have an accurate of 99%, but this is a useless filter, since no relevant tweets will be identified.

Instead, one should use metrics that evaluate the classification of relevant instances in particular. In psychology and some areas of public health this is often called "face validity", since it directly measures whether the classifier achieves its stated aims [Holden, 2010]. The most common metrics used in machine learning are **precision** and **recall**. Precision (also called *positive predictive value*) is the percentage of instances classified as positive that are actually positive. Recall (also called *true positive rate*, *sensitivity*, or *hit rate*) is defined as the percentage of positive instances that were correctly classified as positive. One can think of precision as a type of accuracy, while recall is a measure of coverage. The two metrics are often in competition: recall can be increased by classifying more instances as positive, which may lower precision. The two scores are often summarized by the *F1 score*, which is the harmonic mean of precision and recall.

A common alternative to precision and recall is the **receiver operating characteristic**, also called an ROC curve, which is a curve that plots the true positive rate against the false positive rate. The **area under curve** (AUC) metric is the area under the ROC curve, used to summarize the curve with a concise metric. An AUC of 0.5 is equivalent to random guessing (true positives and false positives are equally likely), while scores significantly above this baseline show that the classifier is making meaningful predictions. While AUC is a popular measure, Hand [2009] found that it is fundamentally incoherent in terms of misclassification costs, and should be avoided.

These metrics require one to know the labels of the instances. If a supervised classifier is being evaluated, then typically one will compute these metrics on the labeled data that was used to train the classifier. If a supervised classifier is used, these evaluation metrics should be computed on out-of-sample test data rather than the training data, for example using cross-validation, as described in the previous subsection. If no data is used to train the filter, such as with human-defined keyword filters or with unsupervised topic modeling, then it is not necessary to evaluate on held-out data, but one will need to label a set of instances in order to compute the evaluation metrics.

For more discussion on evaluating systems for text data, we recommend Resnik and Lin [2010].

4.2   QUALITATIVE ANALYSIS

Most social monitoring is quantitative, used to extract trends or to support predictive modeling. Quantitative analyses typically rely on automated methods in order to process large volumes of data.

Some studies, in contrast, rely on small-scale, manual analysis of data. We refer to such analysis as **qualitative**, in which humans review and characterize raw data. Typically, data is **annotated** to characterize the data under a standard classification system. Annotations are sometimes called *labels* (in the machine learning community) or *codes* (in the medical community).

The goal of qualitative analysis is to understand the content of the social media messages being analyzed, providing a richer understanding of the data than quantitative methods, which provide only aggregate trends. For example, to support the understanding of Twitter-based influenza research, Chew and Eysenbach [2010] and Nagar et al. [2014] performed content analyses of tweets during influenza epidemics by labeled flu-related messages. Both of these studies additionally performed a quantitative analysis, using the annotated tweets to extract temporal trends. Research that combines qualitative and quantitative methods is called **mixed-methods** research.

Other examples of qualitative analysis in social media include characterizing pain-related tweets [Heaivilin et al., 2011], identifying complaints of medical mistakes in Twitter [Nakhasi et al., 2012], and characterizing public responses to poor air quality in Chinese social media [Wang et al., 2015b].

Such studies typically require an initial step of filtering for relevant content, using techniques described in Section 4.1.1, rather than starting with a completely random sample of content.

Annotations from qualitative data analysis can also be used to support machine learning, by using the annotated data to train supervised classifiers (Section 4.1.1). For example, Wang et al. [2015b] used annotations originally created for a qualitative study to then train a supervised classifier to automatically identify more such messages.

Finally, we note that manual analysis can potentially be scaled up with the help of crowdsourcing (Section 3.3.4), although crowd workers will generally not have expertise in the subject area, so this approach is most often used to collect simple annotations that can be straightforwardly described, rather than more complex analysis.

4.2.1   VALIDATION

Evaluating Qualitative Analysis

Like with quantitative research, it is important to be able to characterize the validity and reliability of qualitative analyses, though the methods differ. A general strategy with qualitative research is to have multiple researchers separately perform the same analysis: if multiple people independently arrive at the same conclusions after analyzing the data, then this is evidence that the analysis is consistent.

This strategy is most often used when annotating data, where the quality of the annotations can be measured by how well the annotators agree on the labels. Data annotation is typically conducted by two or more annotators who independently label the same data, following guidelines describing the possible labels. Various metrics exist to measure the agreement between annotators, such as *Cohen's kappa* [Cohen, 1960] or the more general *Fleiss' kappa* [Fleiss, 1971]. For a survey and in-depth discussion of agreement metrics, see Artstein and Poesio [2008].

Annotator agreement scores can be used to quantify the reliability of the annotations, as well as to measure the difficulty of the annotation task, as difficult annotation tasks will have lower agreement. Recognizing that a task is too difficult for annotators can suggest that the task was not well defined and needs refinement, although it can also be a consequence of data that is inherently ambiguous or difficult to interpret (for example, due to sarcasm).

Evaluating Quantitative Systems Qualitatively

Qualitative analyses can also help with understanding the performance of quantitative systems. Tufekci [2014] recommends performing "qualitative pull-outs"—manually inspecting small samples of the research data to check that it is being used and interpreted in the intended way. For example, with influenza surveillance from tweets, a good practice would be to periodically examine a sample of tweets that are being used by the system. Are the tweets actually about an individual being sick (as intended), or is something else being captured, like retweets of a news article? Qualitative checks like these can identify problems that might not be immediately apparent through quantitative metrics, and catching these types of problems early can keep a system from making large errors later.

4.3   STUDY DESIGN

4.3.1   STUDY POPULATION

The first step to studying a population is to ensure you are studying the right population, which means you need to know what population your data is drawn from. In practice, this means ensuring that the data sample is representative of the target population for the research question (or if it is not representative, to be able to characterize in what way it is biased). Health behaviors and outcomes often vary significantly across different groups of people, and research findings should be contextualized by the demographic groups they apply to. This is especially important when studying health, since there are often large disparities in health behaviors and outcomes by population [Shonkoff et al., 2009]. Traditional public health methods for data collection, such as surveys and clinical encounters, include demographic information on the subjects. Demographic variables frequently include location, gender, age, race, ethnicity, income, and can include a variety of categories depending on the domain [Mislove et al., 2011].

Even though public health has a long tradition of using demographics in analyses, there have been few studies that have done so with social media. Three recent examples have started to show how this information can and should be utilized.

Coppersmith et al. [2015b] used gender- and age-matched controls in their broad analysis of mental health disorders on Twitter. By using these controls, they were able to account for other factors related to gender and age that may influence a person's language in relation to their mental state. They used similar controls when designing the CLPsych 2015 Shared Task on Depression and PTSD on Twitter [Coppersmith et al., 2015a]. Similarly, Reis and Culotta [2015] used a matched control group based on various mental health factors, such as depression and anxiety, to measure the effects of exercise on mental health using Twitter. Finally, Weeg et al. [2015] correlated self-reported prevalence rates for 22 diseases with the number of times the diseases were mentioned on Twitter while correcting for demographic bias in the U.S. Twitter population.

One reason there has been relatively little attention to demographics in social monitoring research is that social data often does not include explicit demographic information. For example, Twitter profiles do not contain a field for a person's age and gender; only the user's location is provided, and that is optional. However, progress has been made in developing methods to automatically infer demographics of social media users, which can potentially improve social monitoring.

Inferring Demographic Attributes

Researchers have turned to a variety of automated methods to infer user demographics from their available data. We briefly summarize the most common approaches. For a more detailed summary, see Volkova et al. [2015b].

The most common approach to demographic inference relies on supervised classifiers trained on the **message text** of each user [Burger et al., 2011, Pennacchiotti and Popescu, 2011b, Rao and Yarowsky, 2010, Volkova et al., 2015a]. For example, all of a user's posts are collected into a single document, that is paired with the demographic trait of the user and used for training data. These methods rely on both the topics discussed by a user, and their language use [Rao et al., 2010, Schwartz et al., 2013], in identifying associated traits.

Another source of information about a user's demographics comes from their **social network** [Al Zamal et al., 2012, Bergsma et al., 2013]. The underlying assumption is that users frequently talk to, or are friends with, users who share their demographic traits, e.g., men talk to men, teenagers talk to teenagers, etc. This is known as *homophily*, the tendency of individuals to associate with others who share common bonds or characteristics [McPherson et al., 2001]. In some cases, it may be more valuable to observe a user's friend's comments than the user's own comments [Volkova et al., 2014].

Self-identification can be a reliable source of demographic information. Many users will self-identify in their profile or through explicit statements in content they author [Beller et al., 2014]. Several studies have shown that a user's profile name can be used as a feature in a demographics classifier [Bergsma et al., 2013, Chang et al., 2010, Knowles et al., 2016, Liu and Ruths, 2013, Rao et al., 2011]. Similarly, the location of the user can inform demographics by relying on demographics and location information from Census data [Mohammady and Culotta, 2014].

Finally, **follower lists** can be used to characterize the interests of a user, which are indicative of their demographics. Culotta et al. [2015] combined existing demographic follower information from popular websites (e.g., ESPN, Oprah) with follower lists to infer Twitter user demographic attributes.

Throughout all of these approaches, the most commonly studied demographic categories are age [Nguyen et al., 2013, Pennacchiotti and Popescu, 2011b, Rao et al., 2010] and gender [Alowibdi et al., 2013, Burger et al., 2011, Ciot et al., 2013], followed by race and ethnicity [Bergsma et al., 2013, Pennacchiotti and Popescu, 2011b] and political preference [Pennacchiotti and Popescu, 2011a, Volkova et al., 2014]. Others have considered personality [Quercia et al., 2011, Schwartz et al., 2013], occupation [Sloan et al., 2015], and income level and education [Volkova et al., 2015b].

A separate line of research has studied demographic identification in search queries [Bi et al., 2013], which shares some commonalities with these tasks in social media, but has received less attention due to the restrictions on obtaining search query data grouped by user.

Several research groups have made demographic classification tools and datasets available, mostly for Twitter.

- The **World Wide Well Being Project** hosts several lexica and other resources: `http://www.wwbp.org/data.html`

- Volkova et al. [2015b] provide data and code to accompany their tutorial: `http://www.cs.jhu.edu/~svitlana/`

- Culotta et al. [2015] provide code and data for their system: `https://github.com/tapilab/aaai-2015-demographics`

- **LexHub** hosts tools and datasets for language analysis in the social sciences: `http://lexhub.org/`

- **Demographer** [Knowles et al., 2016] infers demographics from names of Twitter users: `https://bitbucket.org/mdredze/demographer`

Geolocation

Traditional demographics include location, which is provided more consistently in social media than other demographic characteristics. Platforms like Twitter and Facebook allow users to provide a specific set of coordinates with a message, or tag a place (e.g., a point of interest or city).

Unfortunately, this type of location data is rare; only a small percentage of tweets contain coordinates. For example, roughly 1–3% of Twitter messages are geocoded. To increase the amount of geolocated data, researchers have developed a range of methods for automatically inferring location from available user data [Han et al., 2014]. We briefly summarize the most common approaches.

The most straightforward method for determining location relies on user **biographic** information. In many social media platforms, users have "profiles", which can include self-reported locations. Locations may be structured or unstructured. Twitter, for example, allows free-form text in the profile, so users provide locations such as "NYC" or "Baltimore, MD". A challenge with this type of data is resolving different mentions of the same location, such as "NYC" and "New York City," as well as detecting fake locations such as "Candy Land" [Graham et al., 2014, Hecht et al., 2011]. One approach is to create alias dictionaries [Bergsma et al., 2013] that resolve location mentions to structured locations [Dredze et al., 2013]. Kiciman et al. [2014] used geo-tagged data to learn to map profile strings to specific locations.

When users do not explicitly provide their location, it can sometimes be inferred from the textual **content** that users share [Eisenstein et al., 2010, Roller et al., 2012, Wing and Baldridge, 2014, 2011]. This can be done using cues such as linguistic dialects, mentions of geographic features or names of landmarks, and mentions of other local entities such as sports teams. Such approaches are prone to error and may require many messages from users to make accurate inferences. Additionally, the **social network** itself can indicate geolocation [Rahimi et al., 2015a,b] as users are more likely to communicate with other users in the same geographic area [Bergsma et al., 2013].

Geolocation can focus on the user or the specific message. Most research considers the task of user (author) geolocation, the identification of an author's primary (home) location [Cha et al., 2015, Compton et al., 2014, Eisenstein et al., 2010, Han et al., 2014, Jurgens et al., 2015, Rout et al., 2013]. This may be defined as the primary area from where a person tweets, or their home location (where they reside at night). User geolocation systems rely on multiple tweets from each user to identify the location.

The task of tweet geolocation requires the identification of the location where a single tweet was written [Dredze et al., 2013, 2016a, Osborne et al., 2014]. This approach is necessary when geolocation decisions must be made quickly, with limited resources, or when the location of a specific tweet is required. For example, when analyzing a corpus of millions of tweets from millions of users, it may not be feasible to collect a large sample of tweets from each user for user geolocation.

For some platforms—primarily search and browsing logs—the location can be estimated from the IP address of the user. This can provide a location when no information is provided by the user, but IP address-based geolocation is unreliable [Poese et al., 2011].

The efficacy of these methods vary based on platform, and geographic granularity. Overall, they can provide an order of magnitude increase in the number of geocoded messages [Dredze et al., 2013].

As with demographics, a number of tools exist for Twitter geolocation:

- **Carmen** [Dredze et al., 2013] is a Python library that uses a combination of geocoordinates and profile information to provide a structured location for a given tweet: `https://gith ub.com/mdredze/carmen-python`. An older Java version is also available: `https://gi thub.com/mdredze/carmen`

- The **Discussion Graph Tool** from Microsoft Research implements the location method from Kiciman et al. [2014]: `http://research.microsoft.com/dgt/`

- **Twofishes** is a geocoder that translates strings to coordinates: `https://github.com/fou rsquare/fsqio/tree/master/src/jvm/io/fsq/twofishes`

- **pigeo** [Rahimi et al., 2016] is a Python tool that predicts the geolocation for a given text input or Twitter user: `https://github.com/afshinrahimi/pigeo`

- **TextGrounder** [Speriosu et al., 2010] anchors natural language expressions to specific regions of the Earth based on a region-topic model that infers word distributions for each region discussed in a given corpus. `https://github.com/utcompling/textgrounder`

4.3.2   CAUSALITY

A study's conclusions may be causal or merely correlational. Consider the public health example of marijuana legalization. Suppose it was found that states that legalized marijuana have seen increases in marijuana use since legalization. This alone is a correlational relationship between legalization and use. A causal claim might be that marijuana legalization leads to more marijuana use, but perhaps marijuana use would have increased in those states even if it had not been legalized, because it was already gaining in popularity (which led votes to support legalization). To make such a claim, the study would need to be designed in a way to provide stronger evidence of causality.

Most social media research is correlational. Because social data is usually passively monitored—that is, the data is generated organically, without direction from the researchers—the usual ways of designing experiments to determine causality do not apply. The gold standard for experimentation is a randomized controlled trial, in which subjects are randomly assigned to a "treatment" group that receives whatever we want to measure the effect of, vs. a control group that does not. There are many problems for which it is impractical or impossible to create a randomized controlled trial—we can't randomly assign people to live in states that did or did not legalize marijuana, for example. In practice, most social media studies are observational.

Various techniques exist to infer causality even with observational data that is passively collected, including techniques that attempt to simulate the assignment to treatment and control groups. *Matching* techniques create treatment and control groups by collecting data from pairs or strata of subjects that did and did not receive the "treatment" but are otherwise similar in some way. Continuing with the example of marijuana legalization, one might construct a control group by choosing states that did not legalize marijuana but are otherwise as similar as possible to the ones that did—for example, with similar demographics and similar levels of marijuana use prior to legalization. A few studies have used matching in social media research [Cheng et al., 2015, Pavalanathan and Eisenstein, 2016, Reis and Culotta, 2015].

One general purpose matching technique, *propensity score matching* [Rosenbaum and Rubin, 1985], has been widely studied (see Austin [2011] for a survey and tutorial) and found to be effective when applied to online data [Paul, 2017]. This type of matching builds a probability model of the propensity of a subject to receive treatment or not—for example, the probability that a state will legalize marijuana based on its characteristics—and subjects with similar propensities are matched. Two recent studies used propensity score matching to study health in social media. Rehman et al. [2016] measured how one's exposure to public health information affected sentiment toward vaccination, as expressed in Twitter. De Choudhury and Kiciman [2017] measured how types of social support in a Reddit community affected ones future risk of suicidal ideation.

4.3.3   CROSS-SECTIONAL VS. LONGITUDINAL ANALYSIS

A common distinction in observational studies is whether the data is cross-sectional or longitudinal. The difference is perhaps easiest to explain with an example. Suppose you want to estimate the prevalence of influenza over time, measured in weekly intervals, and you do so by sampling 1000 people and determining their illness status. The cross-sectional approach would sample a new set of 1000 people each week, where each week's data would be considered a different cross section of the population. The longitudinal approach would sample 1000 people once, and track them each week. That is, cross-sectional data captures a slice of the study population at a particular point in time (perhaps repeatedly), while longitudinal data makes multiple observations over time from the same population.

In social media, cross-sectional data is easier to obtain, and is generally suitable for tasks like population-level health surveillance, while longitudinal data is generally needed for performing individual-level analyses, or for inferring causality as discussed above. Longitudinal data is used for tasks like measuring how one's long-term behavior has affected their health, or how one's sentiment or awareness has changed over time. Most studies with social media are cross-sectional, though some studies have collected longer-term data on users to understand changes in mental state [De Choudhury and Kiciman, 2017, De Choudhury et al., 2016b], progression in behavior like drinking [Liu et al., 2017], and understanding transitions in phases of illnesses [Paul et al., 2015b, Sidana et al., 2016].

The choice of platform affects which type of data can be collected. With Google Trends, longitudinal data is not available, since only aggregate statistics are released in order to preserve privacy. With Twitter, the streaming API will give a sample that will not include the same population over time. However, Twitter does provide APIs to collect historical tweets from a given user, so one could construct a longitudinal dataset of certain users. The API has limits on how many tweets can be collected per user (the most recent 3,200) and how many users can be downloaded (900 per 15 minutes, at the time of writing),[2] so datasets constructed in this way may be incomplete and smaller than what can be collected with the streaming API. Alternatively, the streaming API allows for collecting all tweets from a set of users in real-time. The most natural platforms for longitudinal data are online communities and discussion forums, where the entire history is publicly available and small enough to download, and where many users actively contribute over time.

---

[2]https://dev.twitter.com/rest/public/rate-limits

CHAPTER 5

Public Health Applications

We now turn to what can be learned about public health from social data. The wide breadth of areas that have been explored reflects the diverse topics covered by social data, and the widespread interest in these uses across public health. This includes monitoring of diseases, both acute and chronic; health-related behaviors, including diet, substance use, and vaccination; environmental factors, including natural disasters and air quality; healthcare quality and safety, including the monitoring of medication side effects; and mental health.

In summarizing the major threads of research in social monitoring for public health, we will show what can be done, rather than going into detail on how a study was done or what was learned. Think of this chapter as a buffet, where the reader can learn a little bit about several topics, rather than focusing in depth on specific studies. The chapter is organized into five main sections covering broad areas of public health, with each section providing an introduction to the area and its importance to public health, followed by a summary of social media research in that area.

We begin each section by framing the problem. What are the goals of each area of public health? What data is needed to support these goals? How is the data typically collected, and what data gaps exist? We then turn toward social data and describe how new research offers a data solution to these problems.

On the next page, you will find a table that summarizes the many different applications that will be explored in this chapter.

5.1 DISEASE SURVEILLANCE

One of the major tasks of public health is surveillance: the continuous, systematic collection, analysis, and interpretation of health-related data. Public health activities rely on surveillance data to plan and implement interventions, and to evaluate the effectiveness of interventions. A common type of surveillance, syndromic surveillance, tracks symptom data from a population to identify and monitor early outbreaks of a disease. This type of surveillance includes identifying outbreaks of rare diseases, which may mandate reporting to a public health agency, or tracking infection rates of common diseases, such as seasonal influenza.

Disease surveillance requires a sophisticated, widespread network of sentinel sites to track infections throughout the population. These networks are time and labor intensive to build and maintain, requiring a significant investment of resources.

Table 5.1: An overview of the social monitoring applications described in this chapter

Section	Application	Summary of Social Monitoring Uses
5.1.1	Influenza surveillance	Tracking seasonal influenza trends, early detection, forecasting, understanding transmission patterns
5.1.2	Other infectious diseases	Tracking the spread of diseases like dengue and West Nile, and awareness of diseases like ebola and Zika
5.1.3	Chronic disease	Tracking geographic patterns in chronic illness, understanding disease progression, discovering correlates of disease
5.2.1	Diet and fitness	Understanding dietary and fitness patterns in different populations, discovering dietary correlates of health outcomes
5.2.2	Substance use	Measuring prevalence of and attitudes toward different substances including tobacco and e-cigarettes, alcohol, and other drugs including prescription drugs
5.2.3	Prevention and awareness	Understanding vaccine behaviors and attitudes (including anti-vaccination sentiment), measuring public awareness of different diseases and public reactions to health guidelines
5.3.1	Disasters and emergencies	Using social data for situational awareness during emergencies such as natural disasters, understanding population behaviors during disasters
5.3.2	Foodborne illness	Identifying cases of foodborne illness through reports on social media including restaurant reviews
5.3.3	Air quality	Measuring public perceptions of air quality, particularly in urban areas with high pollution
5.3.4	Climate change	Understanding people's awareness of and response to climate data
5.3.5	Gun violence	Identifying new instances of gun violence, which is not systematically documented in the U.S.
5.4.1	Healthcare quality	Measuring perceptions and estimating quality of healthcare clinics based on social media reports and reviews of doctors
5.4.2	Medication safety	Detecting drug and medication side effects reported by people online
5.5.1	Depression	Discovering indicators of depression, understanding and predicting depressive episodes, including postpartum depression
5.5.2	Suicide	Understanding suicide risk factors, detecting instances of suicidal ideation
5.5.3	Mood	Inferring emotional states of online users
5.5.4	Other mental illnesses	Understanding patterns in mental illnesses including post-traumatic stress disorder (PTSD), eating disorders, addiction, and schizophrenia

Consider the example of influenza surveillance in the United States as run by the Centers for Disease Control and Prevention (CDC). The CDC uses five different surveillance networks to track influenza-related activity in the United States. Perhaps the most well-known surveillance network is ILINet: the U.S. Outpatient Influenza-Like Illness Surveillance Network, which covers 36 million patient visit each year. ILINet encompasses 2,800 outpatient healthcare providers in all 50 states, as well as Washington D.C., Puerto Rico, and the U.S. Virgin Islands. You can learn more about ILINet on the CDC's website: `https://www.cdc.gov/flu/weekly/overview.htm`.

On a weekly basis, these healthcare centers report the total number of patients seen, and the number of patients that presented with influenza-like illness (ILI). ILI includes patients who have the symptoms of a flu infection, but no other cause is identified. Note that these patients have not necessarily confirmed the infection through laboratory testing, hence influenza-*like* illness. This distinguishes syndromic surveillance from other types of surveillance: the diagnosis is not confirmed, but the symptoms are sufficiently indicative of the disease that they are useful for early detection.

These statistics are aggregated and released on a weekly basis as part of the CDC FluView program, which provides estimates of the influenza rate nationally as well as in ten regions of the United States as defined by the Department of Health and Human Services. FluView estimates are used by the CDC, as well as state and local health agencies to make decisions about influenza response, such as advertising vaccination programs, alerting hospitals to increase staffing and bed availability, and closing schools if outbreaks become severe [Dugas et al., 2012].

ILINet is an excellent program and does a good job of covering the United States on the whole. However, even this comprehensive program leaves a lot of information gaps. Not every provider reports on time, or at all, so coverage gaps can emerge. While coverage is sufficient to provide national and regional numbers, they are not sufficient to provide all state and local jurisdictions with complete pictures of flu activity in their area. For this reason, many areas run their own surveillance systems. Collecting and aggregating thousands of provider reports takes time, which results in a delay of 1-2 weeks in reporting. This delay can be costly when reacting to a large outbreak.

Despite being a strong surveillance system, the gaps in data are limiting. This explains some of the excitement in Google Flu Trends, which promised to help fill in some data gaps, providing early reports and potentially covering finer-grained geographic areas. This is also why there have been so many studies using a variety of social data sources—search queries, Twitter posts, Wikipedia page views—to track influenza.

Most work on disease surveillance using social media has focused on infectious diseases, especially influenza-like illness. A systematic literature review of social media-based disease surveillance found 15 articles about influenza-like illness, 6 about other infectious diseases, and 4 about non-infectious diseases [Charles-Smith et al., 2015], though we will describe many more articles not included in this review.

5.1.1   INFLUENZA

Most digital disease surveillance systems have been for influenza, which is a widespread seasonal virus.

The earliest digital influenza surveillance systems used **search query data**. The use of search query volume as an indicator of influenza prevalence was first demonstrated by Eysenbach [2006], who referred to this approach as "infodemiology." This study was conducted before search trend data was publicly available. To obtain query volumes, Eysenbach purchased Google advertisements for the search queries "flu" and "flu symptoms," and the advertisement tracking system provided statistics about the traffic to those queries. This study found search traffic to be correlated with government surveillance data. Later, Polgreen et al. [2008] demonstrated that search query data from Yahoo could be correlated with influenza prevalence.

In 2008, Google launched Google Flu Trends (GFT) (shown in Figure 5.1), which is perhaps the best-known digital disease surveillance system [Ginsberg et al., 2009]. The original GFT model used a simple univariate regression model (Section 4.1.2) using volumes averaged from several hand-selected queries. However, GFT has been criticized for poor predictive performance, first for underestimating the prevalence of swine flu in 2009-2010, and then for greatly overstating the flu prevalence during the 2012-2013 season [Lazer et al., 2014b, Santillana et al., 2014b]. Google has updated their model multiple times in response to these shortcomings [Cook et al., 2011, Copeland et al., 2013, Stefansen, 2015], and external researchers outside of Google have developed their own flu models using publicly available search data from Google Trends [Preis and Moat, 2014, Santillana et al., 2014b, Wang et al., 2015c, Xu et al., 2010, Yang et al., 2015, Yuan et al., 2013]. As of August 2015, Google no longer publicly posts new Flu trends but continues to share historical data. New trends are shared directly with research teams on request [Google Flu Trends, 2015].

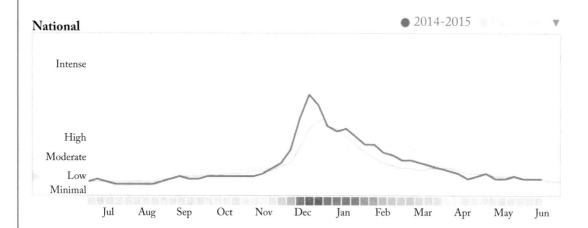

Figure 5.1: A screenshot of the Google Flu Trends system.

Beyond search, many researchers have used data from **Twitter** to monitor influenza. Several researchers first published Twitter-based studies shortly after Google Flu Trends was released [Chew and Eysenbach, 2010, Culotta, 2010, de Quincey and Kostkova, 2010, Lampos and Cristianini, 2010, Signorini et al., 2011]. Later research used more sophisticated models, including with machine learning and natural language processing, to improve Twitter-based estimation [Achrekar et al., 2012, Aramaki et al., 2011, Doan et al., 2012, Lamb et al., 2013, Lampos and Cristianini, 2012, Lampos et al., 2017, Li and Cardie, 2013, Sun et al., 2016, Velardi et al., 2014].

Other web sources have been considered as well, including blogs [Corley et al., 2010] and Wikipedia visits [Generous et al., 2014, McIver and Brownstein, 2014, Priedhorsky et al., 2017]. Nsoesie et al. [2014a] showed that influenza can be estimated by analyzing cancellations of restaurant reservations through OpenTable.

Which data source is best? A comparison of Google, Twitter, and Wikipedia during the 2012-2015 influenza seasons found Google to have the highest sensitivity and positive predictive value, followed by Twitter and then Wikipedia [Sharpe et al., 2016]. Research has also shown that better influenza predictions can be obtained by **combining** signals from multiple web sources [Santillana et al., 2015]. Yang et al. [2017] combined electronic health records with Google Trends data, and Won et al. [2017] combined Google Trends data with a phone survey system.

The majority of influenza research with social media has focused on surveillance in the United States, but some research has conducted surveillance in **other countries**, including the United Kingdom [Doan et al., 2012, Lampos and Cristianini, 2010, Szomszor et al., 2012], Japan [Aramaki et al., 2011], South Korea [Shin et al., 2016], China [Feng and Hossain, 2016, Li and Hu, 2016, Sun et al., 2014, 2017, Yuan et al., 2013, Zhang et al., 2014a], and Portugal and Spain [Prieto et al., 2014]. Paul et al. [2015a] evaluated the Twitter surveillance in ten English-speaking countries, including Australia, New Zealand, and South Africa, finding worse performance outside of North America. Pollett et al. [2017] evaluated Google Flu Trends in several Latin American countries, finding good performance in Mexico but poor performance in many South American countries.

Some research has evaluated surveillance in **fine-grained locations**, including New York City [Broniatowski et al., 2013, Nagar et al., 2014, Sadilek et al., 2012b] and Hong Kong [Xu et al., 2017]; hospital-level surveillance in Baltimore, Maryland [Broniatowski et al., 2015] and Omaha, Nebraska [Araz et al., 2014]; and mass gatherings such as music festivals [Yom-Tov et al., 2014a].

Beyond estimating current prevalence, some researchers have incorporated social data into **forecasting** models, using data from Google Flu Trends [Dugas et al., 2013, Nsoesie et al., 2013, Shaman et al., 2013] and Twitter [Iso et al., 2016, Paul et al., 2014]. Influenza forecasting with social data was the subject of the CDC's "Predict the Flu" contest described in Section 2.2.2 [Biggerstaff et al., 2016].

An important component of influenza forecasting is modeling the **spread** of disease. Sadilek et al. [2012a,b] modeled the spread of influenza using Twitter by looking at social interactions and location proximity. Yom-Tov et al. [2015] showed how Twitter data can be used to estimate parameters of influenza transmission dynamics, namely the secondary attack rate and serial interval. Zhang et al. [2017] also used social media data to estimate parameters of a disease transmission model. Dredze et al. [2016b] and Hawelka et al. [2014] derived global travel data from geolocated tweets, which can be used to forecast the global spread of an infection [Bogoch et al., 2016].

5.1.2 OTHER INFECTIOUS DISEASES

Other infectious diseases have been successfully tracked with social monitoring, albeit to a lesser extent than influenza.

A prominent target of disease surveillance is dengue fever, a flu-like illness in tropical climates, which researchers have tracked using search query volume [Althouse et al., 2011, Chan et al., 2011, Li et al., 2017]. Google Dengue Trends, a spinoff of Google Flu Trends, was developed to estimate dengue prevalence in tropical countries [Gluskin et al., 2014]. Dengue fever has also been examined in Twitter [Gomide et al., 2011].

Other surveillance research includes monitoring Lyme disease through search volume [Seifter et al., 2010], cholera through tweets and news media [Chunara et al., 2012], norovirus (search) [Desai et al., 2012], *E. coli* (tweets) [Diaz-Aviles and Stewart, 2012], malaria (search) [Ocampo et al., 2013], and bubonic plague (tweets) [Da'ar et al., 2016]. Zou et al. [2016] used social media for surveillance of infectious intestinal disease, and Deiner et al. [2016] used search and social media data to analyze the seasonality of conjunctivitis (pink eye).

Research has also examined the utility of social media for surveillance of the 2014 ebola virus outbreak in West Africa [Odlum, 2015b,c, Odlum and Yoon, 2015], although some research has cast doubt on whether social data would have had utility for detecting this outbreak [Yom-Tov, 2015]. While social data may have been limited for surveillance of disease incidence of ebola, a number of researchers have looked at social media to measure public perceptions of the ebola outbreak [Fung et al., 2014, Lazard et al., 2015, Odlum, 2015a, Rodriguez-Morales et al., 2015, Towers et al., 2015].

Similar research has looked at the 2015 Zika virus outbreak in the Americas through social media [Juric et al., 2017, Muppalla et al., 2017]. Multiple studies conducted content analyses of Twitter to understand what is being said about Zika and by whom, to understand public awareness and responses to the outbreak [Miller et al., 2017, Stefanidis et al., 2017]. McGough et al. [2017] used data including search, social media, and news media to forecast Zika.

Resources such as Google Trends and Wikipedia visit logs make it easy to look for trends for a variety of diseases. Some studies have investigated multiple diseases at once, using search volume data [Carneiro and Mylonakis, 2009, Pelat et al., 2009] and Wikipedia browsing data [Generous et al., 2014, Priedhorsky et al., 2017]. These studies analyzed trends for West Nile virus, gastroenteritis, chickenpox, HIV, plague, and tuberculosis, in addition to other diseases already discussed. In perhaps the broadest study, Milinovich et al. [2014] analyzed search volumes related to 64 infectious diseases, finding significant correlations with official monitoring systems for 17 of the diseases.

5.1.3   NON-INFECTIOUS DISEASES AND CHRONIC ILLNESS

While most disease surveillance systems have focused on acute, infectious diseases, there has been some work on social media analysis of chronic conditions.

A number of studies have analyzed search activities related to **cancer** in search engine logs, with the goal of inferring and understanding events and needs experienced by cancer patients [Bader and Theofanos, 2003, Ofran et al., 2012, Paul et al., 2015b, 2016b]. Similar research analyzed patient needs over time in cancer forums [Eschler et al., 2015]. Research with search logs has even shown that cancer can potentially be detected early based on symptoms that people search. Paparrizos et al. [2016a,b] classified diagnoses of pancreatic cancer using search query logs before the date of diagnosis, and found that the classifier could "identify 5% to 15% of cases, while preserving extremely low false-positive rates (0.00001 to 0.0001)."

Researchers have also examined discussions of **pain** in social media [Tighe et al., 2015], including dental pain [Ahlwardt et al., 2014, Heaivilin et al., 2011], back pain [Lee et al., 2016], and migraine headaches [Nascimento et al., 2014].

A variety of both acute and chronic illnesses were examined in Twitter by Yin et al. [2015], including cancer, hypertension, and asthma. Ram et al. [2015] found that tweets and search data can be used to predict asthma-related emergency department visits. Other research has also estimated asthma rates from Twitter data [Dai et al., 2017, Zhang et al., 2016]. Social media has also been analyzed to understand chronic diseases that require regular management, including diabetes [Liu et al., 2016] and human immunodeficiency virus (HIV) [Jin et al., 2016, Young et al., 2014, Young and Wang, 2017].

Others have used social media to infer **indirect** measures of chronic conditions, looking for correlates of the conditions rather than the conditions directly. For example, Fried et al. [2014] found that tweets related to dietary patterns are correlated with rates of diabetes, Gore et al. [2015] found that tweets about nutrition and fitness are predictive of obesity, and Eichstaedt et al. [2015] found that tweets describing stress and emotional states are correlated with rates of heart disease. Culotta [2014] investigated 27 health-related statistics in U.S. counties, finding significant correlations with tweets for six of the health conditions.

Social data has also been used to test **unanswered hypotheses** about various illnesses. For example, Milojevi [2016] used Twitter to test a hypothesis that solar eruptions and geomagnetic storms are triggers of migraine headaches. This is an example of a hypothesis that could not feasibly be tested with traditional data, while Twitter affords the ability measure migraine incidence at the temporal granularity necessary to align with solar eruptions. This study, however, found no association between these two activities. Delir Haghighi et al. [2017] used Twitter reports to understand how changes in weather affect people with fibromyalgia. Moccia et al. [2016] and Simpson et al. [2016] used Google Trends and Twitter, respectively, to provide new evidence that multiple sclerosis has seasonal patterns.

5.1.4   SYSTEMS AND RESOURCES

A number of disease surveillance systems make their data publicly available for others to use. We list some of these systems here. See Brownstein et al. [2009] for a list of other resources.

- **HealthMap.org** tracks news articles related to recent disease epidemics, providing a geographic visualization to monitor diseases around the world.

- **HealthTweets.org** makes Twitter trend data available over time and location [Dredze et al., 2014]. By default, the website provides influenza estimates from the system of Broniatowski et al. [2013] and Lamb et al. [2013]. Other trends are possible upon request.

- **Google Flu Trends** makes available their data in the form of weekly influenza predictions as well as dengue predictions.[1] As of August 2015, the service is no longer operational, but historical data is still available.

- **EpiCaster** is a web-based application for assessing and forecasting disease epidemics, such as influenza and ebola [Deodhar et al., 2015a].[2] It visualizes data from traditional sources as well as web-based sources including Google Flu Trends. A similar system, FluCaster, focuses on flu [Deodhar et al., 2015b].[3]

- **FluTrack.org** provides data and visualizations of flu-related tweets [Chorianopoulos and Talvis, 2016].

- **The Columbia Real-Time Infectious Disease Forecasts** provides weekly ILI forecasts based on CDC and Google data: http://cpid.iri.columbia.edu/.

- **The Now Trending** competition's winning entry shares ongoing statistics about health-related Twitter data: https://nowtrending.hhs.gov/.

5.2   BEHAVIORAL MEDICINE

Human behavior drives many aspects of health. What did you eat for breakfast today? How much alcohol did you drink? Did you get this year's flu shot? All of these are choices individuals make that can have a direct impact on a person's health. These decisions all come together under the broad category of behavioral medicine.

[1] https://www.google.org/flutrends/
[2] http://socialeyes.vbi.vt.edu/epicaster/epicaster.html
[3] http://ndssl.vbi.vt.edu/apps/flucaster/

Behavioral medicine combines a wide range of disciplines to study how people make choices about their health and how these choices affect a person's health and wellbeing. The areas of health covered by behavioral medicine are diverse, because our behavior can have a wide range of effects on health: diet and exercise, substance use, and vaccination, to give a few examples. Behavioral medicine also encompasses many disciplines since human behavior touches many fields of study: epidemiology, psychology, sociology, and nutrition, just to name a few.

The key challenge to collecting data relevant to the study of behavioral medicine topics is that these behaviors take place outside of the doctor's office. While doctors can diagnose an illness, they rely on the self-reports of patients to understand what behaviors may have contributed to the illness.

A myriad of problems arise when relying on this type of information collection. While some people visit a physician when they have a medical issue or for a regular checkup, many do not, and many of the health issues that arise from a behavioral decision may not trigger an office visit, e.g., addiction. If someone does see a physician, we cannot expect a doctor to solicit a wide range of information about health behaviors. A doctor is likely to ask "do you smoke?" but not what types of products or what factors are the greatest barriers to quitting. Even to simple questions like "do you smoke?" a person may not provide an accurate answer. Maybe they do not want to admit that they are a smoker, or they think that a few cigarettes every week does not qualify them as a smoker. Self-reports can be notoriously unreliable [Fisher and Katz, 2000]. Finally, even if doctors are able to collect accurate information on these topics, we lack mechanisms for collecting and aggregating this information. ILINet described in the previous section is a massive undertaking and only collects a small number of data points per provider. Expanding this type of program to include a wider range of health information would be exceedingly difficult and costly.

If not from doctor visits, where does data on behavioral medicine come from? Population surveys provide the primary source of information. For many important areas of behavioral medicine, the government runs large-scale national surveys on a regular basis. Surveys can focus on the questions directly relevant to the behavioral topic, and reach a population inaccessible by working through providers. We've discussed before (Section 2.2) some of the drawbacks of telephone surveys in terms of reliability and population coverage. We'll outline two examples of large surveys critical to understanding population health behaviors in the United States.

The Behavioral Risk Factor Surveillance System (BRFSS)   is the largest telephone survey of the United States population focused on health-related behaviors. BRFSS collects data from all 50 states, Washington, D.C., and 3 U.S. territories. In total, the survey reaches more than 400,000 adults every year and is the primary source of information on a large number of health behaviors, including smoking, obesity, and access to healthcare services.[4]

---

[4]https://www.cdc.gov/brfss/index.html

A survey of this size is not cheap. BRFSS had $18 million in funding in 2015.[5] Even with this level of funding, the survey does not include all questions of interest, as adding a single new question can be expensive. This means that while BRFSS yields a wealth of data each year, there are still data gaps that cannot be addressed by the current survey.[6] [7] For example, the survey cannot reach homes without telephones, which means that people residing in nursing homes are excluded. Self-reports are notoriously unreliable for some types of behavioral questions, such as self-reports of heights and weights [Cameron and Evers, 1990]. Additionally, BRFSS is organized by the CDC but run by individual states, which can vary their survey methods, making comparisons across states challenging.

The National Survey on Drug Use and Health (NSDUH)   is another example of a large, national U.S. survey of health-related behaviors, in this case on the use of tobacco, alcohol, illicit drugs, and mental health.[8] NSDUH involves in-person interviews of tens of thousands of individuals about their use of a wide range of substances. If you ever take the survey (and one of the authors of this book has) you'll discover that it's extremely extensive, covering almost every kind of drug you can imagine. The data is a primary information source for both federal and state health agencies in making decisions about treatment facilities, addiction programs, and prevention efforts.

While NSDUH aims to track the prevalence and emergence of new illicit drugs, it faces the same challenges of all surveys; it must limit what is asked, and how often it can be asked. This means that NSDUH often misses important trends. Bath salts, synthetic stimulants that rose to prominence in the mid-to-late 2000s [Baumann, 2014], were at first unnoticed by the addiction community. It took *years* before bath salts were included in large national surveys, meaning that the community faced a multi-year gap in critical data on this emerging trend.

Similar problems face the current opioid crisis. While deaths from heroin use have skyrocketed in the past decade, NSDUH fails to show a similar increase in the use of such drugs [Casteel, 2017]. Why this gap? Is it because available drugs have dramatically increased in potency, and therefore lethality? Or are heroin users not reporting their use in NSDUH interviews? Even for one of the largest public health crises of our time, we lack basic information on population behaviors.

Since many behavioral trends do not have existing large-scale, up-to-date surveillance systems, and even the best systems have significant gaps, there is a large potential for improvement in using social data to study behavioral medicine [Ayers et al., 2014a].

This section will describe how social monitoring can be used to understand trends in diet and fitness, including weight loss; substance use, including tobacco and drug abuse; and preven-

---

[5]https://www.cdc.gov/chronicdisease/resources/publications/aag/brfss.htm
[6]https://www.ahrq.gov/professionals/quality-patient-safety/quality-resources/tools/asthmaqual/a
sthmacare/appendix-e.html
[7]https://www.cdc.gov/diabetes/statistics/comp/methods.htm
[8]https://nsduhweb.rti.org/respweb/homepage.cfm

tative care, including public awareness of diseases and attitudes toward vaccination. Behavioral medicine is also related to mental health, which we will discuss separately in Section 5.5.

5.2.1 DIET AND FITNESS

Diet and personal fitness are important aspects of behavioral medicine. Studies have found that topics related to diet, nutrition, weight loss, and exercise are commonly discussed in popular platforms including Twitter [Paul and Dredze, 2014], Instagram [Garimella et al., 2016], and Sina Weibo [Wang et al., 2014].

Using public social media, researchers have studied **dietary** habits by analyzing food consumption expressed in Twitter [Abbar et al., 2015] and Instagram [Mejova et al., 2015, Sharma and De Choudhury, 2015]. Fried et al. [2014] found that food-related tweets could be correlated with rates of obesity and diabetes across geography, and Nguyen et al. [2016] that such tweets can be used as indicators of diet and fitness at the granularity of city neighborhoods. Chunara et al. [2013] compared physical activity related interests of Facebook users with obesity rates by area. De Choudhury et al. [2016a] used food content posted on Instagram to understand dietary differences between "food deserts"—locations with limited access to nutritional food—and other locations. Research has also analyzed dietary patterns in search logs [Kusmierczyk et al., 2015, West et al., 2013]. Ayers et al. [2014d] found seasonal patterns in searches for healthy foods, among other healthy behaviors.

Researchers have also studied **exercise** and physical activities in Twitter [Zhang et al., 2013b], including the effect of exercise on mental health [Reis and Culotta, 2015]. Kiciman and Richardson [2015] analyzed goal-oriented tweets, measuring the outcome of fitness goals expressed online, such as marathon training. Akbari et al. [2016] built a classifier to detect tweets that mention actions related to wellness, including exercise, diet, and healthcare utilization. Research even considered the effects of the 2016 Pokémon Go craze on health [LeBlanc and Chaput, 2016], where Althoff et al. [2016] found that it increased physical activity and Ayers et al. [2016d] found that it increased distracted driving.

Many online communities exist to discuss and support **weight loss** and weight management, including discussion forums, chat rooms, and blogs [Chang et al., 2013, Leggatt-Cook and Chamberlain, 2012]. Research has analyzed social media to understand the quality of advice and social support for weight loss in online forums [Hwang et al., 2007, 2010, 2011], as well as Twitter [Pagoto et al., 2014, Turner-McGrievy and Tate, 2013]. Search and browsing logs have also been analyzed to understand how people browse the Web to support their weight loss plans [schraefel et al., 2009].

Temporal and seasonal trends in weight loss (e.g., before and after New Year's) have also been analyzed. Turner-McGrievy and Beets [2015] examined tweets containing hashtags such as #weightloss to estimate levels of interest in weight loss over time.

Research has examined how obesity is perceived and discussed online, finding that derogatory comments and cyberbullying related to weight are prevalent on certain social media platforms, especially on Twitter [Chou et al., 2014, So et al., 2015].

A number of studies have investigated how weight-related social media affects mental health, examining how social media influences weight perception, body image, and self-esteem [Das et al., 2014, Fardouly et al., 2015, Ghaznavi and Taylor, 2015, Lee et al., 2014a, Tiggemann and Slater, 2013]. Research has examined disordered eating in various social media platforms, including Facebook [Walker et al., 2015], Tumblr [De Choudhury, 2015], and Flickr [Yom-Tov et al., 2012]. Yom-Tov and boyd [2014] analyzed search engine activity indicative of anorexic practices, finding temporal correlations with celebrity-related media attention.

5.2.2 SUBSTANCE USE

The use of substances, such as alcohol and tobacco, greatly affects population health. This section will describe social media-based research on the use and abuse of alcohol, tobacco, and other drugs. See Sznitman et al. [2014] for a review of using social media to support substance use research.

Tobacco

Tobacco is one of the most studied areas of public health. Concerted public health efforts have caused smoking rates in the U.S. to drop from over 40% in the 1960s to roughly 17% today [Centers for Disease Control and Prevention, 2014]. Despite this success, the fight against tobacco products continues both in the United States, where smoking kills 480,000 people per year, and internationally, where 6 million people die annually.[9] Critical to ongoing efforts is effective surveillance of tobacco products and prevalence of smoking in specific populations, such as U.S. teenagers.

Tobacco-related topics are discussed in social media [Prier et al., 2011], and social monitoring can support a variety of tasks important for tobacco surveillance.

One use of social media is to measure **sentiment** toward tobacco products [Jain et al., 2015, Myslín et al., 2013]. Tobacco products of particular public health concern recently are electronic cigarettes (e-cigarettes). Researchers have measured interest in e-cigarettes using search query volumes [Ayers et al., 2011a, 2016e] and have examined e-cigarette marketing and sentiment on Twitter [Cole-Lewis et al., 2015, Huang et al., 2014, Lazard et al., 2016]. Ayers et al. [2017] analyze Twitter to understand *why* people use e-cigarettes.

Social media can also be used to promote and support **smoking cessation** and prevention, and researchers have analyzed smoking cessation and online social support [Cobb et al., 2011, Prochaska et al., 2012, Rocheleau et al., 2015].

---

[9]http://www.cdc.gov/tobacco/data_statistics/fact_sheets/fast_facts/

Another use of web data for tobacco surveillance is to analyze and understand **public reaction** to policy changes, which researchers have measured using tweets [Harris et al., 2014b, Lazard et al., 2017] and search queries [Ayers et al., 2011b, 2014b].

Additionally, Tobacco Watcher [Cohen et al., 2015] is a real-time surveillance system that analyzes news media and summarizes tobacco-related content. This system is similar to HealthMap, described at the beginning of Section 5.1.4, with a focus on tobacco.

Alcohol

Alcohol use has also been examined in social media, though to a lesser extent than tobacco. Research has shown that temporal trends in alcohol use can be extracted from Twitter [Aphinyanaphongs et al., 2014, West et al., 2012]. Culotta [2013] found that the volume of alcohol-related tweets is correlated with alcohol sales across the United States. Researchers have also examined alcohol-related content in Facebook [Beullens and Schepers, 2013], particularly among college students [Fournier and Clarke, 2011, Moreno et al., 2012, 2014]. Liu et al. [2017] modeled different stages of alcohol use mentioned in Twitter (planning to use, currently using, reflecting on use).

In contrast to alcohol consumption, Tamersoy et al. [2015] used social media to understand alcohol abstinence.

Marijuana

Legalization of marijuana for non-medical use in several U.S. states has created a public health need for timely information on marijuana use, and social data can potentially provide current insights [Keegan et al., 2017]. Nguyen et al. [2017] showed that marijuana prevalence in different cities can be estimated through Craigslist housing advertisements, which sometimes state whether or not marijuana use is permitted. Twitter has been used to measure sentiment toward marijuana [Cavazos-Rehg et al., 2014, 2015], including a study that examined attitudes toward marijuana before and after legalization in two American states [Thompson et al., 2015]. Sentiment specifically toward medical uses of marijuana has been studied by Dai and Hao [2017].

Prescription and Over-the-counter Drugs

A major public health concern is prescription drug **abuse** (including pain relievers and stimulants), which researchers have begun to monitor using Twitter [Chan et al., 2015, Genes and Chary, 2014, Hanson et al., 2013a,b, Seaman and Giraud-Carrier, 2016]. Other research has examined how social media like Twitter may promote unsafe use of prescription drugs [Mackey et al., 2013], including through the promotion of illegal online pharmacies [Katsuki et al., 2015].

Aside from abuse, researchers have looked at other types of use and **misuse** of medications. For example, Scanfeld et al. [2010] found that many Twitter users appear to use antibiotics incorrectly, and Paul and Dredze [2011] found additional evidence of antibiotic misuse in Twitter.

Paul and Dredze [2011] also examined Twitter mentions of **off-label use** of over-the-counter medications, and Frost et al. [2011] examined off-label use of prescription drugs through PatientsLikeMe, an online community for patients.

Other Illicit Drugs

Figure 5.2: The top words associated with marijuana in an online drug community. The word rankings come from research by Paul and Dredze [2013], who applied topic models to discussion forums to summarize drug information.

Illicit drug use is a public health issue of increasing prominence, due to increased distribution and information-sharing of drugs over the Internet [Wax, 2002]. Record numbers of new drugs have been detected in recent years [European Monitoring Centre for Drugs and Drug Addiction, 2012], yet surveillance of new drugs is particularly difficult, as little is known about these substances, and traditional drug surveys are slow to include novel and emerging drugs [Dunn et al., 2011].

Researchers have started to address this limitation by using social media data to learn about drug trends, particularly for new drugs, and comprehensive drug reviews now commonly include data sources from the Web and social media [Hill and Thomas, 2011]. An important research goal is to identify which drugs are out there, along with information about the drugs such as their effects (positive and negative) and typical dosage. For example, the Psychonaut project [Deluca et al., 2012] is an extensive database of information about new drugs, using information that researchers obtain primarily from dedicated online communities for drug users, such as drugs-forum.com, where users openly discuss drug use under the cloak of pseudonymity [Barratt, 2011]. A number of new drugs have been characterized by reviewing such forums [Corazza et al., 2011, 2012, Gallagher et al., 2012]. While most such studies rely on manual data analysis, natural language processing has also been applied to drug websites to learn about drugs [Chary et al., 2013, Coyle et al., 2012, Paul and Dredze, 2013, Strapparava and Mihalcea, 2017]. Paul et al. [2016a] compared demographic and temporal variability across drugs in drugs-forum.com to official government data (specifically, the NSDUH data described at the beginning of this section), finding high agreement, thus validating the use of this data source for this type of research. Other types of social media have also been used for learning about drug use, such as YouTube videos [Morgan et al., 2010].

In addition to learning the general properties of the drugs, researchers have also analyzed trends in the use of these drugs over time. General interest in various drugs has been measured over time using search queries [Curtis et al., 2015] and tweets [Buntain and Golbeck, 2015]. Ledberg [2015] measured interest in drugs before and after changes in legal status, analyzing drug forums, finding that interest in many substances drops once they are no longer legally available.

5.2.3   DISEASE PREVENTION AND AWARENESS

Population health is influenced by individual behaviors regarding the prevention of disease and reactions to disease outbreaks. This section describes how social media surveillance can help understand vaccination behavior, an important part of public health, as well as more general public awareness of disease.

Vaccination

One of the greatest successes of public health has been large-scale vaccination campaigns, which have eradicated once deadly diseases and dramatically reduced the prevalence of others. While the development of vaccines takes place in a lab, immunization programs lay in the purview of public health. While immunization rates are high for many targeted diseases, they remain low for others. For example, seasonal influenza vaccination rates remain low in the U.S. each year, despite the overall effectiveness and availability of the vaccine.[10] Even for diseases that have traditionally high rates of vaccination, such as measles, mumps and rubella, the trend of vaccine refusal leaves children vulnerable. Only 70% of children between ages 19 and 35 months are up-to-date on immunizations [Bass III, 2015], while some communities in the U.S. have a quarter of school age children with immunization exemptions.[11] Social monitoring is a promising new approach toward addressing these vaccination challenges.

Interest in vaccination can be inferred from online activities. To illustrate this, Figure 5.3 shows the temporal volume of the "flu shot" query taken from Google Trends, which has a different trend than the "flu symptoms" query, which more closely matches a typical flu season curve.

---

[10]http://www.cdc.gov/flu/fluvaxview/
[11]http://www.cdc.gov/vaccines/imz-managers/SchoolVaxView/data-reports/index.html

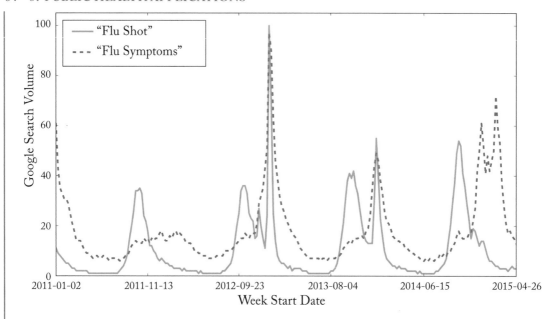

Figure 5.3: Search volumes from Google Trends (`https://google.com/trends/`) for the queries "flu shot" and "flu symptoms." We see that queries for "flu shot" always rise in October, when the influenza vaccine is distributed each year. Sometimes "flu shot" volume also rises later in the winter, in tandem with the peak of the influenza season, which is closely tracked by the "flu symptoms" query volume.

A major research topic of social media-based vaccination research is measuring sentiment, attitudes, and opinions toward vaccination, in order to understand variation in vaccination acceptance and refusal rates. In one of the earliest studies on this topic, Salathé and Khandelwal [2011] inferred sentiment toward the influenza A(H1N1) vaccine from Twitter, finding correlations between sentiment and vaccination rates across geography in the United States. This research was expanded by Salathé et al. [2013a]. Brooks [2014] also examined sentiment toward the H1N1 vaccine in Twitter, but did not find significant correlations with vaccination rates. Huang et al. [2017a] directly classified tweets that mention receipt of the influenza vaccine (e.g., "got my flu shot today"), and find that such tweets are strongly correlated with U.S. vaccine coverage across time and geography.

Smith et al. [2016b] examined Twitter to understand rationales for vaccine refusal, while Dredze et al. [2016c] looked at vaccine misconceptions. Other research has investigated opinions on the human papillomavirus (HPV) vaccine, analyzing Twitter [Dunn et al., 2015, Surian et al., 2016], Sina Weibo [Zhang et al., 2013a], MySpace [Keelan et al., 2010], and YouTube [Briones et al., 2012].

Yom-Tov and Fernandez-Luque [2014] investigated search engine behavior regarding the measles, mumps, and rubella (MMR) vaccine, finding that pro- or anti-vaccination bias is present in queries. More generally, White and Horvitz [2015] showed that biases toward different medical interventions affect how people search for information.

Larson et al. [2013] investigated a variety of vaccination topics by analyzing news media using data from HealthMap (Section 3.5). Chen et al. [2015a] analyzed concerns toward vaccines in China by analyzing Sina Weibo. Broniatowski et al. [2016] measured which factors in the presentation of a vaccine related news article were most compelling to readers, as measured by how often an article was shared.

Public Awareness of Disease

Part of disease surveillance includes the monitoring of **public awareness** of a disease, particularly during epidemics. Studies have found that a population's awareness of disease outbreaks are major factors that affect the disease progression [Funk et al., 2009, Granell et al., 2013, Jones and Salathé, 2009].

Numerous studies have used social media to measure public awareness of, and reaction to, disease epidemics. For example, Signorini et al. [2011] examined tweets that indicated preventative behaviors, such as hand-washing, in response to the swine flu epidemic in 2009. Szomszor et al. [2011] also analyzed tweets during the swine flu epidemic, focusing on public trust of various news sources. Mollema et al. [2015] analyzed tweets to characterize public reactions to the 2013 measles outbreak in the Netherlands. Multiple studies have analyzed reactions in Twitter to the 2014 ebola outbreak in Africa, focusing on anxieties in the United States [Fung et al., 2014, Lazard et al., 2015, Odlum, 2015a, Rodriguez-Morales et al., 2015, Towers et al., 2015]. Concern toward various diseases were measured in Twitter by Ji et al. [2013], and Bakal and Kavuluru [2017] analyzed how health information gets retweeted and diffused in Twitter.

Smith et al. [2016a] compared trends of tweets mentioning influenza infection ("I have the flu") vs. more general mentions ("worried about the next flu season"), finding distinct patterns in the two trends. Non-infection tweets have a sharper rise and fall than infection tweets, with less geographic variability. The study suggested that public awareness of influenza may be driven more by news media than the actual disease prevalence. Smith and Broniatowski [2016] further explored the interaction between disease dynamics, news media, and social media using an agent-based model.

In addition to Twitter, awareness of many different diseases have been analyzed in Chinese social media [Fung et al., 2015], including MERS-CoV and avian influenza A (H7N9) [Fung et al., 2013].

All of these studies used microblogs (Twitter and Sina Weibo), which are generally considered a good type of social media for measuring public opinion at scale, since these platforms encourage everyday users to share opinions with a large audience.

Public awareness of diseases and other health issues is often influenced by news and actions of **celebrities** and public figures. A number of researchers have looked at how celebrity-related news affects attention in social media, regarding health issues including cancer [Ayers et al., 2014c, Noar et al., 2013, 2015], smoking [Sanders-Jackson et al., 2015], eating disorders [Yom-Tov and boyd, 2014], and suicide [Kumar et al., 2015]. Bragazzi et al. [2016] found that actor Harold Ramis' death of vasculitis, an autoimmune disorder, resulted in an increase in vasculitis-related Google searches, tweets, and Wikipedia visits. Ayers et al. [2016c] found that actor Charlie Sheen's public disclosure of human immunodeficiency virus (HIV) led to an increase in HIV-related news media and Google searches, and Allem et al. [2017] found that it also led to a rise in at-home testing.

A common tool for raising public health awareness is through organized **awareness campaigns**. Social data has become a tool for measuring the effectiveness of awareness campaigns. For example, Ayers et al. [2012a, 2016b] and Westmaas et al. [2015] used search and social media data to measure the effect of tobacco awareness days on public attention, and Thackeray et al. [2013] and Bravo and Hoffman-Goetz [2015] examined tweets during cancer awareness campaigns.

Public Response to Guidelines and Policies

Governments and organizations often promote public health through guidelines, advisories, and legal policies, and it is important to understand the public's attitudes and adherence toward such policies. As put by Giabbanelli et al., "Public opinions play an important role in planning policies. A beneficial population intervention may not be publicly acceptable, or policymakers may be over-cautious and believe their constituents do not sufficiently support it. Understanding the feasibility and framing of interventions based on public support is thus an important endeavor for public health" [2016]. Similar to measuring public awareness, social media can provide insights into the public's attitudes toward public health guidelines.

Giabbanelli et al. [2016] analyzed Twitter to characterize public opinion toward proposed taxes on sugary beverages in California. Nastasi et al. [2017] and Khasnavis et al. [2017] used Twitter to understand the public response to screening guidelines for breast cancer and lung cancer, respectively. Researchers have also used social data to understand public opinions on current and proposed regulations of tobacco products [Ayers et al., 2011b, 2014b, Harris et al., 2014b, Lazard et al., 2017].

5.3   ENVIRONMENTAL AND URBAN HEALTH

While the previous section on behavioral medicine focused on choices people make that affect their health, this section focuses on external factors that affect one's health that are largely out of an individual's control: things like pollution, disasters, food quality, and crime. While this is a broad range of issues, they share a common thread: these are topics in which a government, or non-governmental agency, seeks to reach out and learn about a population's experience with these factors, while the population in turn is incentivized to connect with the organization to share information.

In responses to disasters, social media provides a channel of communication, whereby the government can distribute information to the public and individuals can share on-the-ground updates and emergency requests with the government. The same is true of detecting food poisoning events, where the public may wish to report specific instances to food safety regulators. These types of issues have traditionally relied on individuals actively making reports to governments, through services such as 3-1-1 in the United States, rather than using more traditional public health surveillance systems. Recent research has shown how social media can be used as a reporting mechanism [Eshleman and Yang, 2014, Frias-Martinez et al., 2014].

In this section, we will describe how social monitoring can help with emergency management, food safety, air quality monitoring, climate change, and gun violence.

5.3.1   DISASTER AND EMERGENCY RESPONSE

Social media plays an important role in the management of emergencies such as natural disasters. Social media can be used during emergencies in a number of ways, including communication to the public, communication between respondents, and surveillance to monitor the situation.

On the surveillance side, social data has been used extensively for **situational awareness**, the understanding of the events that have taken place and the current public response [Abel et al., 2012, Bennett et al., 2013, Cameron et al., 2012, Power et al., 2014, Tobias, 2011, Verma et al., 2011, Vieweg, 2012, Vieweg et al., 2010, Yin et al., 2012]. Most research on situational awareness has used microblogs as the data source, though Facebook [Gunawong and Jankananon, 2015] and Wikipedia [Steiner, 2014] have also been considered.

In addition to situational awareness, researchers have also found utility in analyzing mood and sentiment during disasters [Buscaldi and Hernandez-Farias, 2015, Doan et al., 2012, Lu et al., 2015].

The bulk of disaster response research with social media has been for natural disasters such as earthquakes and hurricanes, but similar methods can be used to detect other important events such as acts of crime or terrorism. See Imran et al. [2015] for a survey on methodologies for using social media during emergencies.

Natural Disasters

Several studies have shown that microblogs can be used to detect **earthquakes** in real time, including with Twitter [Burks et al., 2014, Crooks et al., 2013, Earle et al., 2012, Robinson et al., 2013, Sakaki et al., 2010, 2013] and Sina Weibo [Robinson et al., 2014]. Social sensors of earthquakes can augment physical sensors with more localized information, as well as with richer reports of damage and impact. Doan et al. [2012] also showed how tweets can measure public response to earthquakes. In addition to detecting earthquakes, social media can also play a crucial role in coordination and management of response [Yates and Paquette, 2011], including search and rescue [Simon et al., 2014a].

Similar to earthquakes, research has shown how social media can be used to monitor and understand **storms**, including hurricanes [Kogan et al., 2015, Mandel et al., 2012, Stowe et al., 2016, Wang et al., 2015a] and tornadoes [Blanford et al., 2014]. Situational awareness is important both during and after storms, and in particular many researchers have used social media to monitor and respond to flooding [Buscaldi and Hernandez-Farias, 2015, Dashti et al., 2014, Fuchs et al., 2013, Gunawong and Jankananon, 2015, Mao et al., 2014, Supian et al., 2017] and waterlogging [Zhang et al., 2014b]. In addition to informal first-hand reports of storms and flooding, researchers have also analyzed how official information is shared through social media [Genes et al., 2014].

Twitter has also been used to detect and monitor **fire events**, such as forest fires [Power et al., 2013, 2015, Slavkovikj et al., 2014].

Other Emergencies and Events

Schulz et al. [2013] demonstrated that car accident incidents can be detected in Twitter, while introducing methods appropriate for detecting **small-scale** incidents, in contrast to large-scale disasters. Also focusing on small-scale incidents, Bendler et al. [2014] showed how Twitter can be monitored to detect reports of crime in neighborhoods. Twitter can also be used as an information source during episodes of cardiac arrest [Bosley et al., 2013].

Researchers have analyzed social media to monitor and understand **shootings and terrorist events**, including the Boston marathon bombings [Cassa et al., 2013], the 2012 massacre in Aurora, Colorado [Page, 2013], and the Westgate Mall attack in Kenya [Simon et al., 2014b]. Rodriguez Jr. [2014] analyzed Twitter to understand the impact of terrorist groups in Africa.

5.3.2   FOODBORNE ILLNESS

Tens of millions of people fall ill to foodborne illness every year in the United States, often from food in restaurants [McCabe-Sellers and Beattie, 2004]. Surveillance of restaurants typically involves a combination of routine inspection and investigations following citizen complaints. Many citizens do not file official reports when catching food poisoning, so passive monitoring of social media is a promising method for increasing the coverage of reported incidents, as people often voice complaints against restaurants on social media [Newkirk et al., 2012].

Researchers have shown that mentions of food poisoning, an indicator of foodborne illness, can be detected in online restaurant reviews from Yelp [Joaristi et al., 2016, Kang et al., 2013, Nsoesie et al., 2014b] as well as messages in Twitter [Ordun et al., 2013]. A Twitter-based system, nEmesis [Sadilek et al., 2013], was deployed in Las Vegas in 2015 as part of a program to flag restaurants for inspection. This system led to a 63% increase in identifying restaurants with health violations compared to a control [Sadilek et al., 2017].

Two well-known food surveillance projects were undertaken by the cities of Chicago and New York. The Chicago Department of Public Health launched a program called FoodBorne Chicago to perform foodborne illness surveillance in social media [Harris et al., 2014a]. This system uses a supervised machine learning classifier to identify messages in Twitter that indicate someone has experienced food poisoning. Authors of identified messages are contacted and asked to submit a report through the program website, www.foodbornechicago.org.

Around the same time, the New York City Department of Health and Mental Hygiene launched a pilot program to investigate reports of foodborne illness in restaurant reviews, using data from Yelp [Harrison et al., 2014]. As with the Chicago program, authors of identified reviews were contacted through Yelp for a followup report. During this study, investigators detected previously undiscovered illness outbreaks.

5.3.3 AIR QUALITY

Research has shown that levels of air pollution can be estimated based on complaints of poor air quality in social media. Researchers have investigated air quality in China through Sina Weibo [Mei et al., 2014, Wang and Bai, 2014, Wang et al., 2015b] and in the United States through Twitter [Riga and Karatzas, 2014]. In contrast to physical sensors of pollutant levels, social media-based analysis measures public **perceptions** of air quality, which is also important to public health, as perceptions of pollution are stronger predictors of willingness to reduce pollution [Zeidner and Shechtera, 1988].

It is also important to understand **public response** to air pollution, which can have an effect on health, such as behaviors to prevent discomfort [Bresnahan et al., 1997]. Wang et al. [2015b] analyzed responses to poor air quality in Sina Weibo, and Zhang et al. [2014c] examined how smartphone applications can be used to measure public response to air pollution outbreaks. A case study of using Sina Weibo to measure public response to air quality was presented by Wang and Bai [2014], focusing on the 2013 Harbin haze disaster.

Chen et al. [2017] combined physical sensor data with social media data to produce forecasts of smog-related hazards.

5.3.4 CLIMATE CHANGE

The potential effects of climate change on the environment are well known, but public health is concerned about its impact on health [Haines et al., 2006]. The World Health Organization considers climate change a significant threat to public health as it can endanger access to safe water, food, and clean air.[12]

The major focus of public health activities around climate change is preparedness [Frumkin et al., 2008], but the primary role of social monitoring in climate change is as a tool in public advocacy. Studies have looked at Twitter to gauge responses to climate change reports

---

[12]http://www.who.int/globalchange/en/

[Newman, 2016] or protest events [Segerberg and Bennett, 2011]. Leas et al. [2016] measured the impact on public awareness of climate change following celebrity advocacy.

5.3.5   GUN VIOLENCE

Gun violence is a major problem in the United States, with gun homicide rates more than 25 times higher than other high-income countries [Grinshteyn and Hemenway, 2016]. Gun violence is not typically thought of as a public health problem, but it is helpful to consider gun violence through the public health framework [Koop and Lundberg, 1992, Matthew Miller, 2013, Mercy et al., 1993, Mozaffarian et al., 2013], as it provides a way of thinking about the problem: population data collection and intervention design.

A particular challenge of research in this area has been a lack of data, caused by a lack of federal funding due to political concerns. Between 2009 and 2012, the CDC spent just over $100,000 annually on firearm injury prevention research [Mayors Against Illegal Guns, 2013], a tiny amount compared to programs like BRFSS ($18 million in 2015).[13] Spending restrictions result from the 1996 Dickey amendment [Public Law, 1996], which led to a 96% drop in gun injury prevention funding within the CDC [Mayors Against Illegal Guns, 2013]. See Ayers et al. [2016a], Jamieson [2013] and Rubin [2016] for a more detailed explanation of funding.

A large gap in available data means greater promise for social monitoring work. Pavlick et al. [2016] used crowdsourcing and natural language processing of news articles to create The Gun Violence Database,[14] a listing of gun violence incidents in the United States. Benton et al. [2016a] used a topic model analysis of gun-related tweets in the year following the Sandy Hook Elementary School shooting to understand perspectives surrounding the debate on guns. In a related study, Benton et al. [2016b] showed that topic models trained on Twitter data could be used to predict the responses in telephone surveys, including on questions related to gun control. Stefanone et al. [2015] studied how images related to gun control spread on Twitter. Finally, Ayers et al. [2016a] used Google search query trends to characterize reactions to mass shootings, including how different types of reactions showed different response patterns.

5.4   HEALTHCARE QUALITY AND SAFETY

Healthcare quality and safety are centered in the clinical patient experience. These interactions take place within the confines of clinics and hospitals, which would suggest that the role of social data is limited. However, the mechanisms for collecting information on these issues are limited, meaning that there is an opportunity for filling in information gaps from online data sources.

Makary and Daniel [2016] argued that medical errors are the third leading cause of death in the United States, trailing behind only heart disease and cancer. While care providers naturally take numerous steps to minimize medical errors while treating patients, such errors still account for a large number of negative outcomes. Hospital-acquired infections, incidents where a patient

---

[13]https://www.cdc.gov/chronicdisease/resources/publications/aag/brfss.htm
[14]http://gun-violence.org/

is admitted to a hospital and then acquires an unrelated infection, were responsible for 722,000 infections and 75,000 deaths during hospitalization in the United States in 2011 [Magill et al., 2014].

A critical step in addressing medical errors is a surveillance system that can identify errors when they occur. Once identified, preventative and mitigating steps can be put into place to improve outcomes. While there is a recognition that patients need to have an active role in such surveillance [Emslie et al., 2002], patient voices often go unheard [Ward and Armitage, 2012], leading to an under-reporting of errors and an omission of an important perspective in delivering care. Alternative methods of data collection that can directly collect information from patients can offer a new method for incorporating the patient's perspective on quality and safety [Greaves et al., 2013, Pronovost et al., 2006].

This section will describe how social data can be used to monitor the quality of healthcare providers as well as the safety of medications.

5.4.1   HEALTHCARE QUALITY

Many patients now share their healthcare experiences online, through general-purpose social media as well as reviews of healthcare providers, creating opportunities for using social media to detect poor care [Greaves et al., 2013]. Examples of doctor reviews are shown in Table 5.2.

Table 5.2: Examples (paraphrased) of anonymous doctor reviews from RateMDs.com, rated on a scale from 1–5, edited to remove names. Research has found that online doctor reviews are predictive of standard healthcare quality metrics [Segal et al., 2012, Wallace et al., 2014].

Rating	Review Body
5.0	I've been seeing Dr. X for years. She listens to all of your concerns and always errs on the side of caution. She's the best!
3.5	I love Dr. X since he HELPs me get well, and he takes many types of insurance. I know he cares and wants to help. The staff is terrible, but he is fantastic.
1.0	This is the worst medical office I've ever been to. They do not have voicemail, and the doctor never returns my messages with the receptionist. NOT RELIABLE AT ALL!!!

López et al. [2012] conducted a qualitative content analysis of a sample of doctor reviews, finding that descriptions of doctors are mostly positive, while sentiment toward systems issues (office and staff) are more mixed. Brody and Elhadad [2010] and Paul et al. [2013] similarly conducted content analyses, but using automated methods, applying topic models to large sets of reviews.

Additional research has shown that online doctor reviews are predictive of healthcare quality. Segal et al. [2012] found that review sentiment is correlated with surgeon volume, and Wallace et al. [2014] found that review sentiment is correlated with followup visit likelihood, both considered proxies for healthcare quality. Mowery et al. [2016] found that Google reviews of nursing homes were correlated with Centers for Medicare and Medicaid Services (CMS) inspection results. Ranard et al. [2016] found Yelp ratings to be correlated with the Hospital Consumer Assessment of Healthcare Providers and Systems (HCAHPS) survey, considered the gold standard for evaluating patient experiences. The authors conclude that online reviews can supplement traditional surveys.

However, Okike et al. [2016] found no correlation between reviews of cardiac surgeons and outcomes (risk-adjusted mortality rates). The authors caution, "Patients using online rating websites to guide their choice of physician should recognize that these ratings may not reflect actual quality of care as defined by accepted metrics."

Doctor reviews have also been analyzed in China [Hao and Zhang, 2016]. Compared to doctor reviews in the United States, Chinese doctor reviews tend to focus more on treatments and less on external aspects like staff [Hao et al., 2017].

Healthcare quality has also been examined in Twitter [Hawkins et al., 2015]. Greaves et al. [2014] analyzed tweets directed at hospitals, finding that most tweets were not about care quality, but among those that were, most were positive. Nakhasi et al. [2012, 2015], in contrast, focused on tweets about negative quality, and characterized tweets describing medical mistakes.

5.4.2   MEDICATION SAFETY

Another important task regarding health safety is **pharmacovigilance**, the monitoring of **adverse drug reactions** (ADRs)—negative side effects to medical use of drugs. Adverse reactions to drugs are often discovered after clinical trials, when drugs enter the market, and health agencies must monitor populations for reports of ADRs [Harpaz et al., 2012]. Traditional pharmacovigilance relies heavily on feedback from patients, who may not always file formal complaints; instead, recent research has investigated monitoring social media and search activity to infer when ADRs have been experienced. See Sarker et al. [2015] and Tricco et al. [2017] for reviews of using social data for pharmacovigilance.

A number of studies have detected ADRs from various types of social media, including health communities and forums [Benton et al., 2011, Leaman and Wojtulewicz, 2010, Nikfarjam and Gonzalez, 2011, Yates et al., 2013], online reviews of drugs [Yates and Goharian, 2013], and Twitter [Bian et al., 2012, Freifeld et al., 2014, Jiang and Zheng, 2013, Nikfarjam et al., 2015, O'Connor et al., 2014, Plachouras et al., 2016]. These systems typically use natural language processing to identify mentions of drugs and ADRs in the user-generated text. Cho et al. [2017] identify when forum users discontinue a medication, which is often due to ADRs experienced by the users.

ADRs have also been mined from search query logs. Yom-Tov and Gabrilovich [2013] mined ADRs from Yahoo search logs. White et al. [2013, 2014] conducted similar studies using Bing search logs, focusing on drug-drug interactions—ADRs that result from *combinations* of drugs [Vilar et al., 2017]. Both of these studies looked for users who searched various symptom terms after searching for the name of a drug, and the studies showed that it is possible to identify ADRs not previously reported. These projects required access to multiple queries within a single user's search history, which is not data that can be publicly obtained through aggregation services like Google Trends. Hence, these studies were done by researchers at Yahoo and Microsoft, who had access to this type of proprietary data.

5.5   MENTAL HEALTH

Mental health, otherwise known as behavioral health, is an area of health with one of the largest gaps between the seriousness of the problem and the little information we have available. This makes it one of the most promising areas of research with social monitoring.

Let's start with what we know. Mental illness is the leading cause of disability in the United States [Kleinman, 2009], with mental illness costing the United States $201 billion annually [Roehrig, 2016]. Suicide is one of the ten leading causes of death in the U.S., and 16% of people will experience depression in their lifetime.[15] Mental illness has a similar global profile, with the World Health Organization reporting mental illnesses the leading causes of disability adjusted life years (DALYs) worldwide [Alwan et al., 2011].

The first step to addressing mental illness is obtaining reliable information and evidence. The WHO's Mental Health Action Plan for the next two decades calls for the strengthening of "information systems, evidence and research." The action plan proposes an ambitious goal: 80% of countries should routinely collect and report a core set of mental health indicators every two years [World Health Organization, 2013].

Treating mental illness happens in the context of a doctor-patient relationship. But while treatments for mental health disorders can be effective, most people diagnosed with a mental disorder go untreated [Kessler et al., 2005]. Public health seeks to reverse this trend on a population level by increasing awareness about mental health, eliminating stigmas and health disparities, and improving access to mental health services [Centers for Disease Control and Prevention (CDC), 2005, U.S. Department of Health and Human Services, 1999]. Additionally, we seek to identify risk factors associated with mental illness, especially those surrounding suicide.

These are ambitious goals, made difficult by large gaps in our understanding of mental health trends in populations [Colpe et al., 2010]. The CDC leads a national effort to collect and maintain surveillance data on mental illness in the United States [Reeves et al., 2011]. Mental health information comes from at least eight different surveillance systems, including the previously described Behavioral Risk Factor Surveillance System (BRFSS). However, none of these systems is focused specifically on mental illness.

As a result, we sometimes lack meaningful data to understand important mental health trends. Consider the case of suicide rates in the U.S. military. Officials noticed increased suicide attempts in the U.S. Army during the wars in Afghanistan and Iraq. However, it took years

[15]https://www.nimh.nih.gov/health/statistics/suicide/index.shtml

to confirm this trend and assemble a study to measure it. The Army Study to Assess Risk and Resilience in Servicemembers (STARRS) program included a longitudinal, retrospective cohort study to identify factors linked to suicide attempts, and to measure the rate of these attempts. The study examined medically documented suicide attempts among active-duty regular Army soldiers from 2004–2009, a time period that included nearly 10,000 suicide attempts. The studies findings were published in 2015, years after this trend first emerged [Ursano et al., 2015].

In response to these data needs, researchers have turned to social data to gain insights into a wide range of mental health disorders. Social data is especially attractive in this case because mental health fundamentally affects behavior, which is exhibited in online behaviors, and social stigma around mental health discourages self-reports. Researchers have begun using publicly posted social media messages as a data source for studying a variety of mental health conditions [De Choudhury, 2013, 2014a]. In addition to general social media platforms like Twitter, mental health support communities are a prominent data source [Cohan et al., 2016, Kavuluru et al., 2016]. These communities serve as important support role, and improvements to how these communities function could improve mental health outcomes.

This section focuses on three of the most prominent areas of research: depression, suicide and mood. See Calvo et al. [2017] for a review of using social media and other text data for various mental health applications.

5.5.1   DEPRESSION

Perhaps due to its high prevalence in the population—nearly 10% of the adult United States population currently suffers from depression [Centers for Disease Control and Prevention, 2010, Kessler et al., 1994]—depression has received the most attention of any condition [De Choudhury et al., 2013c], with research looking at Twitter [Coppersmith et al., 2014b, De Choudhury and Gamon, 2013, Prieto et al., 2014], Reddit [De Choudhury and De, 2014], Facebook [Jelenchick et al., 2013, Moreno et al., 2011], and search query logs [Yang et al., 2010], among others. Depression-related research has looked for indicators of bipolar disorder in Twitter [Flekova et al., 2015], tools for measuring the degree to which a user is depressed [Schwartz et al., 2014], and even predicting oncoming depressive episodes before their onset [De Choudhury and Gamon, 2013]. This diverse range of studies strongly evidences the ability of social data to provide insights into depression in both populations and individuals.

Other work has focused on a specific form of depression: postpartum depression, which affects women after childbirth. De Choudhury et al. [2013a] provided methods for identifying major life changes, such as childbirth, from social media data. De Choudhury et al. [2013b] predicted postpartum changes in emotion and behavior from Twitter, and De Choudhury et al. [2014a] showed similar results for Facebook.

5.5.2 SUICIDE AND SELF-HARM

The relation between social media and suicide is well recognized [Luxton et al., 2012]; suicidal individuals often reach out using social media, or are impacted by their treatment in online communities. While predicting suicide is a notoriously difficult problem, research with social media has looked at population-level trends. Won et al. [2013] used social media data to predict national suicide numbers. Jashinsky et al. [2015] used Twitter to track suicide risk factors. Kumar et al. [2015] relied on Reddit data to measure the Werther effect, the idea that an individual's suicide depicted in the media leads to an increased rate of completed or attempted suicides.

At the individual level, Braithwaite et al. [2016] showed that Twitter users who are at high risk for suicide can be reliably identified with machine learning classifiers. Huang et al. [2017b] analyzed the feeds of 130 Sina Weibo users who committed suicide, looking at temporal shifts in sentiment and content leading up to the time of death. De Choudhury et al. [2016b] identify when users shift from general mental health concerns to suicidal ideation.

Social media has also been used to understand the role of social support for suicidal individuals, for example in suicide watch forums [Kavuluru et al., 2016]. De Choudhury and Kiciman [2017] studied how language and actions used in mental health support communities on Reddit affected suicidal ideation by users in the future.

5.5.3 MOOD

Another common topic of study is the emotional states of individuals, also known as moods, which impact attitudes and behavior [De Choudhury, 2014b, De Choudhury et al., 2012, Golder and Macy, 2011, Hannak et al., 2010, Lampos et al., 2013]. This has extended to measurements of personality [Schwartz et al., 2013], including the development of automated personality assessments from social media [Park et al., 2014] and studying how personality, age, and gender impact mental illnesses [Preoţiuc-Pietro et al., 2015].

5.5.4 OTHER MENTAL HEALTH ISSUES

Beyond these mental health issues, other work has explored a variety of topics, including post-traumatic stress disorder (PTSD) [Coppersmith et al., 2014a], sleep and insomnia patterns [McIver et al., 2015, Tian et al., 2016], stress [Doan et al., 2017, Wang et al., 2016], eating disorders [De Choudhury, 2015, Walker et al., 2015], smoking and drinking problems [Tamersoy et al., 2015], links between exercise and mental health [Reis and Culotta, 2015], schizophrenia [Mitchell et al., 2015], and links between psychological language and heart disease [Eichstaedt et al., 2015]. Coppersmith et al. [2015b] developed general methods for obtaining large collections of data for ten disorders based on users' self-reported diagnoses [Coppersmith et al., 2014b].

Search trends have been used to study patterns in mental health problems at the population level. Ayers et al. [2013] identified seasonal patterns in seeking mental health information on Google, identifying winter peaks across a range of disorders. Similar techniques were used to identify psychological impacts of the Great Recession [Althouse et al., 2014]. At the individual level, Yom-Tov et al. [2014b] analyzed search logs to detect changes in behavior associated with mood disorders.

Additionally, researchers have studied online discussions of mental health issues to understand attitudes and beliefs about mental illness [Reavley and Pilkington, 2014]. This has included studying how people talk about their mental health issues [De Choudhury and De, 2014] and what users are willing to disclose online [Balani and De Choudhury, 2015]. Hwang and Hollingshead [2016] found that people with greater awareness of mental illnesses are less likely to use stigmatizing language on Twitter.

CHAPTER 6

Limitations and Concerns

As with any new source of data, social monitoring raises challenges for research [Babbie, 2016]. What are the limits of how we can use social data? What *should* be the limits? These conversations arise, especially in health, whenever new data sources open new opportunities for research. One challenge to understanding and addressing these limits and concerns are that researchers with computational backgrounds, who are often unfamiliar with existing conversations and practices in health and medicine, are at the forefront of developing new applications and uses for social data in health. Additionally, even researchers with a long history of work in health are unsure of how existing methods and practices apply to social data.

This chapter summarizes the limits and concerns of using social monitoring in health across three areas. First, what are the scientific limitations of using social data in research, and what are the methodological issues that must be addressed in such research? Second, how can information derived from web sources be actioned, and how should systems based on social data be used by practitioners, now and in the future? Third, what are the ethical considerations involved in conducting research with user-generated data? What limits should be placed on the use of these data?

6.1 METHODOLOGICAL LIMITATIONS

A common concern raised about using social data for health research is that the data itself are flawed, and therefore any findings derived from the data, and uses of the data, are necessarily flawed. How can data, created and collected without health applications in mind, with a multitude of poorly understood biases, be considered reliable for making patient and public health decisions?

Critics of these data often point to the high profile failure of Google Flu Trends (GFT) [Lazer et al., 2014b]. As early as 2003, researchers began investigating how people use web search engines to seek health information [Eysenbach and Kohler, 2003, Eysenbach and Köhler, 2004]. This included considering trends in web searches around seasonal influenza as a means of rapid syndromic surveillance [Eysenbach, 2006]. When GFT premiered in 2008 [Watts, 2008], it was hailed as a major step forward in flu surveillance, with the ability to uncover flu outbreaks earlier than current surveillance methods employed by the CDC. The premier features a new website, and a publication of a high profile research paper [Ginsberg et al., 2009]. While the authors were careful to describe their work as a complement to existing surveillance methods, many interpreted the work as the future of infectious disease surveillance.

Perceptions of GFT changed in the wake of the 2012-2013 flu season. That year showed very high rates of infection, which led to officials calling the outbreak a public health emergency. This led to increased coverage of the flu season in the media, and there was widespread concern among the general public. An analysis of GFT during this period, especially during the height of news coverage, showed extremely large increases in the influenza rate [Lazer et al., 2014a]. Yet when compared with the surveillance measures at the CDC, the spike in infection failed to materialize. The common theory is that the general public, faced with scary stories about an outbreak, took to the Web in large numbers in search of information about the flu [Harford, 2014]. Google's algorithms took this increase in searches as an indication of a rise in the infection rate, whereas it was only indicative of increased concern about of the disease.

This explanation is supported by work from the same flu season using Twitter data, which automatically separated tweets describing infection from more general tweets, yielding a more modest rise in infection rates during the same period of increased news coverage [Broniatowski et al., 2013]. Additionally, work with more sophisticated methods using Google's data also mitigated the problems discovered in GFT's system [Martin et al., 2014, Santillana et al., 2014b]. Google itself made updates to its surveillance model in 2013 and 2014, although it has since shut down its public system.

The fallout of this public failure led to criticisms of big data [Harford, 2014, Lazer and Kennedy, 2015], and spurred the creation of clearer guidelines on how new data sources should be used in syndromic surveillance [Althouse et al., 2015]. We can summarize one major conclusion of this criticism: big data is not magic, and it doesn't replace principled models and methods.

We provide the case of GFT as a cautionary tale. Yes, social data can produce new insights and abilities for a range of health problems. However, these opportunities do not come without major methodological challenges that must be addressed to ensure that the data provide reliable and meaningful insights.

Thankfully, while the specific manifestation of challenges posed by these data are new, the types of limitations have long been addressed in earlier work with traditional data sources, such as the reliability and representativeness of the data. This section describes some of the major methodological limitations that arise when using social data for public health research and surveillance, and point to prior and new work on addressing these limitations. We also refer the reader to work that discusses common limitations of social media research in detail: Ruths and Pfeffer [2014], Shah et al. [2015], and Tufekci [2014].

6.1.1   LIMITATIONS OF SELF-REPORTED DATA

Social data is fundamentally a collection of self-reports. Users decide what to write on social platforms, and what they want to enter into a search engine. This problem may be even more acute in some circumstances when self-reports are passive, i.e., the users offer information without prompting, rather than active, e.g., in response to a survey.

Users may **misreport** their health statuses, due to poor memory, over- or under-estimation of health behavior, or incorrect self-diagnosis. Conflations of medical terms in common parlance may mean a misreport. For example, a social media user might state that they have the flu, when in fact the user might have the common cold. One study estimates that approximately 40% of flu tweets are misdiagnoses, and using these tweets without correction worsens surveillance [Mowery, 2016]. In general, self-reported health status is not always reliable compared to objective measurements [Newell et al., 1999, Saunders et al., 2011], and self-perceptions of health can vary across demographic groups and other factors [Brener et al., 2003, Jürges, 2007].

Underreporting is another problem, in that social media users do not always (and in fact, rarely) choose to report their current health status. For example, it is certainly the case that the number of Twitter users who report they have influenza is less than the number of Twitter users who have influenza. Compare the expected underreporting of a common illness like influenza, to sexually transmitted diseases or mental health issues, which are associated with stigmas that discourage public acknowledgement of these illnesses. This is a general limitation of passive surveillance—we only know what users choose to share, and of the public nature of many social media platforms. Furthermore, not only are positive instances (e.g., influenza infection) underreported, but negative instances (e.g., no infection) are often not reported at all. That is, some Twitter users might state that they have the flu, but users almost never state that they do *not* have the flu. This is an example of data missing not at random (MNAR) [Mohan et al., 2013, Rubin, 1976], and a problem of an unknown denominator when estimating prevalence [Chunara et al., 2017, Tufekci, 2014]. Finally, there may also be a bias in the set of people who choose to share such information (discussed in Section 6.1.5), complicating interpretation of the data. Views on privacy differ by age group [Paine et al., 2007], and it is likely that some groups may be more willing to share health information on public platforms.

Another issue with using self-reported data is handling variation in medical **terminology** reported by laypeople on social media. Some users might be limited in reporting an illness if they do not know the name of the illness, and other users might use informal terms (e.g., "flu" rather than "influenza"), so any algorithm that filters for mentions of illness must be able to accommodate variation in terminology. Some research has created mappings between formal and informal terms to address the "terminology gap" between medical professionals and Twitter users [Nie et al., 2014a,b]. Pimpalkhute et al. [2014] used phonetic spelling correction to adjust for the spelling difficulty of drug names. Another approach is to focus on reports of symptoms, rather than mentions of a specific illness, to account for the unreliability of self-diagnosis. This approach has been used for Twitter-based influenza surveillance [Gesualdo et al., 2013, Velardi et al., 2014].

6.1.2   SAMPLING AND SAMPLE SIZE

While data from the Web are often described as big data, the data will shrink upon filtering for relevant content (Section 4.1.1). In most general purpose platforms, only a small percentage of data is related to health, and an even smaller percentage will be related to any one health issue. The small size of relevant data can make it difficult to reliably study health issues that are rare or not commonly discussed, as well as to focus on health in small populations. For example, Paul et al. [2015a] found a correlation between the population of a location and the accuracy of Twitter-based flu surveillance: there are plenty of flu-related tweets across the United States, but few within any one city.

Another issue is that one typically works with smaller samples of original data. For example, most available Twitter data is in the form of a 1% sample of all tweets (Section 3.5). However, Twitter does not publish the details of how the 1% is selected. Statistical models typically assume that data samples are independent and identically distributed, but this assumption is not necessarily true of Twitter samples [Morstatter et al., 2013]. In some cases, like with Facebook, random samples are not available at all, and instead one must collect data filtered for specific keywords, which can further bias the results.

Sampling can be particularly problematic when using data for geospatial analysis or location and demographic inference. In geospatial analysis, random clusters of points in space may be formed by chance when such clusters do not exist in the full data [Jones, 2014, O'Sullivan and Unwin, 2010]. Moreover, it has been observed that geo-tagged tweets are not randomly distributed over the United States population [Malik et al., 2015], and there are confounding factors and biases when inferring location information for Twitter users [Johnson et al., 2017, Pavalanathan and Eisenstein, 2015]. Wood-Doughty et al. [2017] showed how users from different demographic groups have different social media use patterns, which can lead to biases in demographic inference.

Additionally, data collection methods can influence the conclusions drawn from the data. Mac Kim et al. [2016] compared several Twitter data collection techniques and showed how the method can bias demographic inference. Rafail [2017] also compared different methods of sampling Twitter, finding that hashtag-based sampling missed important characteristics of Twitter activity and could be misleading.

In all of these cases, care must be taken to consider where data come from, how they are collected, and how these methods can influence the resulting analyses.

6.1.3 RELIABILITY OF THIRD-PARTY DATA

There are a number of drawbacks to using data that is owned by third parties, such as Twitter and Google.

An important concern with third-party data collection is the effect on scientific **reproducibility**. In some cases, as with search query logs, the raw data is proprietary and cannot be shared with researchers outside of the company that owns the data. Even data that is publicly available at the time of study might not be available in the future. For example, while tweets are publicly available, they cannot be directly shared, per Twitter's terms of use. Instead, researchers can share the identifiers of tweets used in their datasets, which other researchers can download using the Twitter API. However, if a tweet is deleted, then it will not be available when someone tries to access it in the future. This setup protects the users of Twitter, providing users with control over their data, but this protection has the consequence that Twitter datasets typically cannot be recreated exactly.

Another drawback of third-party data is that, since external researchers do not control the data, one must account for potential **changes in a data stream** over time that might affect models using the data. Any web platform will experience changes in usage levels over time. A famous example is MySpace, whose popularity rapidly fell in competition with Facebook. Changes in popularity can skew volume-based measurements of social media data, so data must be appropriately normalized to adjust for variation over time (Section 4.1.2). The demographic composition of a platform's users can also shift over time. For example, Facebook was originally only available to college students, but has since been adopted by all groups.

In addition to changes in *who* uses a platform, there will often be shifts in *how* a platform is used. Often these shifts are in response to changes made to a platform. For example, early Twitter users would retweet (that is, post a previously published tweet) messages by quoting the original tweet and adding the letters "RT" to the beginning. Later, Twitter updated their platform so that retweet functionality is built directly into the system, such that users can retweet a message with the click of a button, and the data API provides information about whether a message is a retweet. Twitter then updated the retweet functionality so that users can add a comment in response to a tweet. More recently, Twitter changed how reply-to messages are structured. Similar changes have been made to how geolocation data is structured and included with tweets. From an engineering perspective, this means developers of systems using tweets must update their systems in response to such changes, in order to correctly process the data. From a scientific perspective, this means analysts must be aware of changes in user behavior that can affect how the data is interpreted.

Updates to platforms can even alter the type of data that is created by users. For example, the design choice of search interfaces can affect the length of queries that users issue [Agapie et al., 2013, Belkin et al., 2003]. Another way search interfaces affect queries is through the query suggestions that most search engines provide, in the form of "autocompletion" (while the user is typing) as well as "related queries" that are suggested in the search results. Search users often use the suggestions to guide and refine their search process, which can bias the queries that are issued [Kato et al., 2013, Niu and Kelly, 2014]. If a search engine were to alter the query suggestion algorithm, then this may in turn alter which queries are commonly searched, which could affect models that use search query volume. As another example, the rapid expansion of Google's voice search capabilities may be changing the way people formulate their queries.

Models that use search or social media should be periodically re-estimated on current data, in order to adjust for inevitable shifts in the data over time. In fact, this was one of the problems with Google Flu Trends discussed above; the original models were not updated over time to account for changes in search trends.

In addition to changes within a platform, one should also be aware of **variation across platforms** and a system's sensitivity to the choice of platform. As discussed in Section 3.3.5, different platforms are used in different ways and by different populations, and so a model that is built using one platform cannot necessarily be applied to another. This fact makes web-based surveillance systems particularly reliant on the stability of the underlying platform. For robust surveillance, a good practice is to compare and combine multiple systems that use different platforms [Santillana et al., 2015].

Finally, researchers cannot assume long-term reliance on third party data sources. Organizations change priorities over time, and may limit or change data access. Initial users of the Twitter streaming API were granted "deca-hose" access (10% data feeds), but this access was later discontinued for new users in favor of the 1% data feed. Similarly, Google Flu Trends no longer makes current influenza estimates publicly available.

While these concerns should not preclude the use of these data, researchers should keep in mind these concerns when making decisions about which data to use, and how to build research efforts and systems around these data sources.

6.1.4   ADVERSARIAL CONCERNS

Data created from the interactions of a large number of people means that a coordinated effort by a group can interfere with the quality of data sources [Lazer et al., 2014b]. While it may not be likely that a group would seek to interfere with a health research project, efforts aimed at other goals could have the side effect of creating data problems for health efforts. For example, political campaigns have been observed to create fake tweets to artificially inflate their popularity in social media [Ratkiewicz et al., 2011]. More commonly, large bot networks on Twitter post tweets to influence people's perceptions around political issues. A common example regarding health is in tobacco. Clark et al. [2016] found that between 70% and 80% of tweets mentioning e-cigarettes were posted by automated accounts, creating problems for understanding the perceptions of the general public around e-cigarettes. The presence of these accounts complicates the analysis of the resulting data. Kim et al. [2016] developed a search filter to retrieve e-cigarette related tweets based on keywords, yet criticism of this work observed that failure to exclude tweets from automated accounts distorts insights derived from the data [Allem and Ferrara, 2016]. Another related example comes from the state of California's awareness around e-cigarettes titled "Still Blowing Smoke." A large counter-campaign titled "Not Blowing Smoke," pushed for by pro-e-cigarette advocacy groups, was referenced more frequently on Twitter [Allem et al., 2016]. The interaction of these two campaigns complicate the understanding of the underlying public's perceptions.

In the case of Google Flu Trends (GFT), one could artificially inflate flu estimates by issuing many flu queries from multiple accounts. While such behavior may not be motivated a desire to corrupt the GFT estimate, such behavior could be used as part of a marketing campaign around medical products for influenza. To address this concern, Google does not share the list of search terms used in the GFT model, and later GFT algorithms attempted to detect "inorganic" spikes in volume for a particular query, to prevent such spikes from influencing the model prediction [Copeland et al., 2013].

6.1.5   BIAS

One of the most common concerns in using social data is that a variety of biases can impact the representativeness of the data [Ruths and Pfeffer, 2014]. Data and analysis bias issues pervade empirical data analysis research. Understanding the source and factors that influence bias aids in addressing and avoiding them. We survey some of the most common sources of bias in using this type of data.

First, since social data originates directly from users, there are a variety of **user-dependent factors** that can influence the data. Users lack domain expertise, so discussions and reports of health issues cannot always be trusted, as discussed in Section 6.1.1. This can be especially problematic with uncommon illnesses and medications, with which users may be unfamiliar, as well as very prevalent conditions, with which the user may mistakenly associate.

The expression of health information can be influenced by the nature of the topic. Some very common conditions may be underrepresented; users may be unlikely to search for the common cold. Some conditions may be underrepresented due to privacy concerns, such as tweets about sexually transmitted diseases. Additionally, external factors can influence which topics appear in the data. A recent suicide in a small community could lead to increased rates of discussion of suicide in that area, or a media report on a new disease could lead users in that area to search for related information. When studying a health topic, researchers must understand factors that influence reporting of the topic.

Second, user **demographics** influence collected data [Goel et al., 2012]. A social media platform may not accurately represent the wider population of interest [Mislove et al., 2011]. The lack of demographic representation is perceived as a widespread limitation of social platforms. However, while the perception of many is that there is a "digital divide" that characterizes social media, this divide has largely disappeared and now most groups are well represented. Recent studies have found that 70% of American adults use social media, and 79% of online American adults use Facebook, the most popular social media platform [Center, 2017, Duggan et al., 2015, Greenwood et al., 2016]. Additionally, social platforms reflect users across gender, education levels, incomes, and urban vs. rural areas. Where divides do exist, social media over-represents certain high-risk groups such as young, urban, and in some cases minority persons. Furthermore, these biases are complementary to the biases in existing survey methods which skew older and less urban.

Additionally, demographics may influence *how* information is shared [Wood-Doughty et al., 2017]. Men may be more likely to search for certain common women's health topics because they are unfamiliar with them. Teenagers may be more willing to share health information because of different opinions about privacy. Different cultural groups may have practices that bias how and when they talk about health [De Choudhury et al., 2017]. Some of these issues can be addressed by carefully controlling samples using the techniques outlined in Section 4.3.1, as well as awareness of known health biases in different populations.

Big data algorithms may also perform less well for some demographic groups. For instance, Johnson et al. [2017] found that most geolocation algorithms for social media are less accurate in rural areas. Furthermore, the bias appears to be part of the algorithm such that it cannot be corrected by oversampling from less populous locations.

Third, social monitoring is typically **passive**, and social data typically does not result from direct questions to users about health. Instead, analyses rely on incidental signals left by other user activities, such as searches for information about a medication, or discussing different diseases. As a result, researchers must infer user intent with regards to the health topic of interest. For example, when a person searches for "flu symptoms," are they searching because they have the flu, or are they trying to learn about flu in preparation for the upcoming flu season? When someone writes "I need a cigarette," does this mean that they are a smoker, or is this statement a colloquialism?

Fourth, the **method of data collection** influences the analytical results. While some platforms allow for an unbiased collection of data, most require collection techniques that bias the data (see Section 3.5 for information on data collection). For example, collecting all tweets that use a specific keyword may omit related messages without the keyword. Facebook allows the collection of public messages, but most messages on a topic may be private. A host of factors beyond this, some beyond a researcher's knowledge and control, can influence data. Some common biases in social media data collection are described in Chunara et al. [2017]. Data validation mechanisms, such as ensuring data conforms to common sense expectations, help safeguard researchers from these types of bias.

Finally, **analytical methods** can introduce bias. This is especially true of statistical, machine learning, and natural language processing algorithms, which can make non-random errors. There has recently been widespread discussion about Fairness, Accountability, and Transparency (FAT) in the machine learning community.[1] For examples, see Caliskan et al. [2017], Hardt et al. [2016], and Misra et al. [2016]. While not unique to social data, we note this concern because of the widespread use of these methods in social monitoring.

In the face of these numerous sources of bias, it can be difficult to believe that social data can successfully produce meaningful health information. Yet numerous studies have repeatedly demonstrated the power of social data in health analysis. The key to success is proper validation (Sections 4.1.4 and 4.2.1), ensuring that results match expectations and information derived from traditional health data sources.

Contextualization of these biases and comparison to other data types places these concerns in perspective. Consider telephone surveys, a bedrock of modern public health research. While results from telephone surveys comprise the primary data source for numerous public health

---

[1]http://www.fatml.org/

topics, they also suffer from numerous biases [Blumberg and Luke, 2007, Iannacchione, 2011, Kempf and Remington, 2007]. Telephone surveys similarly suffer from sampling bias, the most recent issue being landline vs. mobile phones. Other issues include differences in response rates, biases in who responds, how questions are phrased and framed, what order questions are asked, social desirability bias, and outright lying of respondents. Nevertheless, these concerns do not exclude telephone surveys as a data source. To the contrary, proper techniques correct these issues and allow us to derive useful data from these surveys. The same is true of social data [Dredze et al., 2015].

6.2 ACTIONABILITY CONCERNS

We now turn to actionability of public health information obtained from social monitoring systems. What can social media systems be used for? How trustworthy must they be to be actionable? What happens when these systems fail?

We will begin by summarizing how social media systems are currently used by public health and healthcare practitioners. We then discuss the reliability and utility of intelligence derived from these systems, and briefly discuss how this intelligence can be used for interventions and decision-making.

6.2.1 CURRENT USE BY PRACTITIONERS

Social monitoring provides a flexible and effective tool for research, one that has resulted in numerous publications on a variety of health topics. While some studies seek to replicate existing capabilities using social monitoring, many report novel research findings that contribute to the health literature. To date, this has been the primary way in which social monitoring has impacted the health community.

In some areas, research has matured to the point that current practices are impacted. While public health practitioners do not always share information on their use of social monitoring, we provide a few examples.

Several tools exist for influenza surveillance using social data, and public health officials have begun to incorporate these tools into their decision making processes. Influenza policy and decisions are often made by state and local health departments based on a variety of surveillance signals. Several of these agencies review websites that use social monitoring technologies, such as Google Flu Trends [Ginsberg et al., 2009], HealthTweets [Dredze et al., 2014], HealthMap [Freifeld et al., 2008], Sickweather (`sickweather.com`), and the HHS's Now Trending Challenge Site (`nowtrending.hhs.gov`), to name a few.

We reviewed examples of public health departments using social monitoring for food safety (Section 5.3.2). The Chicago effort is ongoing (`www.foodbornechicago.org`). An analysis of the Las Vegas system found "unexpected benefits, including the identification of venues lacking permits, contagious kitchen staff, and fewer customer complaints filed with the Las Vegas health department" [Sadilek et al., 2017].

Social monitoring for disaster response has gained traction. Ushahidi (`ushahidi.com`), Humanity Road (`humanityroad.org`), and other organizations monitor social media during disasters to cull actionable information in real-time, as well as communicate situation updates to people in impacted regions. The American Red Cross operates a Social Media Digital Operations Center[2] for similar purposes.

Tobacco Watcher [Cohen et al., 2015] provides media surveillance for tobacco news to tobacco control groups.

These are just a few examples of how social monitoring techniques already contribute to public health research and policy.

6.2.2   RELIABILITY OF WEB INTELLIGENCE

The actionability of public health systems based on social data is limited by the quality of the data and the reliability of the systems' predictions. Data reliability is particularly important for disease surveillance, where action must be taken promptly to address epidemics. A number of negative consequences can arise from poor predictions of epidemics.

Early detection of disease outbreaks is critical to mitigating the spread and effect of the outbreak. Digital systems failed to detect major public health crises in recent years, including the 2009 swine flu outbreaks in North America [Cook et al., 2011], and the 2014 ebola outbreak in West Africa [Leetaru, 2014]. These are examples of *type II* errors—failing to detect something that happened. While early detection is not the only goal of disease surveillance, failure to do so can cast doubt on the utility of such surveillance systems.

While failing to detect an outbreak has clear consequences, there are also negative consequences of predicting an epidemic that fails to emerge (a *type I* error). Taking unnecessary action to prevent an epidemic, such as undertaking mass immunization, can be costly [Krause, 2006], and campaigns that are perceived as needlessly "alarmist" can erode public trust [Doshi, 2009]. As described earlier, this type of error occurred when Google Flu Trends predicted a record-breaking severe flu season in late 2012. The result was widespread media coverage with statements such as, "Google searches for flu symptoms are at an all-time high. Is it time to panic?" [Boesler, 2013, Oremus, 2013]. The reputation of Google Flu Trends was ultimately hurt after the panic was determined to be warrantless, with headlines such as "Why Google Flu Trends Will Not Replace the CDC Anytime Soon" [Resnick, 2013], and led to more critical inspection by the academic community [Lazer et al., 2014b].

To be clear, these errors happen with traditional surveillance, and are not necessarily worsened by digital surveillance. However, traditional systems are generally well-understood and have been carefully validated, allowing practitioners to appropriately factor in the uncertainty of these systems. There are often validation mechanisms in place around traditional surveillance systems. For example, when areas of the United States report large increases in influenza in-

[2]http://www.redcross.org/news/press-release/The-American-Red-Cross-and-Dell-Launch-
First-Of-Its-Kind-Social-Media-Digital-Operations-Center-for-Humanitarian-Relief

fection rates, the CDC can work with the reporting clinics to validate the reported increase. In order for digital surveillance to be equally actionable, more research will be needed to quantify the reliability and uncertainty of these systems [Groseclose and Buckeridge, 2017].

Validation of social data is still an ongoing research problem. Blouin-Genest and Miller [2017] note that the use of "unofficial" data from social media creates "problems of standardization, control and verification." Bodnar and Salathé [2013] expressed concern with how social media influenza surveillance is validated, finding that systems trained on irrelevant or even randomly generated data can score well under standard validation metrics. This study highlights the need to correct for spatial and temporal autocorrelation (discussed in Section 4.1.4).

Many researchers argue that social monitoring should be done in combination with traditional monitoring, rather than relying on one or the other [Simonsen et al., 2016]. As stated by Salathé [2016], "Despite traditional epidemiology's shortcomings, it is ultimately the generator of ground-truth data against which novel, digital systems need to be validated. It will be prudent of the public health community to build on the strengths of both systems—veracity in traditional epidemiology and velocity and variety in digital epidemiology—in conjunction."

6.2.3   UTILITY OF WEB INTELLIGENCE

Another issue to consider when using social data is how much utility such data offers beyond traditional data. One of the most common uses of social monitoring for public health is the surveillance of influenza in the United States, but as pointed out by Lazer et al. [2014b], simple autoregressive models (Section 4.1.2) using only traditional data are already extremely accurate, so even if social data is perfectly reliable, there is little room for improvement. The CDC publishes influenza prevalence with a one-week delay in the U.S., and while this delay is too long for some tasks (e.g., hospital crowding preparation [Dugas et al., 2012]), the system is sufficiently fast for many purposes. In New York City, influenza prevalence is estimated on a daily basis, so there is little need for realtime social media data [Olson et al., 2013]. Work by Paul et al. [2014] took a different approach to evaluation. Rather than showing correlations between social media data and influenza rates, they demonstrated that adding Twitter data to a forecasting system that already makes use of available traditional CDC surveillance data can improve forecast accuracy more than using either type of data alone.

This does not mean that there is no utility in using social media for influenza surveillance—but there is much more utility in locations that do not conduct formal influenza surveillance, or for which influenza reports are delayed by more than one or two weeks. For example, official influenza reports for South Africa are delayed by at least one month, and data from Twitter can offer significant improvements [Paul et al., 2015a]. Social media data can benefit influenza surveillance in fine-grained locations such as hospitals, for which real-time surveillance is important for planning [Broniatowski et al., 2015], and mass gatherings, at which diseases are not formally monitored [Yom-Tov et al., 2014a].

Moreover, while up-to-date surveillance systems exist for some infectious diseases such as influenza, there are public health issues for which data is severely out of date. For example, the prevalence of behaviors such as smoking is typically estimated through surveys, and these estimates can take a year or more to compile. For this reason, Ayers et al. [2014a] argue that there is more utility in using social media data to study behavioral medicine than in disease surveillance.

More generally, the scientific literature increasingly includes published studies relying on social data. Their impact on health knowledge will be determined through the accumulation of supporting evidence, and through meta-studies that can contextualize results from social data in the larger collection of evidence.

6.2.4   DECISIONS AND INTERVENTIONS

Even if social media systems can deliver novel, reliable information, there is a challenge in determining how to act on this information. Policy makers and public health officials will need to determine the extent to which web-based data sources should be trusted and incorporated into decision models. In areas where social monitoring systems deliver complementary information, such as influenza surveillance, their inclusion in ongoing surveillance will rely on combining multiple information sources in the decision making process. In areas without existing empirical data, where social monitoring systems deliver new information, careful validation and evaluation will be necessary to determine the extent to which the information can be relied on. As discussed in Section 6.2.2, the long-term use of these systems will depend on their use and validation over coming years to better understand how they perform during health crises.

In addition to decisions at the population level, another type of decision involves pursuing interventions with **individuals**. For example, if algorithms can infer that a person has poor mental health [De Choudhury et al., 2013b], should something be done to offer the person support? Some simple, non-controversial interventions are in place on the Web: most major search engines in the United States, for example, will provide the phone number to the National Suicide Prevention Lifeline if a person searches for suicide. However, people might react negatively if such an intervention occurred for non-obvious reasons, such as if a user's long-term behavior was suggestive of suicide risk, even though the user may not have explicitly searched for suicide. How and when to perform such interventions are difficult questions that will need to be addressed. The vast majority of public health research described in Chapter 5 does not involve any type of individual intervention, so these issues have not been well explored.

6.3   ETHICAL CONSIDERATIONS

Using social data to study health raises many ethical challenges [Benton et al., 2017, boyd and Crawford, 2012, Conway, 2014, McKee, 2013, Mikal et al., 2016, Vayena et al., 2015]. Two big ethical concerns arise when monitoring social data for public health: (1) users' data, even if public, are used in ways the users may not have intended; and (2) health data is particularly sensitive information.

The short response to these concerns is that the data under consideration are public (in general), and users agree to share their public data under the terms of service when using social media platforms. Under Institutional Review Board (IRB) guidelines, which govern research ethics in the United States, research can generally be done with social data with an IRB exemption as long as the data are public and there is no interaction with users [Buchanan and Ess, 2009].

However, this response is simplistic. In reality, IRB exemptions of public data were never intended to cover this type of research. Furthermore, while the analyzed data may be public, many users do not behave in a way that suggests they are aware that their data could be shown to a large audience. This is not to say that these guidelines are necessarily wrong, but this is an issue that should be explicitly decided in the community, rather than relying on outdated protocols [O'Connor, 2013].

Therefore, standard IRB procedures should be treated as a starting point, but not an end point in the conversation. Fortunately, the fields of medicine and public health have a long history of ethics research, and current ethics protocols have grown out of decades of research. The community can therefore build off of this experience to develop guidelines for working with social data. A thorough summary of the community's current attitudes toward ethics of social media research is provided by Golder et al. [2017].

Below, we describe in more depth some of the specific ethical concerns with social monitoring, as well as some guidelines for navigating these concerns. For a fuller treatment on relevant issues, we suggest Conway [2014], and see Benton et al. [2017] for a practical guide on research protocols.

6.3.1   PUBLIC DATA

One of the most difficult ethical issues to pin down with social monitoring, particularly for health, is the degree to which data is treated as public data [McKee, 2013]. This question is crucial because research of public data typically does not require informed consent or a full IRB review, and current IRB guidelines treat public social media data this way. However, the issue is more complicated than current IRB guidelines suggest. Users who create public data may not be aware that their data is public, or may not want their public data used for research. Reliance on the complex terms of service of social media platforms may be insufficient. Many social platforms, especially Facebook, have been criticized for having unclear privacy management systems [Liu et al., 2011]. There are a number of ways in which the boundaries between public and private data are unclear in the context of research.

First, users may simply be unaware that their data is publicly accessible, or if they are aware in general, this reality may not be present when they post some content. For example, if a user replies to another user's tweet, they may compose their message intending for a direct conversation, forgetting that the conversation is publicly accessible. Alternatively, users may rely on the "hidden in plain sight" approach, where their messages are public but few people actually see them. There are numerous cases of users who post information to Twitter that they consider private, with the assumption that the people from whom they want to hide the information would never check Twitter.

This same is true of discussion forums and other online communities. Users may have expectations of privacy within the community, thinking that the general public is unlikely to access the forum. Many of these online communities feel private, and users may behave as if they are in a private environment, even if technically the community is accessible to outsiders [Bromseth, 2002].

Second, even if users do not expect privacy in general, they may not wish for their data to be used for all possible purposes. A user may not mind a large group of people viewing their post, but may feel differently if the message is shared on the evening news, or published in an academic article. Online communities can react negatively to having data used for research [Hudson and Bruckman, 2004], although how web users feel about research in general remains an open question. Mikal et al. [2016] conducted interviews with Twitter users with a diagnosed history of depression and found that they held a relatively positive view of using public Twitter data for mental health purposes, provided that results on individuals were aggregated in the analysis.

While many instances of public outrage against this type of research are based on uninformed views of how data is collected, protected, and used, these concerns form some of the primary motivations for informed consent in human subjects research.

Finally, a particularly difficult dilemma arises when public data can be used to infer private information, especially private health information. For example, statistical models and machine learning techniques can be used to infer that a web user has an illness based on the user's public data, even if the user did not share this information explicitly. Private health information, which has legal protections in the United States and elsewhere, can be inferred from data that is publicly available [Horvitz and Mulligan, 2015]. Numerous papers have demonstrated that analysis of social media messages from a user can be used to detect mental health conditions [Coppersmith et al., 2014b, De Choudhury et al., 2013b, Prieto et al., 2014]. These types of inferences fall into a gray area both legally and ethically.

For these reasons, there are strong arguments for treating public data as private, at least in many ways. Even though it may often be reasonable to waive consent from users to use their public data [Hudson and Bruckman, 2004], such research should still be treated as human subjects research, and steps should be taken to protect the participants, such as securing their data [Zimmer, 2010] and putting restrictions on distribution and use [Benton et al., 2017]. Even still, we must seek policies that are not overly restrictive and allow for continued research using social data, balancing privacy concerns and respect for human subjects with the goals of sharing knowledge and making research reproducible. No doubt, this area will continue to be the subject of considerable debate for some time.

6.3.2   USER INTERACTION

Ethical considerations and research protocols change when researchers interact with social media users. If interactions or interventions are involved, then social media research likely requires full IRB review [Benton et al., 2017].

For studies that require the direct recruitment of participating social media users (e.g., [De Choudhury et al., 2014a]), the protocols of IRB review and informed consent are the same as traditional medical research and are therefore relatively straightforward.

Less straightforward is the protocol for interacting with users at a large scale. A well-known example of this scenario is the Facebook emotional contagion study by Kramer et al. [2014]. This study involved hundreds of thousands of Facebook users whose news feeds were altered to contain more or fewer messages expressing positive or negative emotions, and different users were shown different effects. Even though the study was reviewed for ethical concerns, the publication of the study was met with public outrage as many Facebook users felt manipulated, and did not wish to be research subjects. This spurred a debate in the research community as to the ethics of the study, with strong disagreements as to whether the research protocols were ethical. One of the central points of contention was whether the researchers should have attempted to obtain consent from the Facebook users, or if the existing terms of service agreement, which allow for this type of testing, is sufficient.

There is no clear ethical answer as to how to conduct such a study. While many Facebook users were upset, not all academics agreed that the study was unethical. For example, Meyer and Chabris [2015] argue that all users are inherently participating in an experiment by virtue of participating in a social networking platform with unknown effects, and therefore the ethical thing to do is to conduct such research to understand the effect of these platforms. They argue that informed consent was right to be waived for this particular study, because the risk to participants was low and the study could not have been done in the same way if consent was required.

In short, novel uses of social data for health are posing complex ethical questions on data use, the answers to which remain the subject of significant debate. Simple answers, such as "the data is public anyway" are unconvincing given the complexity of many data sets and use cases. Researchers in this area must remain cognizant of these ethical considerations in the design of their studies, and should consistently re-evaluate study goals and protocols as they learn more about their data, and as the conversation in the community progresses.

6.3.3   GUIDELINES FOR ETHICAL RESEARCH

With the above concerns in mind, we offer some practical guidelines for conducting research with social media data. These suggestions largely follow the recommendations of Benton et al. [2017], who synthesize best practices from the research community.

- Social media research should be discussed with Institutional Review Boards (IRBs). IRB feedback can ensure that research is done in the best way possible, and can determine when a study must receive a full IRB approval. IRBs can also suggest safeguards and modifications to research protocols to ensure compliance with best practice.

- In published studies, researchers should clearly state what data was used, whether it was public, if permission was obtained from users, and if the study had IRB approval.

- Obtain informed consent whenever possible.

  While this may be unrealistic in most cases, some data collection settings do provide opportunities for obtaining user consent. Researchers who always assume that consent is unnecessary will miss data settings where it can be collected.

- Safeguard sensitive data. Just because data originates from a public source, does not mean that its collection does not introduce sensitivities. For example, filtering Twitter data to only those messages that indicate suicide attempts or diagnoses of sexually transmitted diseases creates a corpus that contains sensitive information. This data can be protected by restricting access to the data to only those with proper training and a need to access the data, and redistribution can require a data use agreement. Additionally, anonymization could be considered for further protection. Finally, researchers should respect requests to remove data.

- Avoid publishing personally identifiable information (PII), which can include metadata such as usernames and location data. This can include direct quotes from data (e.g., the text of a tweet), since PII can be found by searching the quote on a search engine. Additionally, re-publishing such content without modification may be a violation of the International Committee of Medical Journal Editors [1997] ethics standards and the Association of Internet Researchers [Markham and Buchanan, 2012]. When exact quotes of messages are necessary, researchers should use data that is already well known from public figures or celebrities [Eisenstein, 2013].

- When possible, data—particularly datasets that will be published or shared with other researchers—should be aggregated. For example, if conducting influenza surveillance with Twitter data, it may only be necessary to share the number of influenza-related tweets per day, rather than the tweets themselves.

- Linking data across public sites can reveal information that users did not intend to share. For example, a user may create a public persona on Twitter, and a less identifiable account on a mental health discussion forum. Linking these accounts may assign personal health statements, meant to be confidential, to a public persona. Studies that involve linking should carefully consider the ramifications of such practices and obtain IRB approval.

These suggestions are intended as rules of thumb, and are just some of the many possible good practices that can be considered. For more comprehensive views on ethics of using social media for public health, see Rivers and Lewis [2014], Conway [2014], Vayena et al. [2015], Mikal et al. [2016], and Crowcroft et al. [2017].

CHAPTER 7

Looking Ahead

When we tell people about this kind of research, we often get questions like, "what happens when Twitter shuts down?" It's true that any particular platform like Twitter is unlikely to stick around forever (and one could be forgiven for having the impression that social monitoring requires Twitter specifically, given its dominance in this field!), but that doesn't mean that this type of research hinges on the availability of any particular platform. While specific products come and go, the general form of a technology tends to stick around once it's introduced. Search and email are still ubiquitous, even though most of the popular search engines and email clients of twenty years ago are no longer around. People may no longer use AOL Instant Messenger (AIM), but there are now numerous popular messaging platforms. In the same vein, social networks, (micro)blogs, and online reviews will stick around in some form or another. Social data isn't going anywhere.

Likewise, there's no reason to think that social monitoring is a temporary fad that will lose traction. Its utility has been demonstrated enough times in enough ways that it is clear that this type of data has something powerful to offer, despite the challenges ahead. We are already starting to see social monitoring move beyond proof-of-concept research and be integrated with real systems, as reviewed in Section 6.2.1. We've already learned much about health behaviors from this research. While much of the research described in this book is not yet ready to be adopted into practice, that will undoubtedly improve with continued progress and validation of these techniques. Social monitoring won't replace traditional forms of monitoring, but when combined together, their complementary strengths and weaknesses can play off each other, filling in knowledge gaps and reducing the time and cost of collecting information.

What will social monitoring for public health look like in the coming years? We make three general predictions.

First, we expect the community to branch out to more diverse areas of public health, shifting priorities to areas with the highest data needs. Throughout the book, we've pointed out areas that we think have had too much or too little attention in this community. Flu surveillance has been the most popular public health application for social monitoring—for a lot of good reasons, including high prevalence, high data availability, and established metrics and baselines for validation—but as we pointed out in Section 6.2.3, social data only has so much to offer when you consider that national flu surveillance is already very good. Disease surveillance will benefit from social data more in locations and populations without robust surveillance, and for diseases without so many resources.

Beyond disease surveillance, we think there is especially high potential in social monitoring for problems in behavioral medicine and mental health, which are prime targets for social monitoring. These are issues that affect huge numbers of people but have serious limitations in current monitoring, and depend on everyday attitudes and behaviors that are commonly shared in social data. One area where we especially hope to see more social monitoring is gun violence in the United States (Section 5.3.5), which is a leading cause of death yet there are huge holes in our understanding of this problem, thanks to a lack of standardized monitoring resources. This is a case where social data, on top of the recognition of this type of violence as a public health issue, could make a huge difference.

Second, we are going to see major advancements in the underlying algorithms and technologies that support social monitoring. In the past decade, there have been huge improvements in tasks that fall in the domain of artificial intelligence: things like understanding and transcribing speech, recognizing people and objects in photos, and translating from one language to another. Advances in machine learning, natural language processing, and computer vision are driving these improvements, and it's happening at a faster pace than many expected. These improvements are not just in experiments out of public view; consumer products like Siri and Alexa work noticeably better than even a few years ago.

A major catalyst of these improvements has been a surge of new research in "deep learning," a type of machine learning that uses much larger and more complex models than the types of models described in Section 4.1.1. While many of the ideas of deep learning are rooted in neural network models that have been around for decades, recent improvements in algorithms and computational processing have made these ideas more practical, leading to renewed interest and new discoveries in the capabilities of these models. The authors of this book, who primarily work in machine learning and natural language processing, can attest that there's been a huge increase in the amount of deep learning research in these disciplines just in the past few years. So many people are interested in deep learning, including academic and non-academic researchers and practitioners, that some computer science conferences are even running into problems of overcrowding and sold out registration—problems historically unheard of at technical academic gatherings.

How will these advancements relate to social monitoring? Since social data largely comes in the form of what people say, improvements in automated understanding of human language will lead to more accurate analysis of the data. New algorithms will be better at handling some of the difficulties we've described with text data, such as ambiguity, colloquialisms, and sarcasm (though not perfectly, since even humans struggle with these challenges), and we will have better tools for extracting information like opinions toward vaccines and side effects of drugs from online messages. Media types like images, audio, and video will become more practical as large-scale data sources, as technology gets better at automatically parsing and understanding these types of data. In general, deep learning can improve the ability to make inferences and predictions over traditional statistical models, so we can expect to have more accurate models for detection and forecasting of events like outbreaks.

Third, for all the progress made in the past decade, there remains a wide gap between what is possible with computational methods and the technical skillset common in public health. While computer scientists routinely build algorithms that process millions of messages and produce complex visualizations, public health practitioners often don't even have a way of downloading the right data. Making these methods accessible to non-technical researchers remains a difficult problem. We hope to see more efforts to do so, including better training and tutorials, as well as more user-friendly computational tools.

While we expect to see these trends in social monitoring, we're more excited by what we *can't* predict. Consider the rapid timeline in which this field has popped up. It was less than 20 years ago that researchers first started deeply looking at health information on the Web. It's been 11 years since the first demonstration of social monitoring for health (flu surveillance by Eysenbach [2006]), and 9 years since the launch of Google Flu Trends. Social monitoring started picking up steam as an area of computer science research about 6–8 years ago, and most of the early work (and even much of the current work) was proof-of-concept in nature. The United States federal government started actively promoting this type of health monitoring 3–4 years ago (Section 2.2.2), and the first clear successes of real social monitoring systems were documented 2–3 years ago, when social data was able to alert health inspectors to food safety problems (Section 5.3.2). It's hard to predict where this field will be in 10 years when you consider that this is further away in time than when most of this pioneering work was done.

Whatever happens, it's clear that social data is transforming how public health can be done. As we discovered while writing this book, a lot of creative work is being done in almost every area we can list. It's amazing what has been achieved so far, and as this field continues to advance, we are excited to see the impact it will have on our collective health and wellbeing. Social monitoring will change public health research, and we look forward to participating in the revolution.

Bibliography

Abbar, S., Mejova, Y., and Weber, I. (2015). You tweet what you eat: Studying food consumption through Twitter. In *Conference on Human Factors in Computing Systems (CHI)*. DOI: 10.1145/2702123.2702153. 59

Abel, F., Hauff, C., Houben, G.-J., Stronkman, R., and Tao, K. (2012). Twitcident: Fighting fire with information from social web streams. In *International Conference on World Wide Web (WWW)*. DOI: 10.1145/2187980.2188035. 67

Achrekar, H., Gandhe, A., Lazarus, R., Yu, S., and Liu, B. (2012). Twitter improves seasonal influenza prediction. In *International Conference on Health Informatics*. DOI: 10.5220/0003780600610070. 30, 36, 53

Adler-Milstein, J., DesRoches, C. M., Furukawa, M. F., Worzala, C., Charles, D., Kralovec, P., Stalley, S., and Jha, A. K. (2014). More than half of U.S. hospitals have at least a basic EHR, but stage 2 criteria remain challenging for most. *Health Affairs*, **33**(9), 1664–1671. DOI: 10.1377/hlthaff.2014.0453. 2

Agapie, E., Golovchinsky, G., and Qvarfordt, P. (2013). Leading people to longer queries. In *Conference on Human Factors in Computing Systems (CHI)*. DOI: 10.1145/2470654.2481418. 81

Ahlwardt, K., Heaivilin, N., Gibbs, J., Page, J., Gerbert, B., and Tsoh, J. Y. (2014). Tweeting about pain: Comparing self-reported toothache experiences with those of backaches, earaches and headaches. *Journal of the American Dental Association*, **145**(7), 737–743. 55

Akaike, H. (1974). A new look at the statistical model identification. *IEEE Transactions on Automatic Control*, **19**, 716–723. DOI: 10.1109/tac.1974.1100705. 37

Akbari, M., Hu, X., Liqiang, N., and Chua, T.-S. (2016). From tweets to wellness: Wellness event detection from Twitter streams. In *Conference on Artificial Intelligence (AAAI)*, pages 87–93. 59

Al Zamal, F., Liu, W., and Ruths, D. (2012). Homophily and latent attribute inference: Inferring latent attributes of Twitter users from neighbors. In *International Conference on Weblogs and Social Media (ICWSM)*. 43

Allem, J.-P. and Ferrara, E. (2016). The importance of debiasing social media data to better understand e-cigarette-related attitudes and behaviors. *Journal of Medical Internet Research*, **18**(8). DOI: 10.2196/jmir.6185. 17, 82

Allem, J.-P., Escobedo, P., Chu, K.-H., Soto, D. W., Cruz, T. B., and Unger, J. B. (2016). Campaigns and counter campaigns: Reactions on Twitter to e-cigarette education. *Tobacco Control*. DOI: 10.1136/tobaccocontrol-2015-052757. 82

Allem, J.-P., Leas, E. C., Caputi, T. L., Dredze, M., Althouse, B. M., Noar, S. M., and Ayers, J. W. (2017). The Charlie Sheen effect on rapid in-home human immunodeficiency virus test sales. *Prevention Science*. DOI: 10.1007/s11121-017-0792-2. 66

Alowibdi, J. S., Buy, U., Yu, P., et al. (2013). Language independent gender classification on Twitter. In *Advances in Social Networks Analysis and Mining (ASONAM), IEEE/ACM International Conference on*, pages 739–743. DOI: 10.1145/2492517.2492632. 43

Althoff, T., White, R. W., and Horvitz, E. (2016). Influence of Pokémon Go on physical activity: Study and implications. *Journal of Medical Internet Research*, **18**(12). DOI: 10.2196/jmir.6759. 59

Althouse, B., Allem, J.-P., Childers, M., Dredze, M., and Ayers, J. W. (2014). Population health concerns during the United States' great recession. *American Journal of Preventive Medicine*, **46**(2), 166–170. DOI: 10.1016/j.amepre.2013.10.008. 16, 76

Althouse, B. M., Ng, Y. Y., and Cummings, D. A. T. (2011). Prediction of dengue incidence using search query surveillance. *PLoS Neglected Tropical Diseases*, **5**(8). DOI: 10.1371/journal.pntd.0001258. 54

Althouse, B. M., Scarpino, S. V., Meyers, L. A., Ayers, J. W., Bargsten, M., Baumbach, J., Brownstein, J. S., Castro, L., Clapham, H., Cummings, D. A., et al. (2015). Enhancing disease surveillance with novel data streams: Challenges and opportunities. *EPJ Data Science*, **4**(1), 17. DOI: 10.1140/epjds/s13688-015-0054-0. 78

Alwan, A., et al. (2011). Global status report on noncommunicable diseases 2010. World Health Organization. 73

Aphinyanaphongs, Y., Ray, B., Statnikov, A., and Krebs, P. (2014). Text classification for automatic detection of alcohol use-related tweets. In *International Workshop on Issues and Challenges in Social Computing*. DOI: 10.1109/iri.2014.7051877. 61

Aramaki, E., Maskawa, S., and Morita, M. (2011). Twitter catches the flu: Detecting influenza epidemics using Twitter. In *Empirical Methods in Natural Language Processing (EMNLP)*, pages 1568–1576. 30, 39, 53

Araz, O. M., Bentley, D., and Muelleman, R. L. (2014). Using Google Flu Trends data in forecasting influenza-like-illness related ED visits in Omaha, Nebraska. *American Journal of Emergency Medicine*, **32**(9), 1016–1023. DOI: 10.1016/j.ajem.2014.05.052. 53

Artstein, R. and Poesio, M. (2008). Inter-coder agreement for computational linguistics. *Computer Linguistics*, **34**(4), 555–596. DOI: 10.1162/coli.07-034-r2. 41

Asur, S. and Huberman, B. A. (2010). Predicting the future with social media. In *IEEE/WIC/ACM International Conference on Web Intelligence and Intelligent Agent Technology*. DOI: 10.1109/wi-iat.2010.63. 16

Austin, P. (2011). An introduction to propensity score methods for reducing the effects of confounding in observational studies. *Multivariate Behavior Research*, **46**(3), 399–424. DOI: 10.1080/00273171.2011.568786. 46

Ayers, J. W., Ribisl, K. M., and Brownstein, J. S. (2011a). Tracking the rise in popularity of electronic nicotine delivery systems (electronic cigarettes) using search query surveillance. *American Journal of Preventive Medicine*, **40**(4), 448–453. DOI: 10.1016/j.amepre.2010.12.007. 11, 60

Ayers, J. W., Ribisl, K., and Brownstein, J. S. (2011b). Using search query surveillance to monitor tax avoidance and smoking cessation following the United States' 2009 "SCHIP" cigarette tax increase. *PLoS ONE*, **6**(3). DOI: 10.1371/journal.pone.0016777. 34, 61, 66

Ayers, J. W., Althouse, B. M., Allem, J.-P., Ford, D. E., Ribisl, K. M., and Cohen, J. E. (2012a). A novel evaluation of World No Tobacco Day in Latin America. *Journal of Medical Internet Research*, **3**, e77. DOI: 10.2196/jmir.2148. 66

Ayers, J. W., Althouse, B. M., Allem, J.-P., Childers, M. A., Zafar, W., Latkin, C., Ribisl, K. M., and Brownstein, J. S. (2012b). Novel surveillance of psychological distress during the great recession. *Journal of Affective Disorders*, **142**(1), 323–330. DOI: 10.1016/j.jad.2012.05.005. 16

Ayers, J. W., Althouse, B. M., Allem, J. P., Rosenquist, J. N., and Ford, D. E. (2013). Seasonality in seeking mental health information on Google. *American Journal of Preventive Medicine*, **44**(5), 520–525. DOI: 10.1016/j.amepre.2013.01.012. 75

Ayers, J. W., Althouse, B. M., and Dredze, M. (2014a). Could behavioral medicine lead the web data revolution? *JAMA*, **311**(14), 1399–1400. DOI: 10.1001/jama.2014.1505. 58, 88

Ayers, J. W., Althouse, B. M., Ribisl, K. M., and Emery, S. (2014b). Digital detection for tobacco control: Online reactions to the 2009 U.S. cigarette excise tax increase. *Nicotine Tobacco Research*, **16**(5), 576–583. DOI: 10.1093/ntr/ntt186. 61, 66

Ayers, J. W., Althouse, B. M., Noar, S. M., and Cohen, J. E. (2014c). Do celebrity cancer diagnoses promote primary cancer prevention? *Preventive Medicine*, **58**, 81–84. DOI: 10.1016/j.ypmed.2013.11.007. 66

Ayers, J. W., Althouse, B. M., Johnson, M., Dredze, M., and Cohen, J. E. (2014d). What's the healthiest day? Circaseptan (weekly) rhythms in healthy considerations. *American Journal of Preventive Medicine,*. DOI: 10.1016/j.amepre.2014.02.003. 59

Ayers, J. W., Althouse, B. M., Leas, E. C., Alcorn, T., and Dredze, M. (2016a). Big media data can inform gun violence prevention. In *Bloomberg Data for Good Exchange*. 70

Ayers, J. W., Westmaas, J. L., Leas, E. C., Benton, A., Chen, Y., Dredze, M., and Althouse, B. (2016b). Leveraging big data to improve health awareness campaigns: A novel evaluation of the Great American Smokeout. *JMIR Public Health and Surveillance*. DOI: 10.2196/publichealth.5304. 66

Ayers, J. W., Althouse, B. M., Dredze, M., Leas, E. C., and Noar, S. M. (2016c). News and internet searches about human immunodeficiency virus after Charlie Sheen's disclosure. *JAMA Internal Medicine*. DOI: 10.1001/jamainternmed.2016.0003. 66

Ayers, J. W., Leas, E. C., Dredze, M., Allem, J., Grabowski, J. G., and Hill, L. (2016d). Pokémon Go—a new distraction for drivers and pedestrians. *JAMA Internal Medicine*. DOI: 10.1001/jamainternmed.2016.6274. 59

Ayers, J. W., Althouse, B. M., Allem, J.-P., Leas, E. C., Dredze, M., and Williams, R. S. (2016e). Revisiting the rise of electronic nicotine delivery systems using search query surveillance. *American Journal of Preventive Medicine*, **50**(6), e173–e181. DOI: 10.1016/j.amepre.2015.12.008. 60

Ayers, J. W., Leas, E. C., Allem, J.-P., Benton, A., Dredze, M., Althouse, B. M., Cruz, T. B., and Unger, J. B. (2017). Why do people use electronic nicotine delivery systems (electronic cigarettes)? A content analysis of Twitter, 2012–2015. *PLoS ONE*, **12**(3), 1–8. DOI: 10.1371/journal.pone.0170702. 60

Babbie, R. (2016). *The Practice of Social Research*, 14th ed. Wadsworth Publishing Company. 77

Bader, J. L. and Theofanos, M. F. (2003). Searching for cancer information on the internet: Analyzing natural language search queries. *Journal of Medical Internet Research (Electronic Resource)*, **5**(4). DOI: 10.2196/jmir.5.4.e31. 19, 55

Bakal, G. and Kavuluru, R. (2017). On quantifying diffusion of health information on Twitter. In *IEEE International Conference on Biomedical and Health Informatics*. DOI: 10.1109/bhi.2017.7897311. 65

Balani, S. and De Choudhury, M. (2015). Detecting and characterizing mental health related self-disclosure in social media. In *Conference on Human Factors in Computing Systems (CHI)*, pages 1373–1378, ACM. DOI: 10.1145/2702613.2732733. 76

Baltrusaitis, K., Santillana, M., Crawley, W. A., Chunara, R., Smolinski, M., and Brownstein, S. J. (2017). Determinants of participants' follow-up and characterization of representativeness in Flu Near You, a participatory disease surveillance system. *JMIR Public Health Surveillance*, **3**(2), e18. DOI: 10.2196/publichealth.7304. 20

Barratt, M. J. (2011). Discussing illicit drugs in public internet forums: Visibility, stigma, and pseudonymity. In *International Conference on Communities and Technologies*, pages 159–168. DOI: 10.1145/2103354.2103376. 62

Bartlett, C. and Wurtz, R. (2015). Twitter and public health. *Journal of Public Health Management and Practice*, **21**(4), 375–383. DOI: 10.1097/phh.0000000000000041. 9

Bass III, P. F. (2015). Vaccine refusal. *Contemporary Pediatrics*. 63

Baumann, M. H. (2014). Awash in a sea of "bath salts": Implications for biomedical research and public health. *Addiction*, **109**(10), 1577–1579. DOI: 10.1111/add.12601. 58

Belkin, N. J., Kelly, D., Kim, G., Kim, J.-Y., Lee, H.-J., Muresan, G., Tang, M.-C., Yuan, X.-J., and Cool, C. (2003). Query length in interactive information retrieval. In *Conference on Research and Development in Information Retrieval (SIGIR)*. DOI: 10.1145/860472.860474. 81

Beller, C., Knowles, R., Harman, C., Bergsma, S., Mitchell, M., and Van Durme, B. (2014). I'm a Belieber: Social roles via self-identification and conceptual attributes. In *Association for Computational Linguistics (ACL)*, pages 181–186. DOI: 10.3115/v1/p14-2030. 43

Bendler, J., Brandt, T., Wagner, S., and Neumann, D. (2014). Investigating crime-to-Twitter relationships in urban environments—facilitating a virtual neighborhood watch. In *European Conference on Information Systems*. 68

Bennett, K. J., Olsen, J. M., Harris, S., Mekaru, S., Livinski, A. A., and Brownstein, J. S. (2013). The perfect storm of information: Combining traditional and non-traditional data sources for public health situational awareness during hurricane response. *PLoS Currents*, **5**. DOI: 10.1371/currents.dis.d2800aa4e536b9d6849e966e91488003. 67

Benton, A., Ungar, L., Hill, S., Hennessy, S., Mao, J., Chung, A., Leonard, C. E., and Holmes, J. H. (2011). Identifying potential adverse effects using the web: A new approach to medical hypothesis generation. *Journal of Biomedical Information*, **44**(6), 989–996. DOI: 10.1016/j.jbi.2011.07.005. 72

Benton, A., Hancock, B., Coppersmith, G., Ayers, J. W., and Dredze, M. (2016a). After Sandy Hook Elementary: A year in the gun control debate on Twitter. In *Bloomberg Data for Good Exchange*. 70

Benton, A., Paul, M. J., Hancock, B., and Dredze, M. (2016b). Collective supervision of topic models for predicting surveys with social media. In *Conference on Artificial Intelligence (AAAI)*. 12, 70

Benton, A., Coppersmith, G., and Dredze, M. (2017). Ethical research protocols for social media health research. In *EACL Workshop on Ethics in Natural Language Processing*. 88, 89, 90, 91, 92

Berger, A. L., Pietra, V. J. D., and Pietra, S. A. D. (1996). A maximum entropy approach to natural language processing. *Computer Linguistic*, **22**(1), 39–71. 30

Bergsma, S., Dredze, M., Durme, B. V., Wilson, T., and Yarowsky, D. (2013). Broadly improving user classification via communication-based name and location clustering on Twitter. In *North American Chapter of the Association for Computational Linguistics (NAACL)*. 43, 44, 45

Beullens, K. and Schepers, A. (2013). Display of alcohol use on Facebook: A content analysis. *Cyberpsychology Behavior and Social Networking*, **16**(7), 497–503. DOI: 10.1089/cyber.2013.0044. 61

Bi, B., Shokouhi, M., Kosinski, M., and Graepel, T. (2013). Inferring the demographics of search users: Social data meets search queries. In *International Conference on World Wide Web (WWW)*, pages 131–140. DOI: 10.1145/2488388.2488401. 44

Bian, J., Topaloglu, U., and Yu, F. (2012). Towards large-scale Twitter mining for drug-related adverse events. In *International Workshop on Smart Health and Wellbeing*. DOI: 10.1145/2389707.2389713. 72

Bian, J., Yoshigoe, K., Hicks, A., Yuan, J., He, Z., Xie, M., Guo, Y., Prosperi, M., Salloum, R., and Modave, F. (2016). Mining Twitter to assess the public perception of the "Internet of Things." *PLoS ONE*, **11**(7), 1–14. DOI: 10.1371/journal.pone.0158450. 16

Biggerstaff, M., Alper, D., Dredze, M., Fox, S., Fung, I. C.-H., Hickmann, K. S., Lewis, B., Rosenfeld, R., Shaman, J., Tsou, M.-H., Velardi, P., Vespignani, A., and Finelli, L. (2016). Results from the centers for disease control and prevention's predict the 2013–2014 influenza season challenge. *BMC Infectious Diseases*, **16**(1), 357. DOI: 10.1186/s12879-016-1669-x. 13, 38, 53

Blanford, J. I., Bernhardt, J., Savelyev, A., Wong-Parodi, G., Carleton, A. M., Titley, D. W., and MacEachren, A. M. (2014). Tweeting and tornadoes. In *Conference on Information Systems for Crisis Response and Management (ISCRAM)*. 68

Blei, D. M. and Lafferty, J. D. (2009). Topic models. *Text Mining: Classification, Clustering, and Applications*, **10**(71), 34. 31

Blei, D. M., Ng, A. Y., and Jordan, M. I. (2003). Latent Dirichlet allocation. *The Journal of Machine Learning Research*, **3**, 993–1022. 31

Blouin-Genest, G. and Miller, A. (2017). The politics of participatory epidemiology: Technologies, social media and influenza surveillance in the U.S. *Health Policy and Technology*, **6**(2), 192–197. DOI: 10.1016/j.hlpt.2017.02.001. 87

Blumberg, S. J. and Luke, J. V. (2007). Coverage bias in traditional telephone surveys of low-income and young adults. *Public Opinion Quarterly*, **71**(5), 734–749. DOI: 10.1093/poq/nfm047. 12, 85

Bodnar, T. and Salathé, M. (2013). Validating models for disease detection using Twitter. In *International Conference on World Wide Web (WWW)*. DOI: 10.1145/2487788.2488027. 87

Boesler, M. (2013). The Google Flu chart that's blowing everyone's mind read. http://www.businessinsider.com/google-flu-chart-blowing-everyones-mind-2013-1 86

Bogoch, I. I., Brady, O. J., Kraemer, M., German, M., Creatore, M. I., Kulkarni, M. A., Brownstein, J. S., Mekaru, S. R., Hay, S. I., Groot, E., et al. (2016). Anticipating the international spread of Zika virus from Brazil. *The Lancet*, **387**, 335–336. DOI: 10.1016/s0140-6736(16)00080-5. 54

Bollen, J., Mao, H., and Zeng, X. (2011). Twitter mood predicts the stock market. *Journal of Computational Science*, **2**(1), 1–8. DOI: 10.1016/j.jocs.2010.12.007. 16

Bosley, J. C., Zhao, N. W., Hill, S., Shofer, F. S., Asch, D. A., Becker, L. B., and Merchant, R. M. (2013). Decoding Twitter: Surveillance and trends for cardiac arrest and resuscitation communication. *Resuscitation*, **84**(2), 206–212. DOI: 10.1016/j.resuscitation.2012.10.017. 68

Box, G. E. P. and Jenkins, G. (1990). *Time Series Analysis, Forecasting and Control*. Holden-Day, Incorporated. 37

boyd, D. and Crawford, K. (2012). Critical questions for big data. *Information, Communication and Society*, **15**(5). DOI: 10.1080/1369118x.2012.678878. 88

Bragazzi, N. L., Watad, A., Brigo, F., Adawi, M., Amital, H., and Shoenfeld, Y. (2016). Public health awareness of autoimmune diseases after the death of a celebrity. *Clinical Rheumatology*, pages 1–7. DOI: 10.1007/s10067-016-3513-5. 66

Braithwaite, R. S., Giraud-Carrier, C., West, J., Barnes, D. M., and Hanson, L. C. (2016). Validating machine learning algorithms for Twitter data against established measures of suicidality. *JMIR Mental Health*, **3**(2), e21. DOI: 10.2196/mental.4822. 75

Bravo, C. A. and Hoffman-Goetz, L. (2015). Tweeting about prostate and testicular cancers: What are individuals saying in their discussions about the 2013 Movember Canada campaign? *Journal of Cancer Education*. DOI: 10.1007/s13187-015-0838-8. 66

Brener, N. D., Billy, J. O., and Grady, W. R. (2003). Assessment of factors affecting the validity of self-reported health-risk behavior among adolescents: Evidence from the scientific literature. *Journal of Adolescent Health*, **33**(6), 436–457. DOI: 10.1016/s1054-139x(03)00052-1. 79

Bresnahan, B. W., Dickie, M., and Gerking, S. (1997). Averting behavior and urban air pollution. *Land Economics*, **27**(3), 340–357. DOI: 10.2307/3147172. 69

Briones, R., Nan, X., Madden, K., and Waks, L. (2012). When vaccines go viral: An analysis of HPV vaccine coverage on YouTube. *Health Communication*, **27**(5), 478–485. DOI: 10.1080/10410236.2011.610258. 64

Brody, S. and Elhadad, N. (2010). Detecting salient aspects in online reviews of health providers. In *AMIA Annual Symposium Proceedings*. 31, 71

Bromseth, J. C. H. (2002). Public places—public activities? Methodological approaches and ethical dilemmas in research on computer-mediated communication. In A. Morrison, Ed., *Researching ICTs in Context*, pages 33–61. Inter/Media Report. 90

Broniatowski, D. A., Paul, M. J., and Dredze, M. (2013). National and local influenza surveillance through Twitter: An analysis of the 2012–2013 influenza epidemic. *PLoS ONE*, **8**(12). DOI: 10.1371/journal.pone.0083672. 37, 53, 56, 78

Broniatowski, D. A., Dredze, M., Paul, J. M., and Dugas, A. (2015). Using social media to perform local influenza surveillance in an inner-city hospital: A retrospective observational study. *JMIR Public Health Surveillance*, **1**(1), e5. DOI: 10.2196/publichealth.4472. 36, 53, 87

Broniatowski, D. A., Dredze, M., and Hilyard, K. M. (2016). Effective vaccine communication during the Disneyland measles outbreak. *Vaccine*. DOI: 10.1016/j.vaccine.2016.04.044. 65

Brooks, B. (2014). *Using Twitter Data to Identify Geographic Clustering of Anti-vaccination Sentiments*. Master's thesis, University of Washington. 64

Brownstein, J. S., Freifeld, C. C., and Madoff, L. C. (2009). Digital disease detection—harnessing the web for public health surveillance. *New England Journal of Medicine*, **360**(21), 2153–2157. DOI: 10.1056/nejmp0900702. 13, 56

Buchanan, E. A. and Ess, C. M. (2009). Internet research ethics and the Institutional Review Board: Current practices and issues. *SIGCAS Computers and Society*, **39**(3), 43–49. DOI: 10.1145/1713066.1713069. 89

Budnitz, D. S., Pollock, D. A., Weidenbach, K. N., Mendelsohn, A. B., Schroeder, T. J., and Annest, J. L. (2006). National surveillance of emergency department visits for outpatient adverse drug events. *JAMA*, **296**(15), 1858–1866. DOI: 10.1001/jama.296.15.1858. 11

Buhrmester, M., Kwang, T., and Gosling, S. D. (2011). Amazon's Mechanical Turk a new source of inexpensive, yet high-quality, data? *Perspectives on Psychological Science*, **6**(1), 3–5. DOI: 10.1177/1745691610393980. 20

Buntain, C. and Golbeck, J. (2015). This is your Twitter on drugs: Any questions? In *International Conference on World Wide Web (WWW)*. DOI: 10.1145/2740908.2742469. 63

Burger, J. D., Henderson, J., Kim, G., and Zarrella, G. (2011). Discriminating gender on Twitter. In *Empirical Methods in Natural Language Processing (EMNLP)*, Stroudsburg, PA. 43

Burks, L., Miller, M., and Zadeh, R. (2014). Rapid estimate of ground shaking intensity by combining simple earthquake characteristics with tweets. In *National Conference in Earthquake Engineering*. 67

Burton, S., Morris, R., Dimond, M., Hansen, J., Giraud-Carrier, C., West, J., Hanson, C., and Barnes, M. (2012a). Public health community mining in YouTube. In *International Health Informatics Symposium (SIGHIT)*. DOI: 10.1145/2110363.2110376. 18

Burton, S. H., Tanner, K. W., Giraud-Carrier, C. G., West, J. H., and Barnes, M. D. (2012b). "Right time, right place" health communication on Twitter: value and accuracy of location information. *Journal of Medical Internet Research*, **14**(6). DOI: 10.2196/jmir.2121. 22

Buscaldi, D. and Hernandez-Farias, I. (2015). Sentiment analysis on microblogs for natural disasters management: A study on the 2014 Genoa floodings. In *International Conference on World Wide Web (WWW)*. DOI: 10.1145/2740908.2741727. 67, 68

Caliskan, A., Bryson, J. J., and Narayanan, A. (2017). Semantics derived automatically from language corpora contain human-like biases. *Science*, **356**(6334), 183–186. DOI: 10.1126/science.aal4230. 84

Callison-Burch, C. and Dredze, M. (2010). Creating speech and language data with Amazon's Mechanical Turk. In *Workshop on Creating Speech and Language Data With Mechanical Turk at NAACL-HLT*. 20

Calvo, R. A., Milne, D. N., Hussain, M. S., and Christensen, H. (2017). Natural language processing in mental health applications using non-clinical texts. *Natural Language Engineering*, pages 1–37. DOI: 10.1017/s1351324916000383. 74

Cameron, M. A., Power, R., Robinson, B., and Yin, J. (2012). Emergency situation awareness from Twitter for crisis management. In *International Conference on World Wide Web (WWW)*. DOI: 10.1145/2187980.2188183. 67

Cameron, R. and Evers, S. E. (1990). Self-report issues in obesity and weight management: State of the art and future directions. *Behavioral Assessment*. 58

Carmel, D., Mejer, A., Pinter, Y., and Szpektor, I. (2014). Improving term weighting for community question answering search using syntactic analysis. In *Conference on Information and Knowledge Management (CIKM)*. DOI: 10.1145/2661829.2661901. 29

Carneiro, H. A. and Mylonakis, E. (2009). Google Trends: A web-based tool for real-time surveillance of disease outbreaks. *Clinical Infectious Diseases*, **49**(10), 1557–1564. DOI: 10.1086/630200. 54

Cassa, C. A., Chunara, R., Mandl, K., and Brownstein, J. S. (2013). Twitter as a sentinel in emergency situations: Lessons from the Boston marathon explosions. *PLoS Currents*. DOI: 10.1371/currents.dis.ad70cd1c8bc585e9470046cde334ee4b. 68

Casteel, K. (2017). Data on drug use is disappearing just when we need it most. *Five Thirty Eight*. 58

Cavazos-Rehg, P., Krauss, M., Grucza, R., and Bierut, L. (2014). Characterizing the followers and tweets of a marijuana-focused Twitter handle. *Journal of Medical Internet Research*, **16**(6), e157. DOI: 10.2196/jmir.3247. 61

Cavazos-Rehg, P. A., Krauss, M., Fisher, S. L., Salyer, P., Grucza, R. A., and Bierut, L. J. (2015). Twitter chatter about marijuana. *Journal of Adolescent Health*, **56**(2), 139–145. DOI: 10.1016/j.jadohealth.2014.10.270. 61

Center, P. R. (2017). Social media fact sheet. 83

Centers for Disease Control and Prevention (2010). Current depression among adults—United States, 2006 and 2008. *MMWR Morbidity and Mortality Weekly Report*, **59**(38), 1229. 74

Centers for Disease Control and Prevention (2013). Predict the influenza season challenge. https://www.federalregister.gov/articles/2013/11/25/2013-28198/announcement-of-requirements-and-registration-for-the-predict-the-influenza-season-challenge. Accessed: 2015-06-01. Archived by WebCite at: http://www.webcitation.org/6ZOGoGEOo 38

Centers for Disease Control and Prevention (2014). The health consequences of smoking—50 years of progress: A report of the Surgeon General. *U.S. Department of Health and Human Services*, page 171. 60

Centers for Disease Control and Prevention (CDC) (2005). The role of public health in mental health promotion. *JAMA*, **294**(18), 2293. 73

Cha, M., Gwon, Y., and Kung, H. (2015). Twitter geolocation and regional classification via sparse coding. In *International Conference on Weblogs and Social Media (ICWSM)*. 45

Chamlertwat, W., Bhattarakosol, P., Rungkasiri, T., and Haruechaiyasak, C. (2012). Discovering consumer insight from Twitter via sentiment analysis. *Journal of Universal Computer Science (UCS)*, **18**(8), 973–992. 16

Chan, B., Lopez, A., and Sarkar, U. (2015). The canary in the coal mine tweets: Social media reveals public perceptions of non-medical use of opioids. *PLoS ONE*, **10**(8), e0135072. DOI: 10.1371/journal.pone.0135072. 61

Chan, E. H., Sahai, V., Conrad, C., and Brownstein, J. S. (2011). Using web search query data to monitor dengue epidemics: A new model for neglected tropical disease surveillance. *PLoS Neglected Tropical Diseases*, **5**(5). DOI: 10.1371/journal.pntd.0001206. 54

Chang, J., Rosenn, I., Backstrom, L., and Marlow, C. (2010). Epluribus: Ethnicity on social networks. In *International Conference on Weblogs and Social Media (ICWSM)*. 43

Chang, T., Chopra, V., Zhang, C., and Woolford, S. J. (2013). The role of social media in online weight management: Systematic review. *Journal of Medical Internet Research*, **15**(11), e262. DOI: 10.2196/jmir.2852. 59

Charles-Smith, L. E., Reynolds, T. L., Cameron, M. A., Conway, M., Lau, E. H. Y., Olsen, J. M., Pavlin, J. A., Shigematsu, M., Streichert, L. C., Suda, K. J., and Corley, C. D. (2015). Using social media for actionable disease surveillance and outbreak management: A systematic literature review. *PLoS ONE*, **10**(10), 1–20. DOI: 10.1371/journal.pone.0139701. 51

Chary, M., Genes, N., McKenzie, A., and Manini, A. F. (2013). Leveraging social networks for toxicovigilance. *Journal of Medical Toxicology*, **9**(2), 184–191. DOI: 10.1007/s13181-013-0299-6. 63

Chen, B., Zhang, J. M., Jiang, Z., Shao, J., Jiang, T., Wang, Z., Liu, K., Tang, S., Gu, H., and Jiang, J. (2015a). Media and public reactions toward vaccination during the "hepatitis B vaccine crisis" in China. *Vaccine*, **33**(15), 1780–1785. DOI: 10.1016/j.vaccine.2015.02.046. 65

Chen, J., Chen, H., Wu, Z., Hu, D., and Pan, J. Z. (2017). Forecasting smog-related health hazard based on social media and physical sensor. *Information Systems*, **64**, 281–291. DOI: 10.1016/j.is.2016.03.011. 69

Chen, L., Hossain, K. S. M. T., Butler, P., Ramakrishnan, N., and Prakash, B. A. (2015b). Syndromic surveillance of flu on Twitter using weakly supervised temporal topic models. *Data Mining and Knowledge Discovery*. DOI: 10.1007/s10618-015-0434-x. 31

Cheng, J., Danescu-Niculescu-Mizil, C., and Leskovec, J. (2015). Antisocial behavior in online discussion communities. In *International Conference on Weblogs and Social Media (ICWSM)*. 46

Chew, C. and Eysenbach, G. (2010). Pandemics in the age of Twitter: Content analysis of tweets during the 2009 H1N1 outbreak. *PLoS ONE*, **5**(11), e14118. DOI: 10.1371/journal.pone.0014118. 29, 34, 41, 53

Cho, J. H., Gao, T., and Girju, R. (2017). Identifying medications that patients stopped taking in online health forums. In *IEEE International Conference on Semantic Computing*. DOI: 10.1109/icsc.2017.24. 72

Chorianopoulos, K. and Talvis, K. (2016). Flutrack.org: Open-source and linked data for epidemiology. *Health Informatics Journal*, **22**(4), 962–974. DOI: 10.1177/1460458215599822. 56

Chou, W. Y., Prestin, A., and Kunath, S. (2014). Obesity in social media: A mixed methods analysis. *Translational Behavioral Medicine*, **4**(3), 314–323. DOI: 10.1007/s13142-014-0256-1. 60

Chunara, R., Andrews, J. R., and Brownstein, J. S. (2012). Social and news media enable estimation of epidemiological patterns early in the 2010 Haitian cholera outbreak. *American Journal of Tropical Medicine and Hygiene*, **86**(1), 39–45. DOI: 10.4269/ajtmh.2012.11-0597. 54

Chunara, R., Bouton, L., Ayers, J. W., and Brownstein, J. S. (2013). Assessing the online social environment for surveillance of obesity prevalence. *PLoS ONE*, **8**(4), e61373. DOI: 10.1371/journal.pone.0061373. 59

Chunara, R., Wisk, L. E., and Weitzman, E. R. (2017). Denominator issues for personally generated data in population health monitoring. *American Journal of Preventive Medicine*, **52**(4), 549–553. DOI: 10.1016/j.amepre.2016.10.038. 79, 84

Cioffi-Revilla, C. (2010). Computational social science. *Wiley Interdisciplinary Reviews: Computational Statistics*, **2**(3), 259–271. DOI: 10.1002/wics.95. 16

Ciot, M., Sonderegger, M., and Ruths, D. (2013). Gender inference of Twitter users in non-English contexts. In *Empirical Methods in Natural Language Processing (EMNLP)*, pages 1136–1145. 43

Clark, E. M., Jones, C. A., Williams, J. R., Kurti, A. N., Norotsky, M. C., Danforth, C. M., and Dodds, P. S. (2016). Vaporous marketing: Uncovering pervasive electronic cigarette advertisements on Twitter. *PLoS ONE*, **11**(7), e0157304. DOI: 10.1371/journal.pone.0157304. 82

Cobb, N. K., Graham, A. L., Byron, M. J., Abrams, D. B., and Workshop Participants (2011). Online social networks and smoking cessation: A scientific research agenda. *Journal of Medical Internet Research*, **13**(4). DOI: 10.2196/jmir.1911. 18, 23, 60

Cohan, A., Young, S., and Goharian, N. (2016). Triaging mental health forum posts. In *Workshop on Computational Linguistics and Clinical Psychology (CLPsych)*. DOI: 10.18653/v1/w16-0316. 74

Cohen, J. (1960). A coefficient of agreement for nominal scales. *Educational and Psychological Measurement*, **20**(1), 37–46. DOI: 10.1177/001316446002000104. 41

Cohen, J. E., Ayers, J. W., and Dredze, M. (2015). Tobacco Watcher: Real-time global surveillance for tobacco control. In *World Conference on Tobacco or Health (WCTOH)*. 61, 86

Cole-Lewis, H., Varghese, A., Sanders, A., Schwarz, M., Pugatch, J., and Augustson, E. (2015). Assessing electronic cigarette-related Tweets for sentiment and content using supervised machine learning. *Journal of Medical Internet Research*, **17**(8), e208. DOI: 10.2196/jmir.4392. 60

Colpe, L. J., Freeman, E. J., Strine, T. W., Dhingra, S., McGuire, L. C., Elam-Evans, L. D., and Perry, G. S. (2010). Public health surveillance for mental health. *Preventing Chronic Disease*, **7**(1). 73

Compton, R., Jurgens, D., and Allen, D. (2014). Geotagging one hundred million Twitter accounts with total variation minimization. In *IEEE International Conference on Big Data*, pages 393–401. DOI: 10.1109/bigdata.2014.7004256. 45

Conway, M. (2014). Ethical issues in using Twitter for public health surveillance and research: Developing a taxonomy of ethical concepts from the research literature. *Journal of Medical Internet Research*, **16**(12). DOI: 10.2196/jmir.3617. 88, 89, 93

Cook, C., Heath, F., and Thompson, R. L. (2000). A meta-analysis of response rates in web- or internet-based surveys. *Educational and Psychological Measurement*, **60**(6), 821–836. DOI: 10.1177/00131640021970934. 12

Cook, J., Kenthapadi, K., and Mishra, N. (2013). Group chats on Twitter. In *International Conference on World Wide Web (WWW)*, pages 225–236, New York, ACM. DOI: 10.1145/2488388.2488409. 19

Cook, S., Conrad, C., Fowlkes, A. L., and Mohebbi, M. H. (2011). Assessing Google Flu Trends performance in the United States during the 2009 influenza virus A (H1N1) pandemic. *PLoS ONE*, **6**(8), e23610. DOI: 10.1371/journal.pone.0023610. 52, 86

Copeland, P., Romano, R., Zhang, T., Hecht, G., Zigmond, D., and Stefansen, C. (2013). Google disease trends: An update. In *International Society of Neglected Tropical Diseases*, page 3. 52, 83

Coppersmith, G., Harman, C., and Dredze, M. (2014a). Measuring post traumatic stress disorder in Twitter. In *International Conference on Weblogs and Social Media (ICWSM)*. 75

Coppersmith, G., Dredze, M., and Harman, C. (2014b). Quantifying mental health signals in Twitter. In *ACL Workshop on Computational Linguistics and Clinical Psychology (CLPsych)*. DOI: 10.3115/v1/w14-3207. 74, 75, 90

Coppersmith, G., Dredze, M., Harman, C., Hollingshead, K., and Mitchell, M. (2015a). CLPsych 2015 shared task: Depression and PTSD on Twitter. In *NAACL Workshop on Computational Linguistics and Clinical Psychology (CLPsych)*. DOI: 10.3115/v1/w15-1204. 42

Coppersmith, G., Dredze, M., Harman, C., and Hollingshead, K. (2015b). From ADHD to SAD: Analyzing the language of mental health on Twitter through self-reported diagnoses. In *NAACL Workshop on Computational Linguistics and Clinical Psychology (CLPsych)*. DOI: 10.3115/v1/w15-1201. 42, 75

Corazza, O., Schifano, F., Farre, M., Deluca, P., Davey, Z., Drummond, C., Torrens, M., Demetrovics, Z., Di Furia, L., Flesland, L., and et al. (2011). Designer drugs on the Internet: A phenomenon out-of-control? The emergence of hallucinogenic drug Bromo-Dragonfly. *Current Clinical Pharmacology*, **6**(2), 125–129. DOI: 10.2174/157488411796151129. 62

Corazza, O., Schifano, F., Simonato, P., Fergus, S., Assi, S., Stair, Jacqueline d Corkery, J., Trincas, G., Deluca, P., Davey, Z., Blaszko, U., Demetrovics, Z., Moskalewicz, Jacek a Enea, A., di Melchiorre, G., Mervo, B., di Furia, L., Farre, M., Flesland, L., Pasinetti, Manuela an-Pezzolesi, C., Pisarska, A., Shapiro, H., Siemann, H., Skutle, A., Enea, A., di Melchiorre, G., Sferrazza, E., Torrens, M., van der Kreeft, P., Zummo, D., and Scherbaum, N. (2012). Phenomenon of new drugs on the Internet: The case of ketamine derivative methoxetamine. *Human Psychopharmacology: Clinical and Experimental*, **27**(2), 145–149. DOI: 10.1002/hup.1242. 62

Corley, C. D., Cook, D. J., Mikler, A. R., and Singh, K. P. (2010). Text and structural data mining of influenza mentions in web and social media. *International Journal of Environmental Research and Public Health*, **7**(2), 596–615. DOI: 10.3390/ijerph7020596. 53

Coyle, J. R., Presti, D. E., and Baggott, M. J. (2012). Quantitative analysis of narrative reports of psychedelic drugs. *arXiv*, **1206:0312**. 63

Crawley, A. W., Wójcik, O. P., Olsen, J., Brownstein, J. S., and Smolinski, M. S. (2014). Flu Near You: Comparing crowdsourced reports of influenza-like illness to the CDC outpatient influenza-like illness surveillance network, October 2012 to March 2014. In *Council of State and Territorial Epidemiologists Annual Conference.* 20

Crooks, A., Croitoru, A., Stefanidis, A., and Radzikowski, J. (2013). #earthquake: Twitter as a distributed sensor system. *Transactions in GIS,* **17**(1), 124–147. DOI: 10.1111/j.1467-9671.2012.01359.x. 67

Crowcroft, J., Haddadi, H., and Henderson, T. (2017). *Responsible Research on Social Networks: Dilemmas and Solutions.* Oxford University Press, UK. 93

Culotta, A. (2010). Towards detecting influenza epidemics by analyzing Twitter messages. In *ACM Workshop on Social Media Analytics.* DOI: 10.1145/1964858.1964874. 29, 35, 39, 53

Culotta, A. (2013). Lightweight methods to estimate influenza rates and alcohol sales volume from Twitter messages. *Language Resources and Evaluation,* **47**(1), 217–238. DOI: 10.1007/s10579-012-9185-0. 29, 61

Culotta, A. (2014). Estimating county health statistics with Twitter. In *Conference on Human Factors in Computing Systems (CHI).* DOI: 10.1145/2556288.2557139. 55

Culotta, A., Kumar, N. R., and Cutler, J. (2015). Predicting the demographics of Twitter users from website traffic data. In *Conference on Artificial Intelligence (AAAI).* 43, 44

Curran, J. W., Jaffe, H. W., et al. (2011). AIDS: The early years and CDC's response. *MMWR Surveill Summaries,* **60**(Suppl. 4), 64–9. 11

Curtis, B., Alanis-Hirsch, K., Kaynak, O., Cacciola, J., Meyers, K., and McLellan, A. T. (2015). Using Web searches to track interest in synthetic cannabinoids (a/k/a "herbal incense"). *Drug Alcohol Review,* **34**(1), 105–108. DOI: 10.1111/dar.12189. 63

Da'ar, O. B., Yunus, F., Md Hossain, N., and Househ, M. (2016). Impact of Twitter intensity, time, and location on message lapse of bluebird's pursuit of fleas in Madagascar. *Journal of Infection Public Health.* DOI: 10.1016/j.jiph.2016.06.011. 54

Dai, H. and Hao, J. (2017). Mining social media data on marijuana use for post traumatic stress disorder. *Computers in Human Behavior,* **70**, 282–290. DOI: 10.1016/j.chb.2016.12.064. 61

Dai, H., Lee, B. R., and Hao, J. (2017). Predicting asthma prevalence by linking social media data and traditional surveys. *The ANNALS of the American Academy of Political and Social Science,* **669**(1), 75–92. DOI: 10.1177/0002716216678399. 55

Das, L., Mohan, R., and Makaya, T. (2014). The bid to lose weight: Impact of social media on weight perceptions, weight control and diabetes. *Current Diabetes Review,* **10**(5), 291–297. DOI: 10.2174/1573399810666141010112542. 60

Dashti, S., Palen, L., Heris, M., Anderson, K., Anderson, S., and Anderson, J. (2014). Supporting disaster reconnaissance with social media data: A design-oriented case study of the 2013 Colorado floods. In *Conference on Information Systems for Crisis Response and Management (ISCRAM)*. 68

Davison, K. (1996). The quality of dietary information on the world wide web. *Clinical Performance and Quality Health Care*, **5**(2), 64–66. 16

De Choudhury, M. (2013). Role of social media in tackling challenges in mental health. In *Workshop on Socially-Aware Multimedia*. DOI: 10.1145/2509916.2509921. 74

De Choudhury, M. (2014a). Can social media help us reason about mental health? In *International Conference on World Wide Web (WWW)*, pages 1243–1244. DOI: 10.1145/2567948.2580064. 74

De Choudhury, M. (2014b). You're #happy, i'm #happy: Diffusion of mood expressions on Twitter. In *HCI Korea Conference*. 75

De Choudhury, M. (2015). Anorexia on Tumblr: A characterization study. In *ACM Digital Health Conference*. DOI: 10.1145/2750511.2750515. 60, 75

De Choudhury, M. and De, S. (2014). Mental health discourse on reddit: Self-disclosure, social support, and anonymity. In *International Conference on Weblogs and Social Media (ICWSM)*. 74, 76

De Choudhury, M. and Gamon, M. (2013). Predicting depression via social media. In *International Conference on Weblogs and Social Media (ICWSM)*. 74

De Choudhury, M. and Kiciman, E. (2017). The language of social support in social media and its effect on suicidal ideation risk. In *International Conference on Weblogs and Social Media (ICWSM)*. AAAI. 47, 75

De Choudhury, M., Counts, S., and Gamon, M. (2012). Not all moods are created equal! exploring human emotional states in social media. In *International Conference on Weblogs and Social Media (ICWSM)*. 75

De Choudhury, M., Counts, S., and Horvitz, E. (2013a). Major life changes and behavioral markers in social media: Case of childbirth. In *Conference on Computer Supported Cooperative Work and Social Computing (CSCW)*, pages 1431–1442. ACM. DOI: 10.1145/2441776.2441937. 74

De Choudhury, M., Counts, S., and Horvitz, E. (2013b). Predicting postpartum changes in emotion and behavior via social media. In *Conference on Human Factors in Computing Systems (CHI)*, pages 3267–3276, New York. DOI: 10.1145/2470654.2466447. 74, 88, 90

De Choudhury, M., Counts, S., and Horvitz, E. (2013c). Social media as a measurement tool of depression in populations. In *Web Science Conference*, pages 47–56, ACM. DOI: 10.1145/2464464.2464480. 74

De Choudhury, M., Counts, S., Horvitz, E. J., and Hoff, A. (2014a). Characterizing and predicting postpartum depression from shared Facebook data. In *Conference on Computer Supported Cooperative Work and Social Computing (CSCW)*, pages 626–638. DOI: 10.1145/2531602.2531675. 25, 36, 74, 91

De Choudhury, M., Morris, M. R., and White, R. W. (2014b). Seeking and sharing health information online: Comparing search engines and social media. In *Conference on Human Factors in Computing Systems (CHI)*, pages 1365–1376. DOI: 10.1145/2556288.2557214. 21

De Choudhury, M., Sharma, S., and Kiciman, E. (2016a). Characterizing dietary choices, nutrition, and language in food deserts via social media. In *Conference on Computer Supported Cooperative Work and Social Computing (CSCW)*, pages 1157–1170, New York, ACM. DOI: 10.1145/2818048.2819956. 18, 59

De Choudhury, M., Kiciman, E., Dredze, M., Coppersmith, G., and Kumar, M. (2016b). Discovering shifts to suicidal ideation from mental health content in social media. In *Conference on Human Factors in Computing Systems (CHI)*. DOI: 10.1145/2858036.2858207. 47, 75

De Choudhury, M., Sharma, S. S., Logar, T., Eekhout, W., and Nielsen, R. C. (2017). Gender and cross-cultural differences in social media disclosures of mental illness. In *Conference on Computer Supported Cooperative Work and Social Computing (CSCW)*, pages 353–369, New York, ACM. DOI: 10.1145/2998181.2998220. 84

de Quincey, E. and Kostkova, P. (2010). Early warning and outbreak detection using social networking websites: The potential of Twitter. In *International Conference on Electronic Healthcare*. DOI: 10.1007/978-3-642-11745-9_4. 53

Deiner, M., Lietman, T., McLeod, S., Chodosh, J., and Porco, T. (2016). Surveillance tools emerging from search engines and social media data for determining eye disease patterns. *JAMA Ophthalmology*, **134**(9), 1024–1030. DOI: 10.1001/jamaophthalmol.2016.2267. 54

Delir Haghighi, P., Kang, Y.-B., Buchbinder, R., Burstein, F., and Whittle, S. (2017). Investigating subjective experience and the influence of weather among individuals with fibromyalgia: A content analysis of Twitter. *JMIR Public Health Surveillance*, **3**(1), e4. DOI: 10.2196/publichealth.6344. 55

Deluca, P., Davey, Z., Corazza, O., Di Furia, L., Farre, M., Flesland, L. H., Mannonen, M., Majava, A., Peltoniemi, T., Pasinetti, M., Pezzolesi, C., Scherbaum, N., Siemann, H., Skutle, A., Torrens, M., van der Kreeft, P., Iversen, E., and Schifano, F. (2012). Identifying emerging trends in recreational drug use; outcomes from the Psychonaut Web Mapping

Project. *Progress in Neuro-Psychopharmacology and Biological Psychiatry*, **39**(2), 221–226. DOI: 10.1016/j.pnpbp.2012.07.011. 62

Denecke, K., Krieck, M., Otrusina, L., Smrz, P., Dolog, P., Nejdl, W., Velasco, E., et al. (2013). How to exploit Twitter for public health monitoring. *Methods Information Medicine*, **52**(4), 326–339. DOI: 10.3414/me12-02-0010. 24

Deodhar, S., Chen, J., Wilson, M., Bisset, K., Lewis, B., Barrett, C., and Marathe, M. (2015a). EpiCaster: An integrated web application for situation assessment and forecasting of global epidemics. In *ACM Conference on Bioinformatics, Computational Biology and Health Informatics*. DOI: 10.1145/2808719.2808735. 56

Deodhar, S., Chen, J., Wilson, M., Soundarapandian, M., Bisset, K., Lewis, B., Barrett, C., and Marathe, M. (2015b). Flucaster: A pervasive web application for high resolution situation assessment and forecasting of flu outbreaks. In *International Conference on Healthcare Informatics*, pages 105–114. DOI: 10.1109/ichi.2015.20. 56

Desai, R., Hall, A. J., Lopman, B. A., Shimshoni, Y., Rennick, M., Efron, N., Matias, Y., Patel, M. M., and Parashar, U. D. (2012). Norovirus disease surveillance using Google Internet query share data. *Clinical Infectious Diseases*, **55**(8), e75–78. DOI: 10.1093/cid/cis579. 54

Diaz-Aviles, E. and Stewart, A. (2012). Tracking Twitter for epidemic intelligence: Case study: EHEC/HUS outbreak in Germany, 2011. In *Web Science Conference*. DOI: 10.1145/2380718.2380730. 54

Digrazia, J., McKelvey, K., Bollen, J., and Rojas, F. (2013). More tweets, more votes: Social media as a quantitative indicator of political behavior. *PLoS ONE*, **8**(11), e79449. DOI: 10.1371/journal.pone.0079449. 16

Doan, S., Vo, B. K. H., and Collier, N. (2012). An analysis of Twitter messages in the 2011 Tohoku Earthquake. In *Lecture Notes of the Institute for Computer Sciences, Social-Informatics and Telecommunications Engineering*, volume 91 LNICST, pages 58–66. DOI: 10.1007/978-3-642-29262-0_8. 53, 67

Doan, S., Ritchart, A., Perry, N., Chaparro, D. J., and Conway, M. (2017). How do you #relax when you're #stressed? A content analysis and infodemiology study of stress-related tweets. *JMIR Public Health Surveillance*, **3**(2), e35. DOI: 10.2196/publichealth.5939. 75

Doshi, P. (2009). Calibrated response to emerging infections. *BMJ*, **339**, b3471. DOI: 10.1136/bmj.b3471. 86

Dredze, M. (2012). How social media will change public health. *IEEE Intelligent Systems*, **27**(4), 81–84. DOI: 10.1109/mis.2012.76. 13

Dredze, M., Paul, M. J., Bergsma, S., and Tran, H. (2013). Carmen: A Twitter geolocation system with applications to public health. In *AAAI Workshop on Expanding the Boundaries of Health Informatics Using AI (HIAI)*. 23, 45

Dredze, M., Cheng, R., Paul, M., and Broniatowski, D. (2014). Healthtweets.org: A platform for public health surveillance using Twitter. In *AAAI Workshop on the World Wide Web and Public Health Intelligence*. 56, 85

Dredze, M., Broniatowski, D. A., Smith, M., and Hilyard, K. M. (2015). Understanding vaccine refusal: Why we need social media now. *American Journal of Preventive Medicine*. 12, 85

Dredze, M., Osborne, M., and Kambadur, P. (2016a). Geolocation for Twitter: Timing matters. In *North American Chapter of the Association for Computational Linguistics (NAACL) (short paper)*. DOI: 10.18653/v1/n16-1122. 45

Dredze, M., García-Herranz, M., Rutherford, A., and Mann, G. (2016b). Twitter as a source of global mobility patterns for social good. In *ICML Workshop on #Data4Good: Machine Learning in Social Good Applications*. 54

Dredze, M., Broniatowski, D. A., and Hilyard, K. M. (2016c). Zika vaccine misconceptions: A social media analysis. *Vaccine*. DOI: 10.1016/j.vaccine.2016.05.008. 32, 64

Dredze, M., Wood-Doughty, Z., Quinn, S. C., and Broniatowski, D. A. (2017). Vaccine opponents' use of Twitter during the 2016 U.S. presidential election: Implications for practice and policy. *Vaccine*. DOI: 10.1016/j.vaccine.2017.06.066. 16

Dugas, A. F., Hsieh, Y. H., Levin, S. R., Pines, J. M., Mareiniss, D. P., Mohareb, A., Gaydos, C. A., Perl, T. M., and Rothman, R. E. (2012). Google flu trends: Correlation with emergency department influenza rates and crowding metrics. *Clinical Infectious Diseases*, **54**(4), 463–469. DOI: 10.1093/cid/cir883. 51, 87

Dugas, A. F., Jalalpour, M., Gel, Y., Levin, S., Torcaso, F., Igusa, T., and Rothman, R. E. (2013). Influenza forecasting with Google flu trends. *PLoS ONE*, **8**(2), e56176. DOI: 10.1371/journal.pone.0056176. 36, 53

Duggan, M., Ellison, N. B., Lampe, C., Lenhart, A., and Madden, M. (2015). Demographics of key social networking platforms. http://www.pewinternet.org/2015/01/09/demographics-of-key-social-networking-platforms-2/ 13, 22, 83

Dunn, A. G., Leask, J., Zhou, X., Mandl, K. D., and Coiera, E. (2015). Associations between exposure to and expression of negative opinions about human papillomavirus vaccines on social media: An observational study. *Journal of Medical Internet Research*, **17**(6), e144. DOI: 10.2196/jmir.4343. 64

Dunn, M., Bruno, R., Burns, L., and Roxburgh, A. (2011). Effectiveness of and challenges faced by surveillance systems. *Drug Testing and Analysis*, **3**(9), 635–641. DOI: 10.1002/dta.333. 62

Earle, P. S., Bowden, D. C., and Guy, M. (2012). Twitter earthquake detection: Earthquake monitoring in a social world. *Annals of Geophysics*, **54**(6), 708–715. DOI: 10.4401/ag-5364. 67

Edge, V. L., Pollari, F., Lim, G., Aramini, J., Sockett, P., Martin, S. W., Wilson, J., and Ellis, A. (2004). Syndromic surveillance of gastrointestinal illness using pharmacy over-the-counter sales: A retrospective study of waterborne outbreaks in Saskatchewan and Ontario. *Canadian Journal of Public Health/Revue Canadienne de Sante'e Publique*, pages 446–450. 12

Eichstaedt, J. C., Schwartz, H. A., Kern, M. L., Park, G., Labarthe, D. R., Merchant, R. M., Jha, S., Agrawal, M., Dziurzynski, L. A., Sap, M., Weeg, C., Larson, E. E., Ungar, L. H., and Seligman, M. E. (2015). Psychological language on Twitter predicts county-level heart disease mortality. *Psychological Science*, **26**, 159–169. DOI: 10.1177/0956797614557867. 55, 75

Eisenstein, J. (2013). What to do about bad language on the internet. In *North American Chapter of the Association for Computational Linguistics (NAACL)*, pages 359–369. 92

Eisenstein, J., O'Connor, B., Smith, N. A., and Xing, E. P. (2010). A latent variable model for geographic lexical variation. In *Empirical Methods in Natural Language Processing (EMNLP)*. 16, 45

Emslie, S., Knox, K., and Pickstone, M. (2002). *Improving Patient Safety: Insights from American, Australian, and British healthcare*. Emergency Care Research Institute Europe. DOI: 10.1136/qhc.12.3.235. 71

Eschler, J., Dehlawi, Z., and Pratt, W. (2015). Self-characterized illness phase and information needs of participants in an online cancer forum. In *International Conference on Weblogs and Social Media (ICWSM)*. 55

Eshleman, R. and Yang, H. (2014). "Hey #311, come clean my street!": A spatio-temporal sentiment analysis of Twitter data and 311 civil complaints. In *IEEE International Conference on Big Data and Cloud Computing*. DOI: 10.1109/bdcloud.2014.106. 67

European Monitoring Centre for Drugs and Drug Addiction (2012). Annual report 2012: The state of the drug problem in Europe. *Publications Office of the European Union*. 62

Eysenbach, G. (2002). Infodemiology: The epidemiology of (mis)information. *The American Journal of Medicine*, **113**(9), 763–765. DOI: 10.1016/s0002-9343(02)01473-0. 16

Eysenbach, G. (2006). Infodemiology: Tracking flu-related searches on the web for syndromic surveillance. In *AMIA Annual Symposium Proceedings*, pages 244–248. 52, 77, 97

Eysenbach, G. and Kohler, C. (2003). What is the prevalence of health-related searches on the world wide web? Qualitative and quantitative analysis of search engine queries on the internet. In *AMIA annual symposium proceedings*, volume 2003, page 225. American Medical Informatics Association. 77

Eysenbach, G. and Köhler, C. (2004). Health-related searches on the internet. *JAMA*, **291**(24), 2946–2946. DOI: 10.1001/jama.291.24.2946. 77

Eysenbach, G. and Wyatt, J. (2002). Using the internet for surveys and health research. *Journal of Medical Internet Research*, **4**(2). DOI: 10.2196/jmir.4.2.e13. 12

Fardouly, J., Diedrichs, P. C., Vartanian, L. R., and Halliwell, E. (2015). Social comparisons on social media: The impact of Facebook on young women's body image concerns and mood. *Body Image*, **13**, 38–45. DOI: 10.1016/j.bodyim.2014.12.002. 60

Feng, S. and Hossain, L. (2016). Risk-informed decisions for epidemics. *Journal of Decision Systems*, **25**(sup1), 240–247. DOI: 10.1080/12460125.2016.1187813. 53

Fiesler, C., Dye, M., Feuston, J. L., Hiruncharoenvate, C., Hutto, C. J., Morrison, S., Roshan, P. K., Pavalanathan, U., Bruckman, A. S., Choudhury, M. D., and Gilbert, E. (2017). What (or who) is public?: Privacy settings and social media content sharing. In *Conference on Computer Supported Cooperative Work and Social Computing (CSCW)*, pages 567–580. DOI: 10.1145/2998181.2998223. 21

Fisher, R. and Katz, J. E. (2000). Social-desirability bias and the validity of self-reported values. *Psychology and Marketing*, **17**, 105–120. DOI: 10.1002/(sici)1520-6793(200002)17:2%3C105::aid-mar3%3E3.0.co;2-9. 57

Fleiss, J. L. (1971). Measuring nominal scale agreement among many raters. *Psychological Bulletin*, **76**(5), 378. DOI: 10.1037/h0031619. 41

Flekova, L., Ruppert, E., and Preoţiuc-Pietro, D. (2015). Analysing domain suitability of a sentiment lexicon by identifying distributionally bipolar words. In *EMNLP Workshop on Computational Approaches to Subjectivity, Sentiment and Social Media Analysis*. DOI: 10.18653/v1/w15-2911. 74

Fourney, A., Lafreniere, B., Chilana, P., and Terry, M. (2014). Intertwine: Creating interapplication information scent to support coordinated use of software. In *ACM Symposium on User Interface Software and Technology*. DOI: 10.1145/2642918.2647420. 20

Fournier, A. K. and Clarke, S. W. (2011). Do college students use Facebook to communicate about alcohol? An analysis of student profile pages. *Journal of Psychosocial Research on Cyberspace*, **5**(2). 61

Freeman, B. and Chapman, S. (2007). Is "YouTube" telling or selling you something? Tobacco content on the YouTube video-sharing website. *Tobacco Control*, **16**(3), 207–210. DOI: 10.1136/tc.2007.020024. 18

Freifeld, C. C., Mandl, K. D., Reis, B. Y., and Brownstein, J. S. (2008). HealthMap: Global infectious disease monitoring through automated classification and visualization of internet media reports. *Journal of the American Medical Informatics Association*, **15**(2), 150–157. DOI: 10.1197/jamia.m2544. 85

Freifeld, C. C., Brownstein, J. S., Menone, C. M., Bao, W., Filice, R., Kass-Hout, T., and Dasgupta, N. (2014). Digital drug safety surveillance: Monitoring pharmaceutical products in Twitter. *Drug Safety*, **37**(5), 343–350. DOI: 10.1007/s40264-014-0155-x. 72

Frias-Martinez, V., Sae-Tang, A., and Frias-Martinez, E. (2014). To call, or to tweet? Understanding 3-1-1 citizen complaint behaviors. In *ASE Conference*. 67

Fried, D., Surdeanu, M., Kobourov, S., Hingle, M., and Bell, D. (2014). Analyzing the language of food on social media. In *IEEE International Conference on Big Data*. DOI: 10.1109/bigdata.2014.7004305. 55, 59

Frost, J., Okun, S., Vaughan, T., Heywood, J., and Wicks, P. (2011). Patient-reported outcomes as a source of evidence in off-label prescribing: Analysis of data from PatientsLikeMe. *Journal of Medical Internet Research*, **13**(1), e6. DOI: 10.2196/jmir.1643. 62

Frumkin, H., Hess, J., Luber, G., Malilay, J., and McGeehin, M. (2008). Climate change: The public health response. *American Journal of Public Health*, **98**(3), 435–445. DOI: 10.2105/ajph.2007.119362. 69

Fuchs, G., Andrienko, N., Andrienko, G., Bothe, S., and Stange, H. (2013). Tracing the German centennial flood in the stream of tweets: First lessons learned. In *International Workshop on Crowdsourced and Volunteered Geographic Information*. DOI: 10.1145/2534732.2534741. 68

Fung, I. C., Fu, K. W., Ying, Y., Schaible, B., Hao, Y., Chan, C. H., and Tse, Z. T. (2013). Chinese social media reaction to the MERS-CoV and avian influenza A(H7N9) outbreaks. *Infectious Diseases Poverty*, **2**. DOI: 10.1186/2049-9957-2-31. 65

Fung, I. C., Tse, Z. T., Cheung, C. N., Miu, A. S., and Fu, K. W. (2014). Ebola and the social media. *The Lancet*, **384**(9961), 2207. DOI: 10.1016/s0140-6736(14)62418-1. 54, 65

Fung, I. C., Hao, Y., Cai, J., Ying, Y., Schaible, B. J., Yu, C. M., Tse, Z. T., and Fu, K. W. (2015). Chinese social media reaction to information about 42 notifiable infectious diseases. *PLoS ONE*, **10**(5), e0126092. DOI: 10.1371/journal.pone.0126092. 65

Funk, S., Gilad, E., Watkins, C., and Jansen, V. A. (2009). The spread of awareness and its impact on epidemic outbreaks. *Proc. of the National Academy Sciences U.S.A.*, **106**(16), 6872–6877. DOI: 10.1073/pnas.0810762106. 65

Gallagher, C. T., Assi, S., Stair, J. L., Fergus, S., Corazza, O., and Corkery, John Mand Schifano, F. (2012). 5,6-methylenedioxy-2-aminoindane: From laboratory curiosity to "legal high." *Human Psychopharmacology: Clinical and Experimental*, **27**(2), 106–112. DOI: 10.1002/hup.1255. 62

Garimella, V. R. K., Alfayad, A., and Weber, I. (2016). Social media image analysis for public health. In *Conference on Human Factors in Computing Systems (CHI)*, pages 5543–5547, New York, ACM. DOI: 10.1145/2858036.2858234. 22, 59

Generous, N., Fairchild, G., Deshpande, A., Del Valle, S. Y., and Priedhorsky, R. (2014). Global disease monitoring and forecasting with Wikipedia. *PLoS Computer Biology*, **10**(11), e1003892. DOI: 10.1371/journal.pcbi.1003892. 20, 53, 54

Genes, N. and Chary, M. (2014). Twitter discussions of nonmedical prescription drug use correlate with federal survey data. In *Medicine 2.0 Conference*. 61

Genes, N., Chary, M., and Chason, K. (2014). Analysis of Twitter users' sharing of official New York storm response messages. *Med 2 0*, **3**(1), e1. DOI: 10.2196/med20.3237. 68

Gesualdo, F., Stilo, G., Agricola, E., Gonfiantini, M. V., Pandolfi, E., Velardi, P., and Tozzi, A. E. (2013). Influenza-like illness surveillance on Twitter through automated learning of naïve language. *PLoS ONE*, **8**(12), e82489. DOI: 10.1371/journal.pone.0082489. 79

Ghaznavi, J. and Taylor, L. D. (2015). Bones, body parts, and sex appeal: An analysis of #thinspiration images on popular social media. *Body Image*, **14**, 54–61. DOI: 10.1016/j.bodyim.2015.03.006. 60

Ghenai, A., Mejova, Y., and Fernandez-Luque, L. (2017). Catching Zika fever: Application of crowdsourcing and machine learning for tracking health misinformation on Twitter. In *IEEE International Conference on Healthcare Informatics (ICHI)*. 32

Ghosh, D. D. and Guha, R. (2013). What are we 'tweeting' about obesity? Mapping tweets with topic modeling and geographic information system. *Cartography and Geographic Information Science*, **40**(2), 90–102. DOI: 10.1080/15230406.2013.776210. 31

Giabbanelli, P. J., Adams, J., and Pillutla, V. S. (2016). Feasibility and framing of interventions based on public support: Leveraging text analytics for policymakers. In *International Conference on Social Computing and Social Media (SCSM)*, pages 188–200. DOI: 10.1007/978-3-319-39910-2_18. 66

Ginsberg, J., Mohebbi, M. H., Patel, R. S., Brammer, L., Smolinski, M. S., and Brilliant, L. (2009). Detecting influenza epidemics using search engine query data. *Nature*, **457**(7232), 1012–1014. DOI: 10.1038/nature07634. 29, 35, 52, 77, 85

Gluskin, R. T., Johansson, M. A., Santillana, M., and Brownstein, J. S. (2014). Evaluation of internet-based dengue query data: Google dengue trends. *PLoS Neglected Tropical Diseases*, **8**(2), e2713. DOI: 10.1371/journal.pntd.0002713. 54

Goel, S., Hofman, J. M., Lahaie, S., Pennock, D. M., and Watts, D. J. (2010). Predicting consumer behavior with Web search. *Proc. of the National Academy of Science, U.S.A.*, **107**(41), 17486–17490. DOI: 10.1073/pnas.1005962107. 39

Goel, S., Hofman, J. M., and Sirer, M. I. (2012). Who does what on the Web: A large-scale study of browsing behavior. In *International Conference on Weblogs and Social Media (ICWSM)*. 83

Goldberg, Y. (2017). Neural network methods for natural language processing. *Synthesis Lectures on Human Language Technologies*, **10**(1), 1–309. DOI: 10.2200/s00762ed1v01y201703hlt037. 30

Golder, S., Ahmed, S., Norman, G., and Booth, A. (2017). Attitudes toward the ethics of research using social media: A systematic review. *Journal of Medical Internet Research*, **19**(6), e195. DOI: 10.2196/jmir.7082. 89

Golder, S. A. and Macy, M. W. (2011). Diurnal and seasonal mood vary with work, sleep, and daylength across diverse cultures. *Science*, **333**(6051), 1878–1881. DOI: 10.1126/science.1202775. 75

Gomide, J., Veloso, A., Meira, Jr., W., Almeida, V., Benevenuto, F., Ferraz, F., and Teixeira, M. (2011). Dengue surveillance based on a computational model of spatio-temporal locality of Twitter. In *Web Science Conference*. DOI: 10.1145/2527031.2527049. 54

Goodman, J. K., Cryder, C. E., and Cheema, A. (2013). Data collection in a flat world: The strengths and weaknesses of Mechanical Turk samples. *Journal of Behavioral Decision Making*, **26**(3), 213–224. DOI: 10.1002/bdm.1753. 20

Google Flu Trends (2015). The next chapter for Flu Trends. http://googleresearch.blo gspot.com/2015/08/the-next-chapter-for-flu-trends.html 52

Gore, R. J., Diallo, S., and Padilla, J. (2015). You are what you tweet: Connecting the geographic variation in america's obesity rate to Twitter content. *PLoS ONE*, **10**(9), 1–16. DOI: 10.1371/journal.pone.0133505. 55

Graham, M., Hale, S. A., and Gaffney, D. (2014). Where in the world are you? Geolocation and language identification in Twitter. *The Professional Geographer*, **66**(4), 568–578. DOI: 10.1080/00330124.2014.907699. 44

Grajales III, F. J., Sheps, S., Ho, K., Novak-Lauscher, H., and Eysenbach, G. (2014). Social media: A review and tutorial of applications in medicine and health care. *Journal of Medical Internet Research*, **16**(2), e13. DOI: 10.2196/jmir.2912. 13

Granell, C., Gomez, S., and Arenas, A. (2013). Dynamical interplay between awareness and epidemic spreading in multiplex networks. *Physics Review Letter*, **111**(12), 128701. DOI: 10.1103/physrevlett.111.128701. 65

Greaves, F., Ramirez-Cano, D., Millett, C., Darzi, A., and Donaldson, L. (2013). Harnessing the cloud of patient experience: Using social media to detect poor quality healthcare. *BMJ Quality and Safety*, **22**(3), 251–255. DOI: 10.1136/bmjqs-2012-001527. 71

Greaves, F., Laverty, A. A., Cano, D. R., Moilanen, K., Pulman, S., Darzi, A., and Millett, C. (2014). Tweets about hospital quality: A mixed methods study. *BMJ Quality and Safety*, **23**(10), 838–846. DOI: 10.1136/bmjqs-2014-002875. 72

Greenwood, S., Perrin, A., and Duggan, M. (2016). Social media update 2016. *Pew Research Center*, **11**. 83

Grinshteyn, E. and Hemenway, D. (2016). Violent death rates: The U.S. compared with other high-income OECD countries, 2010. *The American Journal of Medicine*, **129**(3), 266–273. DOI: 10.1016/j.amjmed.2015.10.025. 70

Groseclose, S. L. and Buckeridge, D. L. (2017). Public health surveillance systems: Recent advances in their use and evaluation. *Annual Review of Public Health*, **38**, 57–79. DOI: 10.1146/annurev-publhealth-031816-044348. 87

Gunawong, P. and Jankananon, P. (2015). Flood 2.0: Facebook use and reactions during the 2011/2012 flood in Thailand. *International Journal of Innovation and Learning*, **17**(2), 162–173. DOI: 10.1504/ijil.2015.067405. 67, 68

Haines, A., Kovats, R. S., Campbell-Lendrum, D., and Corvalán, C. (2006). Climate change and human health: Impacts, vulnerability and public health. *Public Health*, **120**(7), 585–596. DOI: 10.1016/j.puhe.2006.01.002. 69

Han, B., Cook, P., and Baldwin, T. (2014). Text-based Twitter user geolocation prediction. *Journal of Artificial Intelligence Research*, pages 451–500. DOI: 10.1613/jair.4200. 23, 44, 45

Hand, D. J. (2009). Measuring classifier performance: A coherent alternative to the area under the ROC curve. *Machine Learning*, **77**(1), 103–123. DOI: 10.1007/s10994-009-5119-5. 40

Hannak, A., Anderson, E., Mislove, A., and Barrett, L. F. (2010). Tweetin' in the rain: Exploring societal-scale effects of weather on mood. *Artificial Intelligence*, pages 479–482. 75

Hanson, C. L., Burton, S. H., Giraud-Carrier, C., West, J. H., Barnes, M. D., and Hansen, B. (2013a). Tweaking and tweeting: Exploring Twitter for nonmedical use of a psychostimulant drug (Adderall) among college students. *Journal of Medical Internet Research*, **15**(4), e62. DOI: 10.2196/jmir.2503. 61

Hanson, L. C., Cannon, B., Burton, S., and Giraud-Carrier, C. (2013b). An exploration of social circles and prescription drug abuse through Twitter. *Journal of Medical Internet Research*, **15**(9), e189. DOI: 10.2196/jmir.2741. 61

Hao, H. and Zhang, K. (2016). The voice of Chinese health consumers: A text mining approach to web-based physician reviews. *Journal of Medical Internet Research*, **18**(5), e108. DOI: 10.2196/jmir.4430. 72

Hao, H., Zhang, K., Wang, W., and Gao, G. (2017). A tale of two countries: International comparison of online doctor reviews between China and the United States. *International Journal of Medical Informatics*, **99**, 37–44. DOI: 10.1016/j.ijmedinf.2016.12.007. 72

Hardt, M., Price, E., Srebro, N., et al. (2016). Equality of opportunity in supervised learning. In *Advances in Neural Information Processing Systems*, pages 3315–3323. 84

Harford, T. (2014). Big data: A big mistake? *Significance*, **11**(5), 14–19. DOI: 10.1111/j.1740-9713.2014.00778.x. 78

Harpaz, R., DuMouchel, W., Shah, N. H., Madigan, D., Ryan, P., and Friedman, C. (2012). Novel data-mining methodologies for adverse drug event discovery and analysis. *Clinical Pharmacology and Therapeutics*, **91**(6), 1010–1021. DOI: 10.1038/clpt.2012.50. 72

Harrell, J. A. and Baker, E. L. (1994). The essential services of public health. *Leadership in Public Health*, **3**(3), 27–31. 9, 10

Harris, J. K., Mueller, N. L., and Snider, D. (2013). Social media adoption in local health departments nationwide. *American Journal of Public Health*, **103**(9), 1700–1707. DOI: 10.2105/ajph.2012.301166. 10

Harris, J. K., Mansour, R., Choucair, B., Olson, J., Nissen, C., and Bhatt, J. (2014a). Health department use of social media to identify foodborne illness—Chicago, Illinois, 2013–2014. *Morbidity and Mortality Weekly Report*, **63**(32), 681–685. 69

Harris, J. K., Moreland-Russell, S., Choucair, B., Mansour, R., Staub, M., and Simmons, K. (2014b). Tweeting for and against public health policy: Response to the Chicago Department of Public Health's electronic cigarette Twitter campaign. *Journal of Medical Internet Research*, **16**(10), e238. DOI: 10.2196/jmir.3622. 61, 66

Harrison, C., Jorder, M., Stern, H., Stavinsky, F., Reddy, V., Hanson, H., Waechter, H., Lowe, L., Gravano, L., and Balter, S. (2014). Using online reviews by restaurant patrons to identify unreported cases of foodborne illness—New York City, 2012–2013. *Morbidity and Mortality Weekly Report*, **63**(20), 441–445. 19, 69

Hawelka, B., Sitko, I., Beinat, E., Sobolevsky, S., Kazakopoulos, P., and Ratti, C. (2014). Geo-located Twitter as proxy for global mobility patterns. *Cartography and Geographic Information Science*, **41**(3), 260–271. DOI: 10.1080/15230406.2014.890072. 54

Hawkins, J. B., Brownstein, J. S., Tuli, G., Runels, T., Broecker, K., Nsoesie, E. O., McIver, D. J., Rozenblum, R., Wright, A., Bourgeois, F. T., and Greaves, F. (2015). Measuring patient-perceived quality of care in U.S. hospitals using Twitter. *Quality and Safety in Health Care*. DOI: 10.1136/bmjqs-2015-004309. 72

Hawn, C. (2009). Take two aspirin and tweet me in the morning: How Twitter, Facebook, and other social media are reshaping health care. *Health Affairs (Millwood)*, **28**(2), 361–368. DOI: 10.1377/hlthaff.28.2.361. 9

Heaivilin, N., Gerbert, B., Page, J. E., and Gibbs, J. L. (2011). Public health surveillance of dental pain via Twitter. *Journal of Dental Research*, **90**(9), 1047–1051. DOI: 10.1177/0022034511415273. 41, 55

Hecht, B., Hong, L., Suh, B., and Chi, E. H. (2011). Tweets from Justin Bieber's heart: The dynamics of the location field in user profiles. In *Conference on Human Factors in Computing Systems (CHI)*. DOI: 10.1145/1978942.1978976. 44

Heffernan, R., Mostashari, F., Das, D., Besculides, M., Rodriguez, C., Greenko, J., Steiner-Sichel, L., Balter, S., Karpati, A., Thomas, P., et al. (2004). New York City syndromic surveillance systems. *Morbidity and Mortality Weekly Report*, pages 25–27. DOI: 10.1037/e307182005-004. 12

Heldman, A. B., Schindelar, J., and Weaver, J. B. (2013). Social media engagement and public health communication: Implications for public health organizations being truly "social." *Public Health Reviews*, **35**(1), 13. DOI: 10.1007/bf03391698. 17

Hill, S., Merchant, R., and Ungar, L. (2013). Lessons learned about public health from online crowd surveillance. *Big Data*, **1**(3), 160–167. DOI: 10.1089/big.2013.0020. 16

Hill, S. L. and Thomas, S. H. L. (2011). Clinical toxicology of newer recreational drugs. *Clinical Toxicology*, **49**(8), 705–719. DOI: 10.3109/15563650.2011.615318. 62

Holden, R. R. (2010). Face validity. *Corsini Encyclopedia of Psychology*. DOI: 10.1002/9780470479216.corpsy0341. 40

Horvitz, E. and Mulligan, D. (2015). Policy forum. Data, privacy, and the greater good. *Science*, **349**(6245), 253–255. DOI: 10.1126/science.aac4520. 90

Hsiao, C.-J., Hing, E., et al. (2012). *Use and Characteristics of Electronic Health Record Systems Among Office-Based Physician Practices, U.S., 2001–2012.* U.S. Department of Health and Human Services, Centers for Disease Control and Prevention, National Center for Health Statistics. 2

Huang, J., Kornfield, R., Szczypka, G., and Emery, S. L. (2014). A cross-sectional examination of marketing of electronic cigarettes on Twitter. *Tobacco Control*, **23**(suppl. 3), iii26–iii30. DOI: 10.1136/tobaccocontrol-2014-051551. 60

Huang, X., Smith, M. C., Paul, M. J., Ryzhkov, D., Quinn, S. C., Broniatowski, D. A., and Dredze, M. (2017a). Examining patterns of influenza vaccination in social media. In *AAAI Joint Workshop on Health Intelligence.* 64

Huang, X., Xing, L., Brubaker, J. R., and Paul, M. J. (2017b). Exploring timelines of confirmed suicide incidents through social media. In *IEEE International Conference on Healthcare Informatics (ICHI).* 75

Hudson, J. M. and Bruckman, A. (2004). "Go away:" Participant objections to being studied and the ethics of chatroom research. *The Information Society*, **20**(2), 127–139. DOI: 10.1080/01972240490423030. 90

Hwang, J. D. and Hollingshead, K. (2016). Crazy mad nutters: The language of mental health. In *Workshop on Computational Linguistics and Clinical Psychology (CLPsych).* DOI: 10.18653/v1/w16-0306. 76

Hwang, K. O., Farheen, K., Johnson, C. W., Thomas, E. J., Barnes, A. S., and Bernstam, E. V. (2007). Quality of weight loss advice on internet forums. *American Journal of Medicine*, **120**(7), 604–609. DOI: 10.1016/j.amjmed.2007.04.017. 59

Hwang, K. O., Ottenbacher, A. J., Green, A. P., Cannon-Diehl, M. R., Richardson, O., Bernstam, E. V., and Thomas, E. J. (2010). Social support in an Internet weight loss community. *International Journal of Medical Informatics*, **79**(1), 5–13. DOI: 10.1016/j.ijmedinf.2009.10.003. 59

Hwang, K. O., Ottenbacher, A. J., Lucke, J. F., Etchegaray, J. M., Graham, A. L., Thomas, E. J., and Bernstam, E. V. (2011). Measuring social support for weight loss in an internet weight loss community. *Journal of Health Communication*, **16**(2), 198–211. DOI: 10.1080/10810730.2010.535106. 59

Hyndman, R. J. and Koehler, A. B. (2006). Another look at measures of forecast accuracy. *International Journal of Forecasting*, pages 679–688. DOI: 10.1016/j.ijforecast.2006.03.001. 37

Iannacchione, V. G. (2011). The changing role of address-based sampling in survey research. *Public Opinion Quarterly*, **75**(3), 556–575. DOI: 10.1093/poq/nfr017. 12, 85

Impicciatore, P., Pandolfini, C., Casella, N., and Bonati, M. (1997). Reliability of health information for the public on the world wide web: Systematic survey of advice on managing fever in children at home. *BMJ*, **314**(7098), 1875. DOI: 10.1136/bmj.314.7098.1875. 16

Imran, M., Castillo, C., Diaz, F., and Vieweg, S. (2015). Processing social media messages in mass emergency: A survey. *ACM Computing Surveys (CSUR)*, **47**(4). DOI: 10.1145/2771588. 67

International Committee of Medical Journal Editors (1997). Uniform requirements for manuscripts submitted to biomedical journals. *New England Journal of Medicine*, **1997**(336), 309–316. 92

Irvine, R. J., Kostakis, C., Felgate, P. D., Jaehne, E. J., Chen, C., and White, J. M. (2011). Population drug use in Australia: A wastewater analysis. *Forensic Science International*, **210**(1), 69–73. DOI: 10.1016/j.forsciint.2011.01.037. 12

Iso, H., Wakamiya, S., and Aramaki, E. (2016). Forecasting word model: Twitter-based influenza surveillance and prediction. In *International Conference on Computational Linguistics (COLING)*. 53

Jain, S., Zhu, S.-H., and Conway, M. (2015). Exploring consumer attitudes towards hookah, cigarettes, and cigars using Twitter. *Tobacco Regulatory Science*, **1**(3), 198–203. DOI: 10.18001/trs.1.3.1. 60

Jamieson, C. (2013). Gun violence research: History of the federal funding freeze. *Psychological Science Agenda*, **27**(2). DOI: 10.1037/e521422013-003. 70

Jashinsky, J., Burton, S. H., Hanson, C. L., West, J., Giraud-Carrier, C., Barnes, M. D., and Argyle, T. (2015). Tracking suicide risk factors through Twitter in the U.S. *Crisis*. DOI: 10.1027/0227-5910/a000234. 75

Jelenchick, L. A., Eickhoff, J. C., and Moreno, M. A. (2013). "Facebook depression?" Social networking site use and depression in older adolescents. *Journal of Adolescent Health*, **52**(1), 128–130. DOI: 10.1016/j.jadohealth.2012.05.008. 74

Ji, X., Chun, S. A., and Geller, J. (2013). Monitoring public health concerns using Twitter sentiment classifications. In *IEEE International Conference on Healthcare Informatics*. DOI: 10.1109/ichi.2013.47. 65

Jiang, K. and Zheng, Y. (2013). Mining Twitter data for potential drug effects. *Advanced Data Mining and Applications*. DOI: 10.1007/978-3-642-53914-5_37. 72

Jin, H., Xianyun, T., Guang, Y., and Fang, H. (2016). Disclosure pattern of self-labeled people living with HIV/AIDS on Chinese social networking site: An exploratory study. *Cyberpsychology, Behavior, and Social Networking*, **19**(8), 516–523. DOI: 10.1089/cyber.2016.0133. 55

Joaristi, M., Serra, E., and Spezzano, F. (2016). Identifying health-violating restaurants with online reviews. In *IEEE-ACM International Conference on Advances in Social Networks Analysis and Mining*. 68

Johnson, I., McMahon, C., Schöning, J., and Hecht, B. (2017). The effect of population and "structural" biases on social media-based algorithms—a case study in geolocation inference across the urban-rural spectrum. In *Conference on Human Factors in Computing Systems (CHI)*. DOI: 10.1145/3025453.3026015. 80, 84

Jones, J. H. and Salathé, M. (2009). Early assessment of anxiety and behavioral response to novel swine-origin influenza A(H1N1). *PLoS ONE*, **4**(12), e8032. DOI: 10.1371/journal.pone.0008032. 65

Jones, T. (2014). The problem with Twitter maps. `http://www.languagejones.com/blog-1/2014/12/24/the-problem-with-{T}witter-maps` 80

Jurgens, D., Finethy, T., McCorriston, J., Xu, Y. T., and Ruths, D. (2015). Geolocation prediction in Twitter using social networks: A critical analysis and review of current practice. In *International Conference on Weblogs and Social Media (ICWSM)*. 45

Jürges, H. (2007). True health vs. response styles: Exploring cross-country differences in self-reported health. *Health Economics*, **16**(2), 163—178. DOI: 10.1002/hec.1134. 79

Juric, R., Kim, I., Panneerselvam, H., and Tesanovic, I. (2017). Analysis of Zika virus tweets: Could hadoop platform help in global health management. In *Hawaii International Conference on System Sciences*. DOI: 10.24251/hicss.2017.395. 32, 54

Kang, J. S., Kuznetsova, P., Luca, M., and Choi, Y. (2013). Where not to eat? Improving public policy by predicting hygiene inspections using online reviews. In *Empirical Methods in Natural Language Processing (EMNLP)*. 68

Kato, M. P., Sakai, T., and Tanaka, K. (2013). When do people use query suggestion? A query suggestion log analysis. *Information Retrieval*, **16**(6), 725–746. DOI: 10.1007/s10791-012-9216-x. 81

Katsuki, T., Mackey, K. T., and Cuomo, R. (2015). Establishing a link between prescription drug abuse and illicit online pharmacies: Analysis of Twitter data. *Journal of Medical Internet Research*, **17**(12), e280. DOI: 10.2196/jmir.5144. 61

Kavuluru, R., Ramos-Morales, M., Holaday, T., Williams, A. G., Haye, L., and Cerel, J. (2016). Classification of helpful comments on online suicide watch forums. In *International Conference on Bioinformatics, Computational Biology, and Health Informatics*, pages 32–40, New York, ACM. DOI: 10.1145/2975167.2975170. 74, 75

Keegan, B. C., Cavazos-Rehg, P., Nguyen, A. N., Savage, S., Kaye, J., De Choudhury, M., and Paul, M. J. (2017). CHI-nnabis: Implications of marijuana legalization for and from human-computer interaction. In *Conference on Human Factors in Computing Systems (CHI)*, pages 1312–1317, New York. DOI: 10.1145/3027063.3051139. 61

Keelan, J., Pavri, V., Balakrishnan, R., and Wilson, K. (2010). An analysis of the Human Papilloma Virus vaccine debate on MySpace blogs. *Vaccine*, **28**(6), 1535–1540. DOI: 10.1016/j.vaccine.2009.11.060. 64

Kempf, A. M. and Remington, P. L. (2007). New challenges for telephone survey research in the 21st century. *Annual Review of Public Health*, **28**, 113–126. DOI: 10.1146/annurev.publhealth.28.021406.144059. 12, 85

Kessler, R. C., McGonagle, K. A., Zhao, S., Nelson, C. B., Hughes, M., Eshleman, S., Wittchen, H.-U., and Kendler, K. S. (1994). Lifetime and 12-month prevalence of DSM-III-R psychiatric disorders in the U.S.: Results from the National Comorbidity Survey. *Archives of General Psychiatry*, **51**(1), 8–19. DOI: 10.1001/archpsyc.1994.03950010008002. 74

Kessler, R. C., Berglund, P., Demler, O., Jin, R., Merikangas, K. R., and Walters, E. E. (2005). Lifetime prevalence and age-of-onset distributions of DSM-IV disorders in the National Comorbidity Survey Replication. *Archives of General Psychiatry*, **62**(6), 593–602. DOI: 10.1001/archpsyc.62.6.593. 73

Khasnavis, S., Rosenkrantz, A. B., and Prabhu, V. (2017). Using Twitter to assess the public response to the United States Preventive Services task force guidelines on lung cancer screening with low dose chest CT. *Journal of Digital Imaging*, **30**(3), 323–327. DOI: 10.1007/s10278-016-9933-6. 66

Kiciman, E. and Richardson, M. (2015). Towards decision support and goal achievement: Identifying action-outcome relationships from social media. In *ACM Conference on Knowledge Discovery and Data Mining (KDD)*. DOI: 10.1145/2783258.2783310. 59

Kiciman, E., Counts, S., Gamon, M., De Choudhury, M., and Thiesson, B. (2014). Discussion graphs: Putting social media analysis in context. In *International Conference on Weblogs and Social Media (ICWSM)*, AAAI. 45

Kim, Y., Huang, J., and Emery, S. (2016). Garbage in, garbage out: Data collection, quality assessment and reporting standards for social media data use in health research, infodemiology and digital disease detection. *Journal of Medical Internet Research*, **18**(2). DOI: 10.2196/jmir.4738. 17, 82

Kleinman, A. (2009). Global mental health: A failure of humanity. *The Lancet*, **374**(9690), 603–604. DOI: 10.1016/s0140-6736(09)61510-5. 73

Knowles, R., Carroll, J., and Dredze, M. (2016). Demographer: Extremely simple name demographics. In *EMNLP Workshop on Natural Language Processing and Computational Social Science*. DOI: 10.18653/v1/w16-5614. 43, 44

Kogan, M., Palen, L., and Anderson, K. M. (2015). Think local, retweet global: Retweeting by the geographically-vulnerable during Hurricane Sandy. In *Conference on Computer Supported Cooperative Work and Social Computing (CSCW)*. DOI: 10.1145/2675133.2675218. 68

Koop, C. E. and Lundberg, G. D. (1992). Violence in America: A public health emergency: Time to bite the bullet back. *JAMA*, **267**(22), 3075–3076. DOI: 10.1001/jama.1992.03480220093036. 70

Koratana, A., Dredze, M., Chisolm, M., Johnson, M., and Paul, M. J. (2016). Studying anonymous health issues and substance use on college campuses with yik yak. In *AAAI Workshop on the World Wide Web and Public Health Intelligence*. 17

Korda, H. and Itani, Z. (2013). Harnessing social media for health promotion and behavior change. *Health Promotion Practice*, **14**(1), 15–23. DOI: 10.1177/1524839911405850. 9

Kramer, A. D., Guillory, J. E., and Hancock, J. T. (2014). Experimental evidence of massive-scale emotional contagion through social networks. *Proc. of the National Academy of Science U.S.A.*, **111**(24), 8788–8790. DOI: 10.1073/pnas.1320040111. 91

Krause, R. (2006). The swine flu episode and the fog of epidemics. *Emerging Infectious Diseases*, **12**(1), 40–43. DOI: 10.3201/eid1201.051132. 86

Kumar, M., Dredze, M., Coppersmith, G., and Choudhury, M. D. (2015). Shifts in suicidal ideation manifested in social media following celebrity suicides. In *Conference on Hypertext and Social Media*. 66, 75

Kusmierczyk, T., Trattner, C., and Norvag, K. (2015). Temporality in online food recipe consumption and production. In *International Conference on World Wide Web (WWW)*. DOI: 10.1145/2740908.2742752. 59

Lamb, A., Paul, M. J., and Dredze, M. (2013). Separating fact from fear: Tracking flu infections on Twitter. In *North American Chapter of the Association for Computational Linguistics (NAACL)*, pages 789–795. 29, 30, 34, 35, 39, 53, 56

Lampos, V. and Cristianini, N. (2010). Tracking the flu pandemic by monitoring the social web. In *The 2nd International Workshop on Cognitive Information Processing, CIP2010*, pages 411–416. DOI: 10.1109/cip.2010.5604088. 29, 34, 53

Lampos, V. and Cristianini, N. (2012). Nowcasting events from the social web with statistical learning. *ACM Transactions on Intelligent Systems and Technology*, **3**(4), 1–22. DOI: 10.1145/2337542.2337557. 53

Lampos, V., Lansdall-Welfare, T., Araya, R., and Cristianini, N. (2013). Analysing mood patterns in the United Kingdom through Twitter content. *arXiv*. 75

Lampos, V., Zou, B., and Cox, I. J. (2017). Enhancing feature selection using word embeddings: The case of flu surveillance. In *International Conference on World Wide Web (WWW)*, pages 695–704. DOI: 10.1145/3038912.3052622. 53

Larson, H. J., Smith, D. M., Paterson, P., Cumming, M., Eckersberger, E., Freifeld, C. C., Ghinai, I., Jarrett, C., Paushter, L., Brownstein, J. S., and Madoff, L. C. (2013). Measuring vaccine confidence: Analysis of data obtained by a media surveillance system used to analyse public concerns about vaccines. *Lancet Infectious Diseases*, **13**(7), 606–613. DOI: 10.1016/s1473-3099(13)70108-7. 65

Lazard, A. J., Scheinfeld, E., Bernhardt, J. M., Wilcox, G. B., and Suran, M. (2015). Detecting themes of public concern: A text mining analysis of the Centers for Disease Control and Prevention's ebola live Twitter chat. *American Journal of Infection Control*. DOI: 10.1016/j.ajic.2015.05.025. 54, 65

Lazard, A. J., Wilcox, G. B., Tuttle, H. M., Glowacki, E. M., and Pikowski, J. (2017). Public reactions to e-cigarette regulations on Twitter: A text mining analysis. *Tobacco Control*. DOI: 10.1136/tobaccocontrol-2016-053295. 61, 66

Lazard, J. A., Saffer, J. A., Wilcox, B. G., Chung, D. A., Mackert, S. M., and Bernhardt, M. J. (2016). E-cigarette social media messages: A text mining analysis of marketing and consumer conversations on Twitter. *JMIR Public Health Surveillance*, **2**(2), e171. DOI: 10.2196/publichealth.6551. 60

Lazer, D. and Kennedy, R. (2015). What we can learn from the epic failure of Google Flu Trends. *Wired*. 78

Lazer, D., Pentland, A. S., Adamic, L., Aral, S., Barabasi, A. L., Brewer, D., Christakis, N., Contractor, N., Fowler, J., Gutmann, M., et al. (2009). Life in the network: The coming age of computational social science. *Science*, **323**(5915), 721. DOI: 10.1126/science.1167742. 16

Lazer, D., Kennedy, R., King, G., and Vespignani, A. (2014a). Google Flu Trends still appears sick: An evaluation of the 2013–2014 flu season. https://gking.harvard.edu/files/gking/files/ssrn-id2408560_2.pdf DOI: 10.2139/ssrn.2408560. 78

Lazer, D., Kennedy, R., King, G., and Vespignani, A. (2014b). The parable of Google Flu: Traps in big data analysis. *Science*, **343**(6167), 1203–1205. DOI: 10.1126/science.1248506. 4, 37, 39, 52, 77, 82, 86, 87

Leaman, R. and Wojtulewicz, L. (2010). Towards internet-age pharmacovigilance: Extracting adverse drug reactions from user posts to health-related social networks. In *Workshop on Biomedical Natural Language Processing*. 72

Leas, E. C., Althouse, B. M., Dredze, M., Obradovich, N., Fowler, J. H., Noar, S. M., Allem, J., and Ayers, J. W. (2016). Big data sensors of organic advocacy: The case of Leonardo DiCaprio and climate change. *PLoS ONE*. DOI: 10.1371/journal.pone.0159885. 70

LeBlanc, A. G. and Chaput, J.-P. (2016). Pokémon Go: A game changer for the physical inactivity crisis? *Preventive Medicine*. DOI: 10.1016/j.ypmed.2016.11.012. 59

Ledberg, A. (2015). The interest in eight new psychoactive substances before and after scheduling. *Drug Alcohol Dependence*, **152**, 73–78. DOI: 10.1016/j.drugalcdep.2015.04.020. 63

Lee, H., McAuley, J. H., Hübscher, M., Allen, H. G., Kamper, S. J., and Moseley, G. L. (2016). Tweeting back: Predicting new cases of back pain with mass social media data. *Journal of the American Medical Informatics Association*, **23**(3), 644. DOI: 10.1093/jamia/ocv168. 55

Lee, H. R., Lee, H. E., Choi, J., Kim, J. H., and Han, H. L. (2014a). Social media use, body image, and psychological well-being: A cross-cultural comparison of Korea and the United States. *Journal of Health Communication*, **19**(12), 1343–1358. DOI: 10.1080/10810730.2014.904022. 60

Lee, J. L., DeCamp, M., Dredze, M., Chisolm, M. S., and Berger, Z. D. (2014b). What are health-related users tweeting? A qualitative content analysis of health-related users and their messages on Twitter. *Journal of Medical Internet Research*, **16**(10), e237. DOI: 10.2196/jmir.3765. 10

Leetaru, K. (2014). Why big data missed the early warning signs of ebola. http://foreignpolicy.com/2014/09/26/why-big-data-missed-the-early-warning-signs-of-ebola/ 86

Leggatt-Cook, C. and Chamberlain, K. (2012). Blogging for weight loss: Personal accountability, writing selves, and the weight-loss blogosphere. *Social Health Illness*, **34**(7), 963–977. DOI: 10.1111/j.1467-9566.2011.01435.x. 59

Lentine, K. L., Schnitzler, M. A., Abbott, K. C., Bramesfeld, K., Buchanan, P. M., and Brennan, D. C. (2009). Sensitivity of billing claims for cardiovascular disease events among kidney transplant recipients. *Clinical Journal of the American Society of Nephrology*, **4**(7), 1213–1221. DOI: 10.2215/cjn.00670109. 12

Li, E. Y., Tung, C.-Y., and Chang, S.-H. (2016). The wisdom of crowds in action: Forecasting epidemic diseases with a web-based prediction market system. *International Journal of Medical Informatics*, **92**, 35–43. DOI: 10.1016/j.ijmedinf.2016.04.014. 20

Li, J. and Cardie, C. (2013). Early stage influenza detection from Twitter. *arXiv*, **arXiv:1309.7340**. 53

Li, Y. and Hu, C. (2016). A method for tracking flu trends through Weibo. *International Journal of Database Theory and Application*, **9**(5), 91–100. DOI: 10.14257/ijdta.2016.9.5.09. 53

Li, Z., Liu, T., Zhu, G., Lin, H., Zhang, Y., He, J., Deng, A., Peng, Z., Xiao, J., Rutherford, S., Xie, R., Zeng, W., Li, X., and Ma, W. (2017). Dengue Baidu search index data can improve the prediction of local dengue epidemic: A case study in Guangzhou, China. *PLOS Neglected Tropical Diseases*, **11**(3), 1–13. DOI: 10.1371/journal.pntd.0005354. 54

Liu, J., Weitzman, E. R., and Chunara, R. (2017). Assessing behavior stage progression from social media data. In *Conference on Computer Supported Cooperative Work and Social Computing (CSCW)*, pages 1320–1333, New York. DOI: 10.1145/2998181.2998336. 47, 61

Liu, W. and Ruths, D. (2013). What's in a name? Using first names as features for gender inference in Twitter. In *AAAI Spring Symposium: Analyzing Microtext*. 43

Liu, Y., Gummadi, K. P., Krishnamurthy, B., and Mislove, A. (2011). Analyzing Facebook privacy settings: User expectations vs. reality. In *ACM SIGCOMM Conference on Internet Measurement Conference*, pages 61–70. DOI: 10.1145/2068816.2068823. 89

Liu, Y., Mei, Q., Hanauer, A. D., Zheng, K., and Lee, M. J. (2016). Use of social media in the diabetes community: An exploratory analysis of diabetes-related tweets. *JMIR Diabetes*, **1**(2), e4. DOI: 10.2196/diabetes.6256. 55

López, A., Detz, A., Ratanawongsa, N., and Sarkar, U. (2012). What patients say about their doctors online: A qualitative content analysis. *Journal of General Internal Medicine*, **27**(6), 685–692. DOI: 10.1007/s11606-011-1958-4. 71

Lu, Y., Hu, X., Wang, F., Kumar, S., Liu, H., and Maciejewski, R. (2015). Visualizing social media sentiment in disaster scenarios. In *International Conference on World Wide Web (WWW)*. DOI: 10.1145/2740908.2741720. 67

Luxton, D. D., June, J. D., and Fairall, J. M. (2012). Social media and suicide: A public health perspective. *American Journal of Public Health*, **102**(S2), S195–S200. DOI: 10.2105/ajph.2011.300608. 75

Mac Kim, S., Wan, S., Paris, C., Jin, B., and Robinson, B. (2016). The effects of data collection methods in Twitter. In *Workshops on Natural Language Processing and Computational Social Science (NLP+CSS)*, page 86. DOI: 10.18653/v1/w16-5611. 80

Mackey, T. K., Liang, B. A., and Strathdee, S. A. (2013). Digital social media, youth, and nonmedical use of prescription drugs: The need for reform. *Journal of Medical Internet Research*, **15**(7), e143. DOI: 10.2196/jmir.2464. 61

Magill, S. S., Edwards, J. R., Bamberg, W., Beldavs, Z. G., Dumyati, G., Kainer, M. A., Lynfield, R., Maloney, M., McAllister-Hollod, L., Nadle, J., et al. (2014). Multistate pointprevalence survey of health care—associated infections. *New England Journal of Medicine*, **370**(13), 1198–1208. DOI: 10.1056/nejmoa1306801. 71

Magruder, S. F., Lewis, S. H., Najmi, A., and Florio, E. (2004). Progress in understanding and using over-the-counter pharmaceuticals for syndromic surveillance. *Morbidity and Mortality Weekly Report*, pages 117–122. DOI: 10.1037/e307182005-022. 12

Makary, M. A. and Daniel, M. (2016). Medical error—the 3rd leading cause of death in the U.S. *BMJ*, **353**. DOI: 10.1136/bmj.i2139. 70

Malik, M., Lamba, H., Nakos, C., and Pfeffer, J. (2015). Population bias in geotagged tweets. In *International Conference on Weblogs and Social Media (ICWSM)*. 80

Mandel, B., Culotta, A., Boulahanis, J., Stark, D., Lewis, B., and Rodrigue, J. (2012). A demographic analysis of online sentiment during Hurricane Irene. In *Workshop on Language in Social Media*, pages 27–36. 68

Mao, M., Pan, S.-L., Hackney, R., Ractham, P., and Kaewkitipong, L. (2014). Constructing the cultural repertoire in a natural disaster: The role of social media in the Thailand flood of 2011. In *Australasian Conference on Information Systems*. 68

Marah, M. and Novotny, T. E. (2011). Geographic patterns of cigarette butt waste in the urban environment. *Tobacco Control*, **20**(Suppl. 1), i42–i44. DOI: 10.1136/tc.2010.042424. 12

Markham, A. and Buchanan, E. (2012). Ethical decision-making and internet research: Version 2.0. recommendations from the AoIR ethics working committee. *Association of Internet Researchers*. 92

Martin, L. J., Xu, B., and Yasui, Y. (2014). Improving Google Flu Trends estimates for the U.S. through transformation. *PLoS ONE*, **9**(12), e109209. DOI: 10.1371/journal.pone.0109209. 78

Matthew Miller, M. (2013). Public health approach to the prevention of gun violence. *The New England Journal of Medicine*, **368**(21), 2033. DOI: 10.1056/nejmsb1302631. 70

Mayors Against Illegal Guns (2013). Access denied: How the gun lobby is depriving police, policy makers, and the public of the data we need to prevent gun violence. 70

McCabe-Sellers, B. J. and Beattie, S. E. (2004). Food safety: Emerging trends in foodborne illness surveillance and prevention. *Journal of the American Diet Association*, **104**(11), 1708–1717. DOI: 10.1016/j.jada.2004.08.028. 68

McCorriston, J., Jurgens, D., and Ruths, D. (2015). Organizations are users too: Characterizing and detecting the presence of organizations on Twitter. In *International Conference on Weblogs and Social Media (ICWSM)*. 17

McGough, S. F., Brownstein, J. S., Hawkins, J. B., and Santillana, M. (2017). Forecasting Zika incidence in the 2016 Latin America outbreak combining traditional disease surveillance with search, social media, and news report data. *PLOS Neglected Tropical Diseases*, **11**(1), 1–15. DOI: 10.1371/journal.pntd.0005295. 54

McIver, D. J. and Brownstein, J. S. (2014). Wikipedia usage estimates prevalence of influenza-like illness in the United States in near real-time. *PLoS Computational Biology*, **10**(4), e1003581. DOI: 10.1371/journal.pcbi.1003581. 20, 53

McIver, D. J., Hawkins, J. B., Chunara, R., Chatterjee, A. K., Bhandari, A., Fitzgerald, T. P., Jain, S. H., and Brownstein, J. S. (2015). Characterizing sleep issues using Twitter. *Journal of Medical Internet Research*, **17**(6). DOI: 10.2196/jmir.4476. 75

McKee, R. (2013). Ethical issues in using social media for health and health care research. *Health Policy*, **110**(2-3), 298–301. DOI: 10.1016/j.healthpol.2013.02.006. 88, 89

McPherson, M., Smith-Lovin, L., and Cook, J. M. (2001). Birds of a feather: Homophily in social networks. *Annual Review of Sociology*, **27**(1), 415–444. DOI: 10.1146/annurev.soc.27.1.415. 43

Mei, S., Li, H., Zhu, X., and Dyer, C. R. (2014). Inferring air pollution by sniffing social media. In *IEEE/ACM International Conference on Advances in Social Network Analysis and Mining*. DOI: 10.1109/asonam.2014.6921638. 69

Mejova, Y., Haddadi, H., Noulas, A., and Weber, I. (2015). #foodporn: Obesity patterns in culinary interactions. In *International Conference on Digital Health*, pages 51–58. DOI: 10.1145/2750511.2750524. 59

Mercy, J. A., Rosenberg, M. L., Powell, K. E., Broome, C. V., and Roper, W. L. (1993). Public health policy for preventing violence. *Health Affairs*, **12**(4), 7–29. DOI: 10.1377/hlthaff.12.4.7. 70

Metzger, K. B., Mostashari, F., and Kerker, B. D. (2005). Use of pharmacy data to evaluate smoking regulations' impact on sales of nicotine replacement therapies in New York City. *American Journal of Public Health*, **95**(6), 1050–1055. DOI: 10.2105/ajph.2004.048025. 12

Meyer, M. N. and Chabris, C. F. (2015). Please, corporations, experiment on us. *New York Times*. 91

Mikal, J., Hurst, S., and Conway, M. (2016). Ethical issues in using Twitter for population-level depression monitoring: A qualitative study. *BMC Medical Ethics*, **17**(1), 1. DOI: 10.1186/s12910-016-0105-5. 88, 90, 93

Milinovich, G. J., Avril, S. M., Clements, A. C., Brownstein, J. S., Tong, S., and Hu, W. (2014). Using internet search queries for infectious disease surveillance: Screening diseases for suitability. *BMC Infectious Diseases*, **14**(1), 3840. DOI: 10.1186/s12879-014-0690-1. 55

Miller, M., Banerjee, T., Muppalla, R., Romine, W., and Sheth, A. (2017). What are people tweeting about Zika? An exploratory study concerning its symptoms, treatment, transmission, and prevention. *JMIR Public Health Surveillance*, **3**(2), e38. DOI: 10.2196/publichealth.7157. 32, 54

Milojevi, S. (2016). Revisiting the connection between solar eruptions and primary headaches and migraines using Twitter. *Science Representations*, **6**, 39769. DOI: 10.1038/srep39769. 55

Mishra, N., Romero, D. M., and Tsaparas, P. (2013). Estimating the relative utility of networks for predicting user activities. In *Conference on Information and Knowledge Management (CIKM)*, pages 1047–1056. DOI: 10.1145/2505515.2505586. 24

Mislove, A., Lehmann, S., Ahn, Y.-y., Onnela, J.-P., and Rosenquist, J. N. (2011). Understanding the demographics of Twitter users. In *International Conference on Weblogs and Social Media (ICWSM)*, pages 554–557. 42, 83

Misra, I., Lawrence Zitnick, C., Mitchell, M., and Girshick, R. (2016). Seeing through the human reporting bias: Visual classifiers from noisy human-centric labels. In *IEEE Conference on Computer Vision and Pattern Recognition*, pages 2930–2939. DOI: 10.1109/cvpr.2016.320. 84

Mitchell, M., Hollingshead, K., and Coppersmith, G. (2015). Quantifying the language of schizophrenia in social media. In *Workshop on Computational Linguistics and Clinical Psychology (CLPsych)*. DOI: 10.3115/v1/w15-1202. 75

Moccia, M., Palladino, R., Falco, A., Saccà, F., Lanzillo, R., and Brescia Morra, V. (2016). Google Trends: New evidence for seasonality of multiple sclerosis. *Journal of Neurology, Neurosurgery and Psychiatry*, **87**(9), 1028–1029. DOI: 10.1136/jnnp-2016-313260. 56

Mohammady, E. and Culotta, A. (2014). Using county demographics to infer attributes of Twitter users. In *Association for Computational Linguistics (ACL)*. DOI: 10.3115/v1/w14-2702. 43

Mohan, K., Pearl, J., and Tian, J. (2013). Graphical models for inference with missing data. In *Advances in Neural Information Processing Systems (NIPS)*, pages 1277–1285. 79

Mollema, L., Harmsen, I. A., Broekhuizen, E., Clijnk, R., De Melker, H., Paulussen, T., Kok, G., Ruiter, R., and Das, E. (2015). Disease detection or public opinion reflection? Content analysis of tweets, other social media, and online newspapers during the measles outbreak in the Netherlands in 2013. *Journal of Medical Internet Research*, **17**(5), e128. DOI: 10.2196/jmir.3863. 65

Moorhead, S. A., Hazlett, D. E., Harrison, L., Carroll, J. K., Irwin, A., and Hoving, C. (2013). A new dimension of health care: Systematic review of the uses, benefits, and limitations of social media for health communication. *Journal of Medical Internet Research*, **15**(4), e85. DOI: 10.2196/jmir.1933. 9, 17

Moreno, M. A., Jelenchick, L. A., Egan, K. G., Cox, E., Young, H., Gannon, K. E., and Becker, T. (2011). Feeling bad on Facebook: Depression disclosures by college students on a social networking site. *Depression and Anxiety*, **28**(6), 447–455. DOI: 10.1002/da.20805. 74

Moreno, M. A., Christakis, D. A., Egan, K. G., Brockman, L. N., and Becker, T. (2012). Associations between displayed alcohol references on Facebook and problem drinking among college students. *Archives of Pediatrics and Adolescent Medicine*, **166**(2), 157–163. DOI: 10.1001/archpediatrics.2011.180. 61

Moreno, M. A., D'Angelo, J., Kacvinsky, L. E., Kerr, B., Zhang, C., and Eickhoff, J. (2014). Emergence and predictors of alcohol reference displays on Facebook during the first year of college. *Computers in Human Behavior*, **30**. DOI: 10.1016/j.chb.2013.07.060. 61

Morgan, E. M., Snelson, C., and Elison-Bowers, P. (2010). Image and video disclosure of substance use on social media websites. *Computers in Human Behavior*, **26**(6), 1405–1411. Online Interactivity: Role of Technology in Behavior Change. DOI: 10.1016/j.chb.2010.04.017. 18, 63

Morstatter, F., Pfeffer, J., Liu, H., and Carley, K. M. (2013). Is the sample good enough? Comparing data from Twitter's streaming API with Twitter's firehose. In *International Conference on Weblogs and Social Media (ICWSM)*. 80

Mowery, J. (2016). Twitter influenza surveillance: Quantifying seasonal misdiagnosis patterns and their impact on surveillance estimates. *Online Journal of Public Health Information*, **8**(3), e198. DOI: 10.5210/ojphi.v8i3.7011. 79

Mowery, J., Andrei, A., Le, E., Jian, J., and Ward, M. (2016). Assessing quality of care and elder abuse in nursing homes via Google Reviews. *Online Journal of Public Health Information*, **8**(3), e201. DOI: 10.5210/ojphi.v8i3.6906. 72

Mozaffarian, D., Hemenway, D., and Ludwig, D. S. (2013). Curbing gun violence: Lessons from public health successes. *JAMA*, **309**(6), 551–552. DOI: 10.1001/jama.2013.38. 70

Muppalla, R., Miller, M., Banerjee, T., and Romine, W. (2017). Discovering explanatory models to identify relevant tweets on Zika. In *IEEE Engineering in Medicine and Biology Society (EMBS)*. 32, 54

Murphy, G. E. (1984). The prediction of suicide: Why is it so difficult? *American Journal of Psychotherapy*. 2

Myslín, M., Zhu, S.-H., Chapman, W., and Conway, M. (2013). Using Twitter to examine smoking behavior and perceptions of emerging tobacco products. *Journal of Medical Internet Research*, **15**(8). DOI: 10.2196/jmir.2534. 60

Nagar, R., Yuan, Q., Freifeld, C. C., Santillana, M., Nojima, A., Chunara, R., and Brownstein, J. S. (2014). A case study of the New York City 2012–2013 influenza season with daily geocoded Twitter data from temporal and spatiotemporal perspectives. *Journal of Medical Internet Research*, **16**(10), e236. DOI: 10.2196/jmir.3416. 41, 53

Nakhasi, A., Passarella, R. J., Bell, S. G., Paul, M. J., Dredze, M., and Pronovost, P. J. (2012). Malpractice and malcontent: Analyzing medical complaints in Twitter. In *AAAI Fall Symposium on Information Retrieval and Knowledge Discovery in Biomedical Text*. 41, 72

Nakhasi, A., Passarella, R. J., Bell, S. G., Paul, M. J., Dredze, M., and Pronovost, P. J. (2015). The potential of Twitter as a data source for patient safety. *Journal of Patient Safety*. DOI: 10.1097/pts.0000000000000253. 72

Nascimento, T. D., DosSantos, M. F., Danciu, T., DeBoer, M., van Holsbeeck, H., Lucas, S. R., Aiello, C., Khatib, L., Bender, M. A., Zubieta, J. K., and et al. (2014). Real-time sharing and expression of migraine headache suffering on Twitter: A cross-sectional infodemiology study. *Journal of Medical Internet Research*, **16**(4), e96. DOI: 10.2196/jmir.3265. 55

Nastasi, A., Bryant, T., Canner, J. K., Dredze, M., Camp, M. S., and Nagarajan, N. (2017). Breast cancer screening and social media: A content analysis of evidence use and guideline opinions on Twitter. *Journal of Cancer Education*, pages 1–8. DOI: 10.1007/s13187-017-1168-9. 66

Neiger, B. L., Thackeray, R., Burton, S. H., Thackeray, C. R., and Reese, J. H. (2013). Use of Twitter among local health departments: An analysis of information sharing, engagement, and action. *Journal of Medical Internet Research*, **15**(8), e177. DOI: 10.2196/jmir.2775. 10

Newell, S. A., Girgis, A., Sanson-Fisher, R. W., and Savolainen, N. J. (1999). The accuracy of self-reported health behaviors and risk factors relating to cancer and cardiovascular disease in the general population: A critical review. *American Journal of Preventive Medicine*, **17**(3), 211–229. DOI: 10.1016/s0749-3797(99)00069-0. 79

Newkirk, R. W., Bender, J. B., and Hedberg, C. W. (2012). The potential capability of social media as a component of food safety and food terrorism surveillance systems. *Foodborne Pathogens and Disease*, **9**(2), 120–124. DOI: 10.1089/fpd.2011.0990. 68

Newman, T. P. (2016). Tracking the release of IPCC AR5 on Twitter: Users, comments, and sources following the release of the Working Group I summary for policymakers. *Public Understanding of Science*. DOI: 10.1177/0963662516628477. 70

Nguyen, A., Nguyen, L., Nguyen, D., Le, U., and Tran, T. (2017). 420 friendly: Revealing marijuana use via Craigslist rental ads. In *AAAI Joint Workshop on Health Intelligence*. 61

Nguyen, C. Q., Li, D., Meng, H.-W., Kath, S., Nsoesie, E., Li, F., and Wen, M. (2016). Building a national neighborhood dataset from geotagged Twitter data for indicators of happiness, diet, and physical activity. *JMIR Public Health Surveillance*, **2**(2), e158. DOI: 10.2196/publichealth.5869. 59

Nguyen, D., Gravel, R., Trieschnigg, D., and Meder, T. (2013). "How old do you think i am?" A study of language and age in Twitter. In *International Conference on Weblogs and Social Media (ICWSM)*. 43

Nie, L., Zhao, Y.-L., Akbari, M., Shen, J., and Chua, T.-S. (2014a). Bridging the vocabulary gap between health seekers and healthcare knowledge. *IEEE Transactions on Knowledge and Data Engineering*. DOI: 10.1109/tkde.2014.2330813. 79

Nie, L., Akbari, M., Li, T., and Chua, T.-S. (2014b). A joint local-global approach for medical terminology assignment. In *SIGIR Workshop on Medical Information Retrieval*, pages 24–27. 79

Nikfarjam, A. and Gonzalez, G. H. (2011). Pattern mining for extraction of mentions of adverse drug reactions from user comments. In *AMIA Annual Symposium*, pages 1019–26. 72

Nikfarjam, A., Sarker, A., O'Connor, K., Ginn, R., and Gonzalez, G. (2015). Pharmacovigilance from social media: Mining adverse drug reaction mentions using sequence labeling with word embedding cluster features. *Journal of the American Medical Informatics Association*. DOI: 10.1093/jamia/ocu041. 72

Niu, X. and Kelly, D. (2014). The use of query suggestions during information search. *Information Processing and Management*, **50**(1), 218–234. DOI: 10.1016/j.ipm.2013.09.002. 81

Noar, S. M., Ribisl, K. M., Althouse, B. M., Willoughby, J. F., and Ayers, J. W. (2013). Using digital surveillance to examine the impact of public figure pancreatic cancer announcements on media and search query outcomes. *Journal of the National Cancer Institute of Monographs*, **2013**(47), 188–194. DOI: 10.1093/jncimonographs/lgt017. 66

Noar, S. M., Althouse, B. M., Ayers, J. W., Francis, D. B., and Ribisl, K. M. (2015). Cancer information seeking in the digital age: effects of Angelina Jolie's prophylactic mastectomy announcement. *Medical Decision Making*, **35**(1), 16–21. DOI: 10.1177/0272989x14556130. 66

Nsoesie, E., Mararthe, M., and Brownstein, J. (2013). Forecasting peaks of seasonal influenza epidemics. *PLoS Currents*, **5**, 1–13. DOI: 10.1371/currents.outbreaks.bb1e879a23137022ea79a8c508b030bc. 53

Nsoesie, E. O., Buckeridge, D. L., and Brownstein, J. S. (2014a). Guess who's not coming to dinner? Evaluating online restaurant reservations for disease surveillance. *Journal of Medical Internet Research*, **16**(1), e22. DOI: 10.2196/jmir.2998. 53

Nsoesie, E. O., Kluberg, S. A., and Brownstein, J. S. (2014b). Online reports of foodborne illness capture foods implicated in official foodborne outbreak reports. *Prevention Medicine*, **67**, 264–269. DOI: 10.1016/j.ypmed.2014.08.003. 68

Ocampo, A. J., Chunara, R., and Brownstein, J. S. (2013). Using search queries for malaria surveillance, Thailand. *Malaria Journal*, **12**(1), 390. DOI: 10.1186/1475-2875-12-390. 54

O'Connor, B., Balasubramanyan, R., Routledge, B. R., and Smith, N. A. (2010). From tweets to polls: Linking text sentiment to public opinion time series. In *International Conference on Weblogs and Social Media (ICWSM)*. 16

O'Connor, D. (2013). The apomediated world: Regulating research when social media has changed research. *The Journal of Law, Medicine and Ethics*, **41**(2), 470–483. DOI: 10.1111/jlme.12056. 89

O'Connor, K., Pimpalkhute, P., Nikfarjam, A., Ginn, R., Smith, K. L., and Gonzalez, G. (2014). Pharmacovigilance on Twitter? Mining tweets for adverse drug reactions. *AMIA Annual Symposium Proceedings*, **2014**, 924–933. 72

Odlum, M. (2015a). Analysis of public perceptions about ebola to inform health information messages: Content and trend analysis of tweets. In *Annual Meeting of the American Public Health Association*. 54, 65

Odlum, M. (2015b). Early epidemic detection of ebola through tweet analysis: Nigeria as a case study. In *Annual Meeting of the American Public Health Association*. 54

Odlum, M. (2015c). How Twitter can support early warning systems in ebola outbreak surveillance. In *Annual Meeting of the American Public Health Association*. 54

Odlum, M. and Yoon, S. (2015). What can we learn about the Ebola outbreak from tweets? *American Journal of Infection Control*, **43**(6), 563–571. DOI: 10.1016/j.ajic.2015.02.023. 54

Ofran, Y., Paltiel, O., Pelleg, D., Rowe, J. M., and Yom-Tov, E. (2012). Patterns of information-seeking for cancer on the internet: An analysis of real world data. *PLoS ONE*, **7**(9). DOI: 10.1371/journal.pone.0045921. 55

Okike, K., Peter-Bibb, K. T., Xie, C. K., and Okike, N. O. (2016). Association between physician online rating and quality of care. *Journal of Medical Internet Research*, **18**(12), e324. DOI: 10.2196/jmir.6612. 72

Olson, D. R., Konty, K. J., Paladini, M., Viboud, C., and Simonsen, L. (2013). Reassessing Google Flu Trends data for detection of seasonal and pandemic influenza: A comparative epidemiological study at three geographic scales. *PLoS Computational Biology*, **9**(10). DOI: 10.1371/journal.pcbi.1003256. 87

Ordun, C., Blake, J. W., Rosidi, N., Grigoryan, V., Reffett, C., Aslam, S., Gentilcore, A., Cyran, M., Shelton, M., , and Klenk, J. (2013). Open source health intelligence (oshint) for foodborne illness event characterization. *Online Journal of Public Health Informatics*, **5**(1), e128. DOI: 10.5210/ojphi.v5i1.4442. 68

Oremus, W. (2013). Google Flu Trends predicts worst season on record. `http://www.slate.com/articles/technology/technology/2013/01/flu_shot_time_google_flu_trends_predicts_worst_season_on_record.html` 86

Orenstein, W. A., Papania, M. J., and Wharton, M. E. (2004). Measles elimination in the United States. *Journal of Infectious Diseases*, **189**(Suppl. 1), S1–S3. DOI: 10.1086/377693. 1

Osborne, M. and Dredze, M. (2014). Facebook, Twitter and Google Plus for breaking news: Is there a winner? In *International Conference on Weblogs and Social Media (ICWSM)*. 21

Osborne, M., Moran, S., McCreadie, R., Von Lunen, A., Sykora, M. D., Cano, E., Ireson, N., Macdonald, C., Ounis, I., He, Y., et al. (2014). Real-time detection, tracking, and monitoring of automatically discovered events in social media. In *Association for Computational Linguistics (ACL)*. DOI: 10.3115/v1/p14-5007. 45

O'Sullivan, D. and Unwin, D. J. (2010). *The Pitfalls and Potential of Spatial Data*, pages 33–54. John Wiley & Sons, Inc. DOI: 10.1002/9780470549094.ch2. 80

Page, R. E. (2013). *What We Tweet About in Chaos: Framing, Twitter, and the 2012 Aurora Massacre*. Master's thesis, Texas Tech University. 68

Pagoto, S., Schneider, K. L., Evans, M., Waring, M. E., Appelhans, B., Busch, A. M., Whited, M. C., Thind, H., and Ziedonis, M. (2014). Tweeting it off: Characteristics of adults who tweet about a weight loss attempt. *Journal of the American Medical Informatics Association*, **21**(6), 1032–1037. DOI: 10.1136/amiajnl-2014-002652. 59

Paine, C., Reips, U.-D., Stieger, S., Joinson, A., and Buchanan, T. (2007). Internet users' perceptions of "privacy concerns" and "privacy actions." *International Journal of Human–Computer Studies*, **65**(6), 526–536. DOI: 10.1016/j.ijhcs.2006.12.001. 79

Paolacci, G., Chandler, J., and Ipeirotis, P. G. (2010). Running experiments on Amazon Mechanical Turk. *Judgment and Decision Making*, **5**(5), 411–419. 20

Paparrizos, J., White, R. W., and Horvitz, E. (2016a). Detecting devastating diseases in search logs. In *ACM Conference on Knowledge Discovery and Data Mining (KDD)*, pages 559–568. DOI: 10.1145/2939672.2939722. 55

Paparrizos, J., White, R. W., and Horvitz, E. (2016b). Screening for pancreatic adenocarcinoma using signals from web search logs: Feasibility study and results. *Journal of Oncology Practice*, **12**(8), 737–744. DOI: 10.1200/jop.2015.010504. 55

Park, G., Schwartz, H. A., Eichstaedt, J. C., Kern, M. L., Stillwell, D. J., Kosinski, M., Ungar, L. H., and Seligman, M. E. (2014). Automatic personality assessment through social media language. *Journal of Personality and Social Psychology*, **108**, 934–952. DOI: 10.1037/pspp0000020. 75

Parker, J., Yates, A., Goharian, N., and Frieder, O. (2015). Health-related hypothesis generation using social media data. *Social Network Analysis and Mining*, **5**(1). DOI: 10.1007/s13278-014-0239-8. 13

Paul, M. and Dredze, M. (2013). Drug extraction from the web: Summarizing drug experiences with multi-dimensional topic models. In *North American Chapter of the Association for Computational Linguistics (NAACL)*. 62, 63

Paul, M., Dredze, M., Broniatowski, D., and Generous, N. (2015a). Worldwide influenza surveillance through Twitter. In *AAAI Workshop on the World Wide Web and Public Health Intelligence*. 53, 80, 87

Paul, M. J. (2017). Feature selection as causal inference: Experiments with text classification. In *Conference on Computational Natural Language Learning (CoNLL)*. 46

Paul, M. J. and Dredze, M. (2011). You are what you Tweet: Analyzing Twitter for public health. In *International Conference on Weblogs and Social Media (ICWSM)*. xvii, 30, 31, 32, 61

Paul, M. J. and Dredze, M. (2014). Discovering health topics in social media using topic models. *PLoS ONE*, **9**(8), e103408. DOI: 10.1371/journal.pone.0103408. 31, 59

Paul, M. J., Wallace, B., and Dredze, M. (2013). What affects patient (dis)satisfaction? Analyzing online doctor ratings with a joint topic-sentiment model. In *AAAI Workshop on Expanding the Boundaries of Health Informatics Using AI (HIAI)*. 71

Paul, M. J., Dredze, M., and Broniatowski, D. (2014). Twitter improves influenza forecasting. *PLoS Currents Outbreaks*. DOI: 10.1371/currents.outbreaks.90b9ed0f59bae4ccaa683a39865d9117. 35, 36, 39, 53, 87

Paul, M. J., White, R. W., and Horvitz, E. (2015b). Diagnoses, decisions, and outcomes: Web search as decision support for cancer. In *International Conference on World Wide Web (WWW)*. DOI: 10.1145/2736277.2741662. 47, 55

Paul, M. J., Chisolm, M. S., Johnson, M. W., Vandrey, R. G., and Dredze, M. (2016a). Assessing the validity of online drug forums as a source for estimating demographic and temporal trends in drug use. *Journal of Addiction Medicine*, **10**(5), 324–330. DOI: 10.1097/adm.0000000000000238. 63

Paul, M. J., White, R. W., and Horvitz, E. (2016b). Search and breast cancer: On episodic shifts of attention over life histories of an illness. *ACM Transactions on the Web*, **10**(2). DOI: 10.1145/2893481. 55

Pavalanathan, U. and Eisenstein, J. (2015). Confounds and consequences in geotagged Twitter data. In *Empirical Methods in Natural Language Processing (EMNLP)*. DOI: 10.18653/v1/d15-1256. 80

Pavalanathan, U. and Eisenstein, J. (2016). Emoticons vs. emojis on Twitter: A causal inference approach. In *AAAI Spring Symposium on Observational Studies through Social Media and Other Human-Generated Content*. 46

Pavlick, E., Ji, H., Pan, X., and Callison-Burch, C. (2016). The gun violence database: A new task and data set for NLP. In *Empirical Methods in Natural Language Processing (EMNLP)*. DOI: 10.18653/v1/d16-1106. 70

Pelat, C., Turbelin, C., Bar-Hen, A., Flahault, A., and Valleron, A. J. (2009). More diseases tracked by using Google Trends. *Emerging Infectious Diseases*, **15**(8), 1327–1328. DOI: 10.3201/eid1508.090299. 54

Pennacchiotti, M. and Popescu, A.-M. (2011a). Democrats, Republicans and Starbucks afficionados: User classification in Twitter. In *ACM Conference on Knowledge Discovery and Data Mining (KDD)*, pages 430–438, ACM. DOI: 10.1145/2020408.2020477. 43

Pennacchiotti, M. and Popescu, A.-M. (2011b). A machine learning approach to Twitter user classification. In *International Conference on Weblogs and Social Media (ICWSM)*, pages 281–288. 43

Pennebaker, J. W., Francis, M. E., and Booth, R. J. (2001). Linguistic inquiry and word count: LIWC 2001. *Mahway: Lawrence Erlbaum Associates*, **71**, 2001. 29

Pimpalkhute, P., Patki, A., Nikfarjam, A., and Gonzalez, G. (2014). Phonetic spelling filter for keyword selection in drug mention mining from social media. In *AMIA Summits on Translational Science*. 79

Plachouras, V., Leidner, J. L., and Garrow, A. G. (2016). Quantifying self-reported adverse drug events on Twitter: Signal and topic analysis. In *International Conference on Social Media and Society*. DOI: 10.1145/2930971.2930977. 72

Poese, I., Uhlig, S., Kaafar, M. A., Donnet, B., and Gueye, B. (2011). IP geolocation databases: Unreliable? *SIGCOMM Computer Communication Review*, **41**(2), 53–56. DOI: 10.1145/1971162.1971171. 45

Polgreen, P. M., Nelson, F. D., and Neumann, G. R. (2007). Use of prediction markets to forecast infectious disease activity. *Clinical Infectious Diseases*, **44**(2), 272–279. DOI: 10.1086/510427. 20

Polgreen, P. M., Chen, Y., Pennock, D. M., and Nelson, F. D. (2008). Using internet searches for influenza surveillance. *Clinical Infectious Diseases*, **47**(11), 1443–1448. DOI: 10.1086/593098. 52

Pollett, S., Boscardin, W. J., Azziz-Baumgartner, E., Tinoco, Y. O., Soto, G., Romero, C., Kok, J., Biggerstaff, M., Viboud, C., and Rutherford, G. W. (2017). Evaluating Google Flu Trends in Latin America: Important lessons for the next phase of digital disease detection. *Clinical Infectious Diseases*, **64**(1), 34. DOI: 10.1093/cid/ciw657. 53

Power, R., Robinson, B., and Ratcliffe, D. (2013). Finding fires with Twitter. In *Australian Language Technology Association Workshop*. 68

Power, R., Robinson, B., Colton, J., and Cameron, M. (2014). Emergency situation awareness: Twitter case studies. In *Information Systems for Crisis Response and Management in Mediterranean Countries*, Springer. DOI: 10.1007/978-3-319-11818-5_19. 67

Power, R., Robinson, B., Colton, J., and Cameron, M. (2015). A case study for monitoring fires with Twitter. In *Conference on Information Systems for Crisis Response and Management (ISCRAM)*. 68

Preis, T. and Moat, H. S. (2014). Adaptive nowcasting of influenza outbreaks using Google searches. *Royal Society Open Science*, **1**(2). DOI: 10.1098/rsos.140095. 36, 52

Preoțiuc-Pietro, D., Eichstaedt, J., Park, G., Sap, M., Smith, L., Tobolsky, V., Schwartz, H. A., and Ungar, L. H. (2015). The role of personality, age and gender in tweeting about mental illnesses. In *NAACL Workshop on Computational Linguistics and Clinical Psychology (CLPsych)*. DOI: 10.3115/v1/w15-1203. 75

Priedhorsky, R., Osthus, D., Daughton, A. R., Moran, K. R., Generous, N., Fairchild, G., Deshpande, A., and Del Valle, S. Y. (2017). Measuring global disease with Wikipedia: Success, failure, and a research agenda. In *Conference on Computer Supported Cooperative Work and Social Computing (CSCW)*, pages 1812–1834. DOI: 10.1145/2998181.2998183. 53, 54

Prier, K. W., Smith, M. S., Giraud-Carrier, C., and Hanson, C. L. (2011). Identifying health-related topics on Twitter: An exploration of tobacco-related tweets as a test topic. In *International Conference on Social Computing, Behavioral-cultural Modeling and Prediction*, pages 18–25. DOI: 10.1007/978-3-642-19656-0_4. 31, 60

Prieto, V. M., Matos, S., Álvarez, M., Cacheda, F., and Oliveira, J. L. (2014). Twitter: A good place to detect health conditions. *PLoS ONE*, **9**(1), e86191. DOI: 10.1371/journal.pone.0086191. 30, 53, 74, 90

Prochaska, J. J., Pechmann, C., Kim, R., and Leonhardt, J. M. (2012). Twitter=quitter? An analysis of Twitter quit smoking social networks. *Tobacco Control*, **21**(4), 447–449. DOI: 10.1136/tc.2010.042507. 60

Pronovost, P. J., Thompson, D. A., Holzmueller, C. G., Lubomski, L. H., Dorman, T., Dickman, F., Fahey, M., Steinwachs, D. M., Engineer, L., Sexton, J. B., Wu, A. W., and Morlock, L. L. (2006). Toward learning from patient safety reporting systems. *Journal of Critical Care*, **21**(4), 305–315. DOI: 10.1016/j.jcrc.2006.07.001. 71

Public Law (1996). *PUBLIC LAW 104–208—SEPT. 30, 1996: Omnibus Consolidated Appropriations Act, 1997*. 104th Congress. 70

Quercia, D., Kosinski, M., Stillwell, D., and Crowcroft, J. (2011). Our Twitter profiles, our selves: Predicting personality with Twitter. In *International Conference on Social Computing (SocialCom)*, pages 180–185. DOI: 10.1109/passat/socialcom.2011.26. 44

Rafail, P. (2017). Nonprobability sampling and Twitter. *Social Science Computer Review*. DOI: 10.1177/0894439317709431. 29, 80

Rahimi, A., Vu, D., Cohn, T., and Baldwin, T. (2015a). Exploiting text and network context for geolocation of social media users. In *North American Chapter of the Association for Computational Linguistics (NAACL)*. DOI: 10.3115/v1/n15-1153. 45

Rahimi, A., Cohn, T., and Baldwin, T. (2015b). Twitter user geolocation using a unified text and network prediction model. In *Association for Computational Linguistics (ACL)*. DOI: 10.3115/v1/p15-2104. 45

Rahimi, A., Cohn, T., and Baldwin, T. (2016). Pigeo: A python geotagging tool. In *Association for Computational Linguistics (ACL): Systems Demonstrations*, pages 127–132. DOI: 10.18653/v1/p16-4022. 46

Ram, S., Zhang, W., Williams, M., and Pengetnze, Y. (2015). Predicting asthma-related emergency department visits using big data. *IEEE Journal of Biomedical and Health Informatics*. DOI: 10.1109/jbhi.2015.2404829. 55

Ramage, D., Rosen, E., Chuang, J., Manning, C. D., and McFarland, D. A. (2009). Topic modeling for the social sciences. In *Advances in Neural Information Processing Systems (NIPS)*. 31

Ranard, B. L., Werner, R. M., Antanavicius, T., Schwartz, H. A., Smith, R. J., Meisel, Z. F., Asch, D. A., Ungar, L. H., and Merchant, R. M. (2016). Yelp reviews of hospital care can supplement and inform traditional surveys of the patient experience of are. *Health Affairs (Millwood)*, **35**(4), 697–705. DOI: 10.1377/hlthaff.2015.1030. 72

Rao, D. and Yarowsky, D. (2010). Detecting latent user properties in social media. In *NIPS MLSN Workshop*. 43

Rao, D., Yarowsky, D., Shreevats, A., and Gupta, M. (2010). Classifying latent user attributes in Twitter. In *Workshop on Search and Mining User-generated Contents*. DOI: 10.1145/1871985.1871993. 23, 43

Rao, D., Paul, M., Fink, C., Yarowsky, D., Oates, T., and Coppersmith, G. (2011). Hierarchical Bayesian models for latent attribute detection in social media. In *International Conference on Weblogs and Social Media (ICWSM)*. 43

Ratkiewicz, J., Conover, M., Meiss, M., Gonçalves, B., Flammini, A., and Menczer, F. (2011). Detecting and tracking political abuse in social media. In *International Conference on Weblogs and Social Media (ICWSM)*. 82

Reavley, N. J. and Pilkington, P. D. (2014). Use of Twitter to monitor attitudes toward depression and schizophrenia: An exploratory study. *PeerJ*, **2**, e647. DOI: 10.7717/peerj.647. 76

Reeves, W. C., Pratt, L. A., Thompson, W., Dhingra, S. S., McKnight-Eily, L. R., Harrison, L., D'Angelo, D. V., Williams, L., Morrow, B., Gould, D., et al. (2011). Mental illness surveillance among adults in the U.S. *Morbidity and Mortality Weekly Report (MMWR)*. 73

Rehman, N., Liu, J., and Chunara, R. (2016). Using propensity score matching to understand the relationship between online health information sources and vaccination sentiment. In *AAAI Spring Symposium on Observational Studies through Social Media and Other Human-Generated Content*. 46

Reis, V. L. D. and Culotta, A. (2015). Using matched samples to estimate the effects of exercise on mental health from Twitter. In *Conference on Artificial Intelligence (AAAI)*. 42, 46, 59, 75

Resnick, B. (2013).   Why Google Flu Trends will not replace the CDC anytime
soon.   `http://www.nationaljournal.com/healthcare/why-google-flu-trends-wi`
`ll-not-replace-cdc-anytime-soon-20130125` 86

Resnik, P. and Lin, J. (2010). *Evaluation of NLP Systems*, pages 271–295. Wiley-Blackwell.
DOI: 10.1002/9781444324044.ch11. 40

Riga, M. and Karatzas, K. (2014). Investigating the relationship between social media content
and real-time observations for urban air quality and public health. In *International Conference
on Web Intelligence, Mining and Semantics (WIMS14)*. DOI: 10.1145/2611040.2611093. 69

Rivers, C. M. and Lewis, B. L. (2014).   Ethical research standards in a world of big data.
F1000Research, **3**(38). DOI: 10.12688/f1000research.3-38.v1. 93

Robinson, B., Power, R., and Cameron, M. (2013).   A sensitive Twitter earthquake de-
tector.   In *International Conference on World Wide Web (WWW)*, pages 999–1002. DOI:
10.1145/2487788.2488101. 67

Robinson, B., Bai, H., Power, R., and Lin, X. (2014). Developing a Sina Weibo incident monitor
for disasters. In *Australian Language Technology Association Workshop*. 67

Rocheleau, M., Sadasivam, R. S., Baquis, K., Stahl, H., Kinney, R. L., Pagoto, S. L., and Hous-
ton, T. K. (2015). An observational study of social and emotional support in smoking cessation Twitter accounts: Content analysis of tweets. *Journal of Medical Internet Research*, **17**(1),
e18. DOI: 10.2196/jmir.3768. 60

Rodriguez Jr., R. M. (2014). *A Spatial Analysis of Boko Haram and Al-Shabaab References in Social
Media in Sub-Saharan Africa.* Master's thesis, George Mason University. 68

Rodriguez-Morales, A. J., Castaneda-Hernandez, D. M., and McGregor, A. (2015).   What
makes people talk about Ebola on social media? A retrospective analysis of Twitter use. *Travel
Medicine and Infectious Disease*, **13**(1), 100–101. DOI: 10.1016/j.tmaid.2014.11.004. 54, 65

Roehrig, C. (2016). Mental disorders top the list of the most costly conditions in the U.S.: $201
billion. *Health Affairs*. DOI: 10.1377/hlthaff.2015.1659. 73

Roller, S., Speriosu, M., Rallapalli, S., Wing, B., and Baldridge, J. (2012).   Supervised text-
based geolocation using language models on an adaptive grid. In *Empirical Methods in Natural
Language Processing (EMNLP)*. 45

Rosenbaum, P. and Rubin, D. (1985). Constructing a control group using multivariate matched
sampling methods that incorporate the propensity score. *The American Statistician*, **39**, 33–38.
DOI: 10.1017/cbo9780511810725.019. 46

Rout, D., Bontcheva, K., Preoţiuc-Pietro, D., and Cohn, T. (2013). Where's @wally?: A classification approach to geolocating users based on their social ties. In *ACM Conference on Hypertext and Social Media*, pages 11–20, ACM. DOI: 10.1145/2481492.2481494. 45

Rubin, D. B. (1976). Inference and missing data. *Biometrika*, **63**, 581—592. DOI: 10.2307/2335739. 79

Rubin, R. (2016). Tale of 2 agencies: CDC avoids gun violence research but NIH funds it. *JAMA*, **315**(16), 1689–1692. DOI: 10.1001/jama.2016.1707. 70

Ruths, D. and Pfeffer, J. (2014). Social media for large studies of behavior. *Science*, **346**(6213), 1063–1064. DOI: 10.1126/science.346.6213.1063. 78, 83

Sadilek, A., Kautz, H., and Silenzio, V. (2012a). Modeling spread of disease from social interactions. In *International Conference on Weblogs and Social Media (ICWSM)*, pages 322–329. 23, 36, 54

Sadilek, A., Kautz, H., and Silenzio, V. (2012b). Predicting disease transmission from geotagged micro-blog data. In *Conference on Artificial Intelligence (AAAI)*. 23, 36, 53, 54

Sadilek, A., Brennan, S., Kautz, H., and Silenzio, V. (2013). nEmesis: Which restaurants should you avoid today? In *AAAI Conference on Human Computation and Crowdsourcing*. 68

Sadilek, A., Kautz, H., DiPrete, L., Labus, B., Portman, E., Teitel, J., and Silenzio, V. (2017). Deploying nEmesis: Preventing foodborne illness by data mining social media. *AI Magazine*, **38**(1), 37–48. DOI: 10.1609/aimag.v38i1.2711. 68, 85

Safran, C., Bloomrosen, M., Hammond, W. E., Labkoff, S., Markel-Fox, S., Tang, P. C., and Detmer, D. E. (2007). Toward a national framework for the secondary use of health data: An American Medical Informatics Association white paper. *Journal of the American Medical Informatics Association*, **14**(1), 1–9. DOI: 10.1197/jamia.m2273. 2

Sakaki, T., Okazaki, M., and Matsuo, Y. (2010). Earthquake shakes Twitter users: Real-time event detection by social sensors. In *International Conference on World Wide Web (WWW)*, page 851. DOI: 10.1145/1772690.1772777. 67

Sakaki, T., Okazaki, M., and Matsuo, Y. (2013). Tweet analysis for real-time event detection and earthquake reporting system development. *IEEE Transactions on Knowledge and Data Engineering*, **25**(4), 919–931. DOI: 10.1109/tkde.2012.29. 67

Salathé, M. (2016). Digital pharmacovigilance and disease surveillance: Combining traditional and big-data systems for better public health. *The Journal of Infectious Diseases*, **214**(4), S399. DOI: 10.1093/infdis/jiw281. 87

Salathé, M. and Khandelwal, S. (2011). Assessing vaccination sentiments with online social media: Implications for infectious disease dynamics and control. *PLoS Computational Biology*, 7(10), e1002199. DOI: 10.1371/journal.pcbi.1002199. 64

Salathé, M., Bengtsson, L., Bodnar, T. J., Brewer, D. D., Brownstein, J. S., Buckee, C., Campbell, E. M., Cattuto, C., Khandelwal, S., Mabry, P. L., and Vespignani, A. (2012). Digital epidemiology. *PLoS Computational Biology*, 8(7), e1002616. DOI: 10.1371/journal.pcbi.1002616. 13

Salathé, M., Vu, D. Q., Khandelwal, S., and Hunter, D. R. (2013a). The dynamics of health behavior sentiments on a large online social network. *EPJ Data Science*, 2(1). DOI: 10.1140/epjds16. 64

Salathé, M., Freifeld, C. C., Mekaru, S. R., Tomasulo, A. F., and Brownstein, J. S. (2013b). Influenza a (h7n9) and the importance of digital epidemiology. *The New England Journal of Medicine*, pages 1–3. DOI: 10.1056/nejmp1307752. 13

Sanders-Jackson, A., Brown, C. G., and Prochaska, J. J. (2015). Applying linguistic methods to understanding smoking-related conversations on Twitter. *Tobacco Control*, 24(2), 136–138. DOI: 10.1136/tobaccocontrol-2013-051243. 66

Santillana, M. (2017). Editorial commentary: Perspectives on the future of internet search engines and biosurveillance systems. *Clinical Infectious Diseases*, 64(1), 42. DOI: 10.1093/cid/ciw660. 28

Santillana, M., Nsoesie, E. O., Mekaru, S. R., Scales, D., and Brownstein, J. S. (2014a). Using clinicians' search query data to monitor influenza epidemics. *Clinical Infectious Diseases*, 59(10), 1446–1450. DOI: 10.1093/cid/ciu647. 19

Santillana, M., Zhang, D. W., Althouse, B. M., and Ayers, J. W. (2014b). What can digital disease detection learn from (an external revision to) Google Flu Trends? *American Journal of Preventive Medicine*, 47(3), 341–347. DOI: 10.1016/j.amepre.2014.05.020. 52, 78

Santillana, M., Nguyen, A. T., Dredze, M., Paul, M. J., Nsoesie, E. O., and Brownstein, J. S. (2015). Combining search, social media, and traditional data sources to improve influenza surveillance. *PLoS Computational Biology*. DOI: 10.1371/journal.pcbi.1004513. 53, 82

Sarker, A., Ginn, R., Nikfarjam, A., O'Connor, K., Smith, K., Jayaraman, S., Upadhaya, T., and Gonzalez, G. (2015). Utilizing social media data for pharmacovigilance: A review. *Journal of Biomedical Informatics*, 54, 202–212. DOI: 10.1016/j.jbi.2015.02.004. 72

Saunders, T. J., Prince, S. A., and Tremblay, M. S. (2011). Clustering of children's activity behaviour: The use of self-report vs. direct measures. *International Journal of Behavioral Nutrition and Physical Activity*, 8, 48. DOI: 10.1186/1479-5868-8-48. 79

Scanfeld, D., Scanfeld, V., and Larson, E. L. (2010). Dissemination of health information through social networks: Twitter and antibiotics. *American Journal of Infection Control*, **38**(3), 182–188. DOI: 10.1016/j.ajic.2009.11.004. 61

schraefel, m.c., White, R. W., André, P., and Tan, D. (2009). Investigating web search strategies and forum use to support diet and weight loss. In *Conference on Human Factors in Computing Systems (CHI)*, pages 3829–3834. DOI: 10.1145/1520340.1520579. 20, 59

Schulz, A., Ristoski, P., and Paulheim, H. (2013). I see a car crash: Real-time detection of small scale incidents in microblogs. In *Extended Semantic Web Conference*. DOI: 10.1007/978-3-642-41242-4_3. 68

Schwartz, G. E. (1978). Estimating the dimension of a model. *Annals of Statistics*, **6**(2), 461–464. DOI: 10.1214/aos/1176344136. 37

Schwartz, H. A. and Ungar, L. H. (2015). Data-driven content analysis of social media: A systematic overview of automated methods. *The ANNALS of the American Academy of Political and Social Science*, **659**, 78–94. DOI: 10.1177/0002716215569197. 24

Schwartz, H. A., Eichstaedt, J. C., Kern, M. L., Dziurzynski, L., Ramones, S. M., Agrawal, M., Shah, A., Kosinski, M., Stillwell, D., Seligman, M. E., and Ungar, L. H. (2013). Personality, gender, and age in the language of social media: The open-vocabulary approach. *PLoS ONE*, **8**(9), e73791. DOI: 10.1371/journal.pone.0073791. 16, 25, 43, 44, 75

Schwartz, H. A., Eichstaedt, J., Kern, M. L., Park, G., Sap, M., Stillwell, D., Kosinski, M., and Ungar, L. (2014). Towards assessing changes in degree of depression through Facebook. In *Workshop on Computational Linguistics and Clinical Psychology (CLPsych)*. DOI: 10.3115/v1/w14-3214. 74

Seaman, I. and Giraud-Carrier, C. (2016). Prevalence and attitudes about illicit and prescription drugs on Twitter. In *IEEE International Conference on Healthcare Informatics (ICHI)*, pages 14–17. DOI: 10.1109/ichi.2016.98. 61

Segal, J., Sacopulos, M., Sheets, V., Thurston, I., Brooks, K., and Puccia, R. (2012). Online doctor reviews: Do they track surgeon volume, a proxy for quality of care? *Journal of Medical Internet Research*, **14**(2), e50. DOI: 10.2196/jmir.2005. 71

Segerberg, A. and Bennett, W. L. (2011). Social media and the organization of collective action: Using Twitter to explore the ecologies of two climate change protests. *The Communication Review*, **14**(3), 197–215. DOI: 10.1080/10714421.2011.597250. 70

Seifter, A., Schwarzwalder, A., Geis, K., and Aucott, J. (2010). The utility of "Google Trends" for epidemiological research: Lyme disease as an example. *Geospatial Health*, **4**(2), 135–137. DOI: 10.4081/gh.2010.195. 54

Shah, D. V., Cappella, J. N., and Neuman, W. R. (2015). Big data, digital media, and computational social science: Possibilities and perils. *The Annals of the American Academy of Political and Social Science*, **659**(1), 6–13. DOI: 10.1177/0002716215572084. 78

Shaman, J., Karspeck, A., Yang, W., Tamerius, J., and Lipsitch, M. (2013). Real-time influenza forecasts during the 2012–2013 season. *Nature Communications*, **4**, 2837. DOI: 10.1038/ncomms3837. 53

Shapiro, D. N., Chandler, J., and Mueller, P. A. (2013). Using Mechanical Turk to study clinical populations. *Clinical Psychological Science*, page 2167702612469015. DOI: 10.1177/2167702612469015. 20

Sharma, S. and De Choudhury, M. (2015). Detecting and characterizing nutritional information of food and ingestion content in Instagram. In *International Conference on World Wide Web (WWW)*. DOI: 10.1145/2740908.2742754. 59

Sharpe, D. J., Hopkins, S. R., Cook, L. R., and Striley, W. C. (2016). Evaluating Google, Twitter, and Wikipedia as tools for influenza surveillance using Bayesian change point analysis: A comparative analysis. *JMIR Public Health Surveillance*, **2**(2), e161. DOI: 10.2196/publichealth.5901. 53

Shin, S.-Y., Kim, T., Seo, D.-W., Sohn, C. H., Kim, S.-H., Ryoo, S. M., Lee, Y.-S., Lee, J. H., Kim, W. Y., and Lim, K. S. (2016). Correlation between national influenza surveillance data and search queries from mobile devices and desktops in South Korea. *PLoS ONE*, **11**(7), 1–10. DOI: 10.1371/journal.pone.0158539. 53

Shonkoff, J. P., Boyce, W. T., and McEwen, B. S. (2009). Neuroscience, molecular biology, and the childhood roots of health disparities: Building a new framework for health promotion and disease prevention. *JAMA*, **301**(21), 2252–2259. DOI: 10.1001/jama.2009.754. 42

Sidana, S., Mishra, S., Amer-Yahia, S., Clausel, M., and Amini, M.-R. (2016). Health monitoring on social media over time. In *Conference on Research and Development in Information Retrieval (SIGIR)*, pages 849–852, New York, ACM. DOI: 10.1145/2911451.2914697. 47

Signorini, A., Segre, A. M., and Polgreen, P. M. (2011). The use of Twitter to track levels of disease activity and public concern in the U.S. during the influenza a H1N1 pandemic. *PLoS ONE*, **6**(5), e19467. DOI: 10.1371/journal.pone.0019467. 53, 65

Simon, T., Adini, B., El-Hadid, M., Goldberg, A., and Aharonson-Daniel, L. (2014a). The race to save lives: Demonstrating the use of social media for search and rescue operations. *PLoS Currents*, **6**. DOI: 10.1371/currents.dis.806848c38f18c6b7b0037fae3cd4edc5. 68

Simon, T., Goldberg, A., Aharonson-Daniel, L., Leykin, D., and Adini, B. (2014b). Twitter in the cross fire—the use of social media in the Westgate Mall terror attack in Kenya. *PLoS ONE*, **9**(8), e104136. DOI: 10.1371/journal.pone.0104136. 68

Simonsen, L., Gog, J. R., Olson, D., and Viboud, C. (2016). Infectious disease surveillance in the big data era: Towards faster and locally relevant systems. *The Journal of Infectious Diseases*, **214**(4), S380. DOI: 10.1093/infdis/jiw376. 87

Simpson, A., Pereira, M., Cooper, S., and Ramagopalan, S. V. (2016). Seasonality of tweets related to multiple sclerosis. *Journal of Neurology, Neurosurgery and Psychiatry*. DOI: 10.1136/jnnp-2016-313941. 56

Sinnott, R. O. and Chen, W. (2016). Estimating crowd sizes through social media. In *IEEE International Conference on Pervasive Computing and Communication Workshops (PerCom Workshops)*, pages 1–6. DOI: 10.1109/percomw.2016.7457123. 16

Slavkovikj, V., Verstockt, S., Hoecke, S. V., and de Walle, R. V. (2014). Review of wildfire detection using social media. *Fire Safety Journal*, **68**, 109–118. DOI: 10.1016/j.firesaf.2014.05.021. 68

Sloan, L., Morgan, J., Burnap, P., and Williams, M. (2015). Who tweets? Deriving the demographic characteristics of age, occupation and social class from Twitter user meta-data. *PLoS ONE*, **10**(3), 1–20. DOI: 10.1371/journal.pone.0115545. 44

Smith, M., Broniatowski, D. A., Paul, M. J., and Dredze, M. (2016a). Towards real-time measurement of public epidemic awareness: Monitoring influenza awareness through Twitter. In *AAAI Spring Symposium on Observational Studies through Social Media and Other Human-generated Content*. 65

Smith, M., Broniatowski, D. A., and Dredze, M. (2016b). Using Twitter to examine social rationales for vaccine refusal. In *International Engineering Systems Symposium (CESUN)*. 64

Smith, M. C. and Broniatowski, D. A. (2016). Modeling influenza by modulating flu awareness. In *International Conference on Social, Cultural, and Behavioral Modeling (SBP-BRiMS)*, pages 262–271. DOI: 10.1007/978-3-319-39931-7_25. 65

Smith-Bindman, R., Quale, C., Chu, P. W., Rosenberg, R., and Kerlikowske, K. (2006). Can Medicare billing claims data be used to assess mammography utilization among women ages 65 and older? *Medical Care*, **44**(5), 463–470. DOI: 10.1097/01.mlr.0000207436.07513.79. 12

Smolinski, M. S., Crawley, A. W., Baltrusaitis, K., Chunara, R., Olsen, J. M., Wójick, O., Santillana, M., Nguyen, A. T., and Brownstein, J. S. (2015). Flu Near You: Crowdsourced symptom reporting spanning two influenza seasons. *American Journal of Public Health*. DOI: 10.2105/ajph.2015.302696. 20

So, J., Prestin, A., Lee, L., Wang, Y., Yen, J., and Chou, W.-Y. S. (2015). What do people like to "share" about obesity? A content analysis of frequent retweets about obesity on Twitter. *Health Communication*. DOI: 10.1080/10410236.2014.940675. 60

Speriosu, M., Brown, T., Moon, T., Baldridge, J., and Erk, K. (2010). Connecting language and geography with region-topic models. In *Proc. Workshop on Computational Models of Spatial Language Interpretation (COSLI)*. 46

Stanfill, S. B., Connolly, G. N., Zhang, L., Jia, L. T., Henningfield, J. E., Richter, P., Lawler, T. S., Ayo-Yusuf, O. A., Ashley, D. L., and Watson, C. H. (2011). Global surveillance of oral tobacco products: Total nicotine, unionised nicotine and tobacco-specific N-nitrosamines. *Tobacco Control*, **20**(3), e2. DOI: 10.1136/tc.2010.037465. 11

Stefanidis, A., Vraga, E., Lamprianidis, G., Radzikowski, J., Delamater, L. P., Jacobsen, H. K., Pfoser, D., Croitoru, A., and Crooks, A. (2017). Zika in Twitter: Temporal variations of locations, actors, and concepts. *JMIR Public Health Surveillance*, **3**(2), e22. DOI: 10.2196/publichealth.6925. 32, 54

Stefanone, M. A., Saxton, G. D., Egnoto, M. J., Wei, W., and Fu, Y. (2015). Image attributes and diffusion via Twitter: The case of #guncontrol. In *System Sciences (HICSS), 48th Hawaii International Conference on*, pages 1788–1797, IEEE. DOI: 10.1109/hicss.2015.216. 70

Stefansen, C. (2015). Google Flu Trends gets a brand new engine. `http://googleresearch.b logspot.com/2014/10/google-flu-trends-gets-brand-new-engine.html`. Accessed: 2015-06-01. Archived by WebCite at: `http://www.webcitation.org/6ZPoiUZqq` 52

Steiner, T. (2014). Comprehensive Wikipedia monitoring for global and realtime natural disaster detection. In *ISWC Developers Workshop*. 67

Stone, M. (1977). An asymptotic equivalence of choice of model by cross-validation and akaike's criterion. *Journal of Royal Statistical Society*, **39**, 44–47. 39

Stowe, K., Paul, M., Palmer, M., Palen, L., and Anderson, K. (2016). Identifying and categorizing disaster-related tweets. In *EMNLP Workshop on Natural Language Processing for Social Media (SocialNLP)*. DOI: 10.18653/v1/w16-6201. 68

Strapparava, C. and Mihalcea, R. (2017). A computational analysis of the language of drug addiction. In *European Chapter of the Association for Computational Linguistics (EACL)*. 63

Sun, X., Ye, J., and Ren, F. (2014). Real time early-stage influenza detection with emotion factors from Sina Microblog. In *5th Workshop on South and Southeast Asian NLP*. DOI: 10.3115/v1/w14-5511. 53

Sun, X., Ye, J., and Ren, F. (2016). Detecting influenza states based on hybrid model with personal emotional factors from social networks. *Neurocomputing*, **210**, 257–268. SI:Behavior Analysis In {SN}. DOI: 10.1016/j.neucom.2016.01.107. 53

Sun, X., Ren, F., and Ye, J. (2017). Trends detection of flu based on ensemble models with emotional factors from social networks. *IEEJ Transactions on Electrical and Electronic Engineering*, **12**(3), 388–396. DOI: 10.1002/tee.22389. 53

Supian, M. N. A. A., Razak, F. A., and Bakar, S. A. (2017). Twitter communication during 2014 flood in Malaysia: Informational or emotional? In *4th International Conference on Mathematical Sciences*. DOI: 10.1063/1.4980883. 68

Surian, D., Nguyen, Q. D., Kennedy, G., Johnson, M., Coiera, E., and Dunn, G. A. (2016). Characterizing Twitter discussions about HPV vaccines using topic modeling and community detection. *Journal of Medical Internet Research*, **18**(8), e232. DOI: 10.2196/jmir.6045. 64

Sznitman, S. R., Taubman, D., and Lewis, N. (2014). Analyzing Twitter as an opportunity to understand substance use. *Drugs in Europe: Change and Continuity*, pages 103–122. DOI: 10.2139/ssrn.2566850. 60

Szomszor, M., Kostkova, P., and St. Louis, C. (2011). Twitter informatics: Tracking and understanding public reaction during the 2009 swine flu pandemic. In *IEEE International Conference on Web Intelligence and Intelligent Agent Technology*. DOI: 10.1109/wi-iat.2011.311. 65

Szomszor, M., Kostkova, P., and de Quincey, E. (2012). #swineflu: Twitter predicts swine flu outbreak in 2009. In *Electronic Healthcare*, volume 69, pages 18–26. DOI: 10.1007/978-3-642-23635-8_3. 53

Tamersoy, A., De Choudhury, M., and Chau, P. (2015). Characterizing smoking and drinking abstinence from social media. In *ACM Conference on Hypertext and Social Media*. DOI: 10.1145/2700171.2791247. 61, 75

Tausczik, Y., Faasse, K., Pennebaker, J. W., and Petrie, K. J. (2012). Public anxiety and information seeking following the H1N1 outbreak: Blogs, newspaper articles, and Wikipedia visits. *Health Communication*, **27**(2), 179–185. DOI: 10.1080/10410236.2011.571759. 20

Thackeray, R., Neiger, B. L., Hanson, C. L., and McKenzie, J. F. (2008). Enhancing promotional strategies within social marketing programs: Use of web 2.0 social media. *Health Promotion Practice*, **9**(4), 338–343. DOI: 10.1177/1524839908325335. 17

Thackeray, R., Burton, S. H., Giraud-Carrier, C., Rollins, S., and Draper, C. R. (2013). Using Twitter for breast cancer prevention: An analysis of Breast Cancer Awareness Month. *BMC Cancer*, **13**, 508. DOI: 10.1186/1471-2407-13-508. 66

Thompson, L., Rivara, F. P., and Whitehill, J. M. (2015). Prevalence of marijuana-related traffic on Twitter, 2012–2013: A content analysis. *Cyberpsychology, Behavior, and Social Networking*, **18**(6), 311–319. DOI: 10.1089/cyber.2014.0620. 61

Thompson, P., Bryan, C., and Poulin, C. (2014). Predicting military and veteran suicide risk: Cultural aspects. In *ACL Workshop on Computational Linguistics and Clinical Psychology (CLPsych)*. DOI: 10.3115/v1/w14-3201. 36

Tian, X., Yu, G., and He, F. (2016). An analysis of sleep complaints on Sina Weibo. *Computers in Human Behavior*, **62**, 230–235. DOI: 10.1016/j.chb.2016.04.014. 75

Tiggemann, M. and Slater, A. (2013). NetGirls: The Internet, Facebook, and body image concern in adolescent girls. *International Journal of Eat Disorders*, **46**(6), 630–633. DOI: 10.1002/eat.22141. 60

Tighe, P. J., Goldsmith, R. C., Gravenstein, M., Bernard, H. R., and Fillingim, R. B. (2015). The painful tweet: Text, sentiment, and community structure analyses of tweets pertaining to pain. *Journal of Medical Internet Research*, **17**(4), e84. DOI: 10.2196/jmir.3769. 55

Tobias, E. (2011). Using Twitter and other social media platforms to provide situational awareness during an incident. *Journal of Business Continuity and Emergency Planning*, **5**(3), 208–23. 67

Towers, S., Afzal, S., Bernal, G., Bliss, N., Brown, S., Espinoza, B., Jackson, J., Judson-Garcia, J., Khan, M., Lin, M., Mamada, R., Moreno, V. M., Nazari, F., Okuneye, K., Ross, M. L., Rodriguez, C., Medlock, J., Ebert, D., and Castillo-Chavez, C. (2015). Mass media and the contagion of fear: The case of ebola in America. *PLoS ONE*, **10**(6), e0129179. DOI: 10.1371/journal.pone.0129179. 54, 65

Tricco, A. C., Zarin, W., Lillie, E., Pham, B., and Straus, S. E. (2017). Utility of social media and crowd-sourced data for pharmacovigilance: A scoping review protocol. *BMJ Open*, **7**(1). DOI: 10.1136/bmjopen-2016-013474. 72

Tse, R., Zhang, L. F., Lei, P., and Pau, G. (2017). Social network based crowd sensing for intelligent transportation and climate applications. *Mobile Networks and Applications*. DOI: 10.1007/s11036-017-0832-y. 16

Tufekci, Z. (2014). Big questions for social media big data: Representativeness, validity and other methodological pitfalls. In *International Conference on Weblogs and Social Media (ICWSM)*. 42, 78, 79

Tumasjan, A., Sprenger, T. O., Sandner, P. G., and Welpe, I. M. (2010). Predicting elections with Twitter: What 140 characters reveal about political sentiment. In *International Conference on Weblogs and Social Media (ICWSM)*. 16

Tung, C.-y., Chou, T.-C., and Lin, J.-w. (2015). Using prediction markets of market scoring rule to forecast infectious diseases: A case study in Taiwan. *BMC Public Health*, **15**(1), 766. DOI: 10.1186/s12889-015-2121-7. 20

Turner-McGrievy, G. M. and Beets, M. W. (2015). Tweet for health: Using an online social network to examine temporal trends in weight loss-related posts. *Translational Behavioral Medicine*, **5**(2), 160–166. DOI: 10.1007/s13142-015-0308-1. 59

Turner-McGrievy, G. M. and Tate, D. F. (2013). Weight loss social support in 140 characters or less: Use of an online social network in a remotely delivered weight loss intervention. *Translational Behavioral Medicine*, **3**(3), 287–294. DOI: 10.1007/s13142-012-0183-y. 59

Ursano, R. J., Kessler, R. C., Stein, M. B., Naifeh, J. A., Aliaga, P. A., Fullerton, C. S., Sampson, N. A., Kao, T.-C., Colpe, L. J., Schoenbaum, M., et al. (2015). Suicide attempts in the U.S. army during the wars in Afghanistan and Iraq, 2004–2009. *JAMA Psychiatry*. DOI: 10.1001/jamapsychiatry.2015.0987. 74

U.S. Department of Health and Human Services (1999). Mental health: A report of the Surgeon General. 73

van Nuijs, A. L., Castiglioni, S., Tarcomnicu, I., Postigo, C., de Alda, M. L., Neels, H., Zuccato, E., Barcelo, D., and Covaci, A. (2011). Illicit drug consumption estimations derived from wastewater analysis: A critical review. *Science of the Total Environment*, **409**(19), 3564–3577. DOI: 10.1016/j.scitotenv.2010.05.030. 12

Vance, K., Howe, W., and Dellavalle, R. P. (2009). Social internet sites as a source of public health information. *Dermatologic Clinics*, **27**(2), 133–136. DOI: 10.1016/j.det.2008.11.010. 18

Vayena, E., Salathé, M., Madoff, L. C., and Brownstein, J. S. (2015). Ethical challenges of big data in public health. *PLoS Computational Biology*, **11**(2), e1003904. DOI: 10.1093/eur-pub/ckv169.024. 88, 93

Velardi, P., Stilo, G., Tozzi, A. E., and Gesualdo, F. (2014). Twitter mining for fine-grained syndromic surveillance. *Artificial Intelligence Medicine*, **61**(3), 153–163. DOI: 10.1016/j.artmed.2014.01.002. 53, 79

Verma, S., Vieweg, S., Corvey, W. J., Palen, L., Martin, J. H., Palmer, M., Schram, A., and Anderson, K. M. (2011). Natural language processing to the rescue? Extracting "situational awareness" tweets during mass emergency. In *International Conference on Weblogs and Social Media (ICWSM)*, pages 385–392. 67

Vieweg, S. (2012). Twitter communications in mass emergency: Contributions to situational awareness. In *Conference on Computer Supported Cooperative Work and Social Computing (CSCW)*, pages 227–230. DOI: 10.1145/2141512.2141584. 67

Vieweg, S., Hughes, A. L., Starbird, K., and Palen, L. (2010). Microblogging during two natural hazards events: What Twitter may contribute to situational awareness. In *Conference on Human Factors in Computing Systems (CHI)*. DOI: 10.1145/1753326.1753486. 67

Vilar, S., Friedman, C., and Hripcsak, G. (2017). Detection of drug-drug interactions through data mining studies using clinical sources, scientific literature and social media. *Briefings in Bioinformatics*. DOI: 10.1093/bib/bbx010. 72

Volkova, S., Coppersmith, G., and Van Durme, B. (2014). Inferring user political preferences from streaming communications. In *Association for Computational Linguistics (ACL)*. DOI: 10.3115/v1/p14-1018. 43, 44

Volkova, S., Bachrach, Y., Armstrong, M., and Sharma, V. (2015a). Inferring latent user properties from texts published in social media. In *AAAI Conference on Artificial Intelligence (AAAI)*, Austin, TX. 43

Volkova, S., Van Durme, B., Yarowsky, D., and Bachrach, Y. (2015b). Social media predictive analytics. In *North American Chapter of the Association for Computational Linguistics (NAACL): Tutorial*. DOI: 10.3115/v1/n15-4005. 43, 44

Walker, M., Thornton, L., De Choudhury, M., Teevan, J., Bulik, C., Levinson, C., and Zerwas, S. (2015). Facebook use and disordered eating in college-aged women. *Journal of Adolescent Health*. DOI: 10.1016/j.jadohealth.2015.04.026. 60, 75

Wallace, B. C., Paul, M. J., Sarkar, U., Trikalinos, T. A., and Dredze, M. (2014). A large-scale quantitative analysis of latent factors and sentiment in online doctor reviews. *Journal of the American Medical Informatics Association (JAMIA)*. DOI: 10.1136/amiajnl-2014-002711. 71

Wang, H., Hovy, E., and Dredze, M. (2015a). The hurricane Sandy Twitter corpus. In *AAAI Workshop on the World Wide Web and Public Health Intelligence*. 68

Wang, S. and Bai, H. (2014). A case study on micro-blog communication characteristics related to haze during the Harbin haze disaster. In *International Conference on Management Science and Engineering*. DOI: 10.1109/icmse.2014.6930218. 69

Wang, S., Paul, M. J., and Dredze, M. (2014). Exploring health topics in Chinese social media: An analysis of Sina Weibo. In *AAAI Workshop on the World Wide Web and Public Health Intelligence*. 31, 59

Wang, S., Paul, J. M., and Dredze, M. (2015b). Social media as a sensor of air quality and public response in China. *Journal of Medical Internet Research*, **17**(1), e22. DOI: 10.2196/jmir.3875. 41, 69

Wang, W., Hernandez, I., Newman, D. A., He, J., and Bian, J. (2016). Twitter analysis: Studying US weekly trends in work stress and emotion. *Applied Psychology*, **65**(2), 355–378. DOI: 10.1111/apps.12065. 75

Wang, Z., Chakraborty, P., Mekaru, S. R., Brownstein, J. S., Ye, J., and Ramakrishnan, N. (2015c).   Dynamic poisson autoregression for influenza-like-illness case count prediction.   In *ACM Conference on Knowledge Discovery and Data Mining (KDD)*. DOI: 10.1145/2783258.2783291. 52

Ward, J. K. and Armitage, G. (2012). Can patients report patient safety incidents in a hospital setting? A systematic review. *BMJ Quality and Safety*, **21**(8), 685–699. DOI: 10.1136/bmjqs-2011-000213. 71

Watts, G. (2008).   Google watches over flu.   *BMJ: British Medical Journal*, **337**. DOI: 10.1136/bmj.a3076. 77

Wax, P. (2002). Just a click away: Recreational drug web sites on the Internet. *Pediatrics*, **109**(6). DOI: 10.1542/peds.109.6.e96. 62

Weeg, C., Schwartz, H. A., Hill, S., Merchant, R. M., Arango, C., and Ungar, L. (2015). Using Twitter to measure public discussion of diseases: A case study. *JMIR Public Health and Surveillance*, **1**(1), e6. DOI: 10.2196/publichealth.3953. 42

Welser, H. T., Smith, M., Fisher, D., and Gleave, E. (2008). Distilling digital traces: Computational social science approaches to studying the internet. *Handbook of Online Research Methods*, pages 116–140. DOI: 10.4135/9780857020055.n7. 15

West, J. H., Hall, P. C., Prier, K., Hanson, C. L., Giraud-Carrier, C., Neeley, E. S., and Barnes, M. D. (2012). Temporal variability of problem drinking on Twitter. *Open Journal of Preventative Medicine*, **2**(1). DOI: 10.4236/ojpm.2012.21007. 61

West, R., White, R. W., and Horvitz, E. (2013). From cookies to cooks: Insights on dietary patterns via analysis of web usage logs. In *International Conference on World Wide Web (WWW)*, Republic and Canton of Geneva, Switzerland. DOI: 10.1145/2488388.2488510. 59

Westmaas, J. L., Ayers, J. W., Dredze, M., and Althouse, B. M. (2015). Evaluation of the Great American Smokeout by digital surveillance. In *Society of Behavioral Medicine*. 66

White, R. W. and Horvitz, E. (2015). Belief dynamics and biases in web search. *ACM Transactions on Information Systems*. DOI: 10.1145/2746229. 65

White, R. W., Tatonetti, N. P., Shah, N. H., Altman, R. B., and Horvitz, E. (2013). Web-scale pharmacovigilance: Listening to signals from the crowd. *Journal of the American Medical Informatics Association*, **20**(3), 404–8. DOI: 10.1136/amiajnl-2012-001482. 72

White, R. W., Harpaz, R., Shah, N. H., DuMouchel, W., and Horvitz, E. (2014).   Toward enhanced pharmacovigilance using patient-generated data on the internet. *Clinical Pharmacology and Therapeutics*, **96**(2), 239–246. DOI: 10.1038/clpt.2014.77. 72

Wicks, P., Vaughan, T. E., Massagli, M. P., and Heywood, J. (2011). Accelerated clinical discovery using self-reported patient data collected online and a patient-matching algorithm. *National Biotechnology*, **29**(5), 411–414. DOI: 10.1038/nbt.1837. 19

Williams, S. A., Terras, M., and Warwick, C. (2013). How Twitter is studied in the medical professions: A classification of Twitter papers indexed in PubMed. *Med 2 0*, **2**(2), e2. DOI: 10.2196/med20.2269. 13

Wing, B. and Baldridge, J. (2014). Hierarchical discriminative classification for text-based geolocation. In *Empirical Methods in Natural Language Processing (EMNLP)*, pages 336–348. DOI: 10.3115/v1/d14-1039. 45

Wing, B. P. and Baldridge, J. (2011). Simple supervised document geolocation with geodesic grids. In *Association for Computational Linguistics (ACL)*. 45

Won, H.-H., Myung, W., Song, G.-Y., Lee, W.-H., Kim, J.-W., Carroll, B. J., and Kim, D. K. (2013). Predicting national suicide numbers with social media data. *PLoS ONE*, **8**(4), e61809. DOI: 10.1371/journal.pone.0061809. 75

Won, M., Marques-Pita, M., Louro, C., and Gonçalves-Sá, J. (2017). Early and real-time detection of seasonal influenza onset. *PLoS Computational Biology*, **13**(2), 1–20. DOI: 10.1371/journal.pcbi.1005330. 53

Wood-Doughty, Z., Smith, M., Broniatowski, D., and Dredze, M. (2017). How does Twitter user behavior vary across demographic groups? In *ACL Workshop on Natural Language Processing and Computational Social Science*. 80, 83

World Health Organization (2013). Mental health action plan 2013–2020. 73

Xu, Q., Gel, Y. R., Ramirez Ramirez, L. L., Nezafati, K., Zhang, Q., and Tsui, K.-L. (2017). Forecasting influenza in Hong Kong with Google search queries and statistical model fusion. *PLoS ONE*, **12**(5), 1–17. DOI: 10.1371/journal.pone.0176690. 53

Xu, W., Han, Z. W., and Ma, J. (2010). A neural netwok based approach to detect influenza epidemics using search engine query data. In *International Conference on Machine Learning and Cybernetics*. DOI: 10.1109/icmlc.2010.5580851. 52

Yang, A. C., Huang, N. E., Peng, C.-K., and Tsai, S.-J. (2010). Do seasons have an influence on the incidence of depression? The use of an internet search engine query data as a proxy of human affect. *PLoS ONE*, **5**(10), e13728. DOI: 10.1371/journal.pone.0013728. 74

Yang, S., Santillana, M., and Kou, S. C. (2015). Accurate estimation of influenza epidemics using Google search data via ARGO. *Proc. of the National Academy of Sciences*. DOI: 10.1073/pnas.1515373112. 52

Yang, S., Santillana, M., Brownstein, J. S., Gray, J., Richardson, S., and Kou, S. C. (2017). Using electronic health records and internet search information for accurate influenza forecasting. *BMC Infectious Diseases*, **17**(1), 332. DOI: 10.1186/s12879-017-2424-7. 53

Yates, A. and Goharian, N. (2013). ADRTrace: Detecting expected and unexpected adverse drug reactions from user reviews on social media sites. In *European Conference on Advances in Information Retrieval*, Berlin, Heidelberg. DOI: 10.1007/978-3-642-36973-5_92. 19, 72

Yates, A., Coharian, N., and Frieder, O. (2013). Extracting adverse drug reactions from forum posts and linking them to drugs. In *SIGIR Workshop on Health and Discovery*. 72

Yates, D. and Paquette, S. (2011). Emergency knowledge management and social media technologies: A case study of the 2010 Haitian earthquake. *International Journal of Information Management*, **31**(1), 6–13. DOI: 10.1016/j.ijinfomgt.2010.10.001. 68

Yin, J., Lampert, A., Cameron, M., Robinson, B., and Power, R. (2012). Using social media to enhance emergency situation awareness. *IEEE Intelligent Systems*, **27**(6), 52–59. DOI: 10.1109/mis.2012.6. 67

Yin, Z., Fabbri, D., Rosenbloom, S. T., and Malin, B. (2015). A scalable framework to detect personal health mentions on Twitter. *Journal of Medical Internet Research*, **17**(6), e138. DOI: 10.2196/jmir.4305. 30, 55

Yom-Tov, E. (2015). Ebola data from the internet: An opportunity for syndromic surveillance or a news event? In *5th International Conference on Digital Health*. DOI: 10.1145/2750511.2750512. 54

Yom-Tov, E. and boyd, d. (2014). On the link between media coverage of anorexia and pro-anorexic practices on the web. *International Journal in Eat Disorder*, **47**(2), 196–202. DOI: 10.1002/eat.22195. 60, 66

Yom-Tov, E. and Fernandez-Luque, L. (2014). Information is in the eye of the beholder: Seeking information on the MMR vaccine through an Internet search engine. *AMIA Annual Symposium Proceedings*, **2014**, 1238–1247. 64

Yom-Tov, E. and Gabrilovich, E. (2013). Postmarket drug surveillance without trial costs: Discovery of adverse drug reactions through large-scale analysis of web search queries. *Journal of Medical Internet Research*, **15**(6), e124. DOI: 10.2196/jmir.2614. 72

Yom-Tov, E., Fernandez-Luque, L., Weber, I., and Crain, S. P. (2012). Pro-anorexia and pro-recovery photo sharing: A tale of two warring tribes. *Journal of Medical Internet Research*, **14**(6), e151. DOI: 10.2196/jmir.2239. 60

Yom-Tov, E., Borsa, D., Cox, I. J., and McKendry, R. A. (2014a). Detecting disease outbreaks in mass gatherings using Internet data. *Journal of Medical Internet Research*, **16**(6), e154. DOI: 10.2196/jmir.3156. 53, 87

Yom-Tov, E., White, W. R., and Horvitz, E. (2014b). Seeking insights about cycling mood disorders via anonymized search logs. *Journal of Medical Internet Research*, **16**(2), e65. DOI: 10.2196/jmir.2664. 76

Yom-Tov, E., Johansson-Cox, I., Lampos, V., and Hayward, A. C. (2015). Estimating the secondary attack rate and serial interval of influenza-like illnesses using social media. *Influenza Other Respiratory Viruses*, **9**(4), 191–199. DOI: 10.1111/irv.12321. 54

Yoo, I. and Mosa, A. S. M. (2015). Analysis of PubMed user sessions using a full-day PubMed query log: A comparison of experienced and nonexperienced PubMed users. *JMIR Medical Informatics*, **3**(3), e25. DOI: 10.2196/medinform.3740. 19

Yoon, S., Elhadad, N., and Bakken, S. (2013). A practical approach for content mining of Tweets. *American Journal of Preventive Medicine*, **45**(1), 122–129. DOI: 10.1016/j.amepre.2013.02.025. 24, 33

Young, S. D., Rivers, C., and Lewis, B. (2014). Methods of using real-time social media technologies for detection and remote monitoring of HIV outcomes. *Preventive Medicine*, **63**, 112–115. DOI: 10.1016/j.ypmed.2014.01.024. 55

Young, S. D., Yu, W., and Wang, W. (2017). Toward automating HIV identification: Machine learning for rapid identification of HIV-related social media data. *Journal of Acquired Immune Deficiency Syndromes*, **74**, S128–S131. DOI: 10.1097/qai.0000000000001240. 55

Yuan, Q., Nsoesie, E. O., Lv, B., Peng, G., Chunara, R., and Brownstein, J. S. (2013). Monitoring influenza epidemics in China with search query from Baidu. *PLoS ONE*, **8**(5). DOI: 10.1371/journal.pone.0064323. 52, 53

Zeidner, M. and Shechtera, M. (1988). Psychological responses to air pollution: Some personality and demographic correlates. *Journal of Environmental Psychology*, **8**(3), 191–208. DOI: 10.1016/s0272-4944(88)80009-4. 69

Zhang, C., Gotsis, M., and Jordan-Marsh, M. (2013a). Social media microblogs as an HPV vaccination forum. *Human Vaccines and Immunotherapeutics*, **9**(11), 2483–2489. DOI: 10.4161/hv.25599. 64

Zhang, F., Luo, J., Li, C., Wang, X., and Zhao, Z. (2014a). Detecting and analyzing influenza epidemics with social media in China. In *Advances in Knowledge Discovery and Data Mining*, pages 90–101. DOI: 10.1007/978-3-319-06608-0_8. 53

Zhang, N., Campo, S., Janz, K. F., Eckler, P., Yang, J., Snetselaar, L. G., and Signorini, A. (2013b). Electronic word of mouth on Twitter about physical activity in the U.S.: exploratory infodemiology study. *Journal of Medical Internet Research*, **15**. DOI: 10.2196/jmir.2870. 59

Zhang, N., Zheng, G., Chen, H., Chen, X., and Chen, J. (2014b). Monitoring urban waterlogging disaster using social sensors. In *Chinese Semantic Web and Web Science Conference*, pages 227–236. DOI: 10.1007/978-3-662-45495-4_20. 68

Zhang, Q., Perra, N., Perrotta, D., Tizzoni, M., Paolotti, D., and Vespignani, A. (2017). Forecasting seasonal influenza fusing digital indicators and a mechanistic disease model. In *International Conference on World Wide Web (WWW)*, pages 311–319, Republic and Canton of Geneva, Switzerland. DOI: 10.1145/3038912.3052678. 54

Zhang, W., Ram, S., Burkart, M., and Pengetnze, Y. (2016). Extracting signals from social media for chronic disease surveillance. In *International Conference on Digital Health Conference*, pages 79–83, New York, ACM. DOI: 10.1145/2896338.2897728. 55

Zhang, W. M., Ho, S. C., Fang, P., Lu, Y., and Ho, C. R. (2014c). Usage of social media and smartphone application in assessment of physical and psychological well-being of individuals in times of a major air pollution crisis. *JMIR mHealth uHealth*, **2**(1), e16. DOI: 10.2196/mhealth.2827. 69

Zimmer, M. (2010). "But the data is already public": On the ethics of research in Facebook. ethics and Information Technology, **12**(4), 313–325. DOI: 10.1007/s10676-010-9227-5. 90

Zou, B., Lampos, V., Gorton, R., and Cox, I. J. (2016). On infectious intestinal disease surveillance using social media content. In *International Conference on Digital Health Conference*, pages 157–161, New York, ACM. DOI: 10.1145/2896338.2896372. 54

Zuccato, E., Chiabrando, C., Castiglioni, S., Bagnati, R., and Fanelli, R. (2008). Estimating community drug abuse by wastewater analysis. *Environmental Health Perspectives*, **116**(8), 1027. DOI: 10.1289/ehp.11022. 12

Authors' Biographies

MICHAEL J. PAUL

Michael J. Paul is an assistant professor in Information Science at the University of Colorado, Boulder. He develops data science techniques for analyzing and organizing large text datasets, used for applications in health science and computational epidemiology. His work was among the first to identify the broad set of health issues that can be studied in Twitter, and his research has advanced the state of the art in influenza surveillance on multiple occasions. He is a former Twitter intern, and his work with Mark Dredze was featured in a video as part of the *Twitter Stories* series.[1] He obtained his Ph.D. in Computer Science from Johns Hopkins University in 2015. See his website for more information: `http://www.michaeljpaul.com`

MARK DREDZE

Mark Dredze is an associate professor in Computer Science at Johns Hopkins University. He is affiliated with the Center for Language and Speech Processing, the Human Language Technology Center of Excellence, and the Malone Center for Engineering in Healthcare. His work focuses on developing machine learning models for natural language processing (NLP) applications. He has pioneered new applications of these technologies in public health informatics, including work with social media data, biomedical articles, and clinical texts. His work is regularly covered by major media outlets, including NPR, *The New York Times*, and CNN. He obtained his Ph.D. in Computer Science from the University of Pennsylvania in 2009. See his website for more information: `http://www.dredze.com`

---

[1]`https://www.youtube.com/watch?v=HmDIh-YSOGI`

Printed in the United States
by Baker & Taylor Publisher Services